Bombshells

UNITED

Volume 3
TAPS

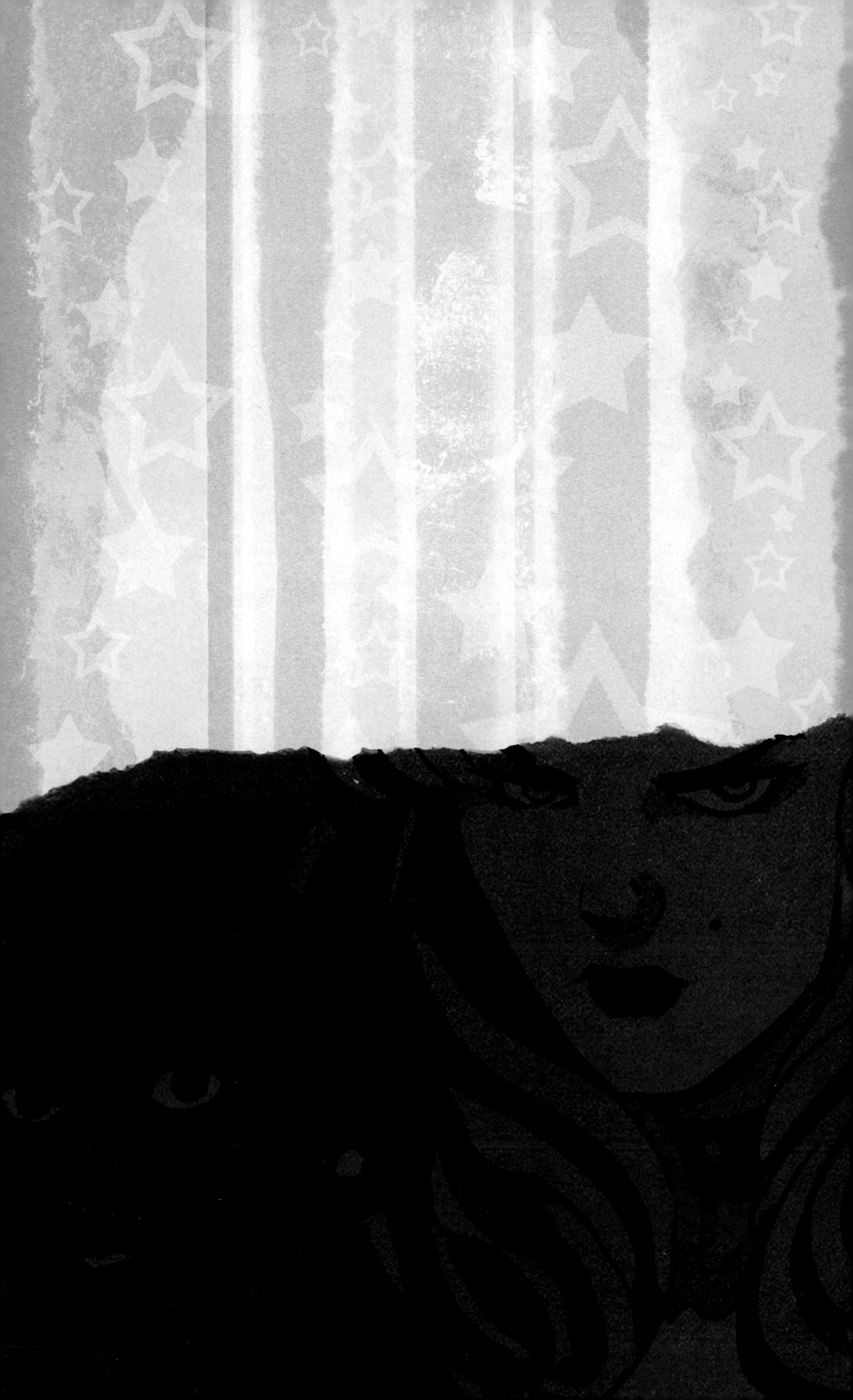

Bombshells UNITED

Volume 3
TAPS

MARGUERITE BENNETT
writer

SANDY JARRELL
DAVID HAHN
ANEKE
SIYA OUM
MARGUERITE SAUVAGE
artists

J. NANJAN
KELLY FITZPATRICK
MARGUERITE SAUVAGE
colorists

WES ABBOTT
letterer

TERRY and RACHEL DODSON
collection cover artists

SUPERGIRL based on the characters created by JERRY SIEGEL and JOE SHUSTER.
By special arrangement with the Jerry Siegel family.

KRISTY QUINN Editor – Original Series
JEB WOODARD Group Editor – Collected Editions
TYLER-MARIE EVANS Editor – Collected Edition
STEVE COOK Design Director – Books
SHANNON STEWART Publication Design

BOB HARRAS Senior VP – Editor-in-Chief, DC Comics
PAT McCALLUM Executive Editor, DC Comics

DAN DiDIO Publisher * JIM LEE Publisher & Chief Creative Officer
AMIT DESAI Executive VP – Business & Marketing Strategy, Direct to Consumer & Global Franchise Management
BOBBIE CHASE VP & Executive Editor, Young Reader & Talent Development * MARK CHIARELLO Senior VP – Art, Design & Collected Editions
JOHN CUNNINGHAM Senior VP – Sales & Trade Marketing * BRIAR DARDEN VP – Business Affairs
ANNE DePIES Senior VP – Business Strategy, Finance & Administration * DON FALLETTI VP – Manufacturing Operations
LAWRENCE GANEM VP – Editorial Administration & Talent Relations * ALISON GILL Senior VP – Manufacturing & Operations
JASON GREENBERG VP – Business Strategy & Finance * HANK KANALZ Senior VP – Editorial Strategy & Administration
JAY KOGAN Senior VP – Legal Affairs * NICK J. NAPOLITANO VP – Manufacturing Administration
LISETTE OSTERLOH VP – Digital Marketing & Events * EDDIE SCANNELL VP – Consumer Marketing
COURTNEY SIMMONS Senior VP – Publicity & Communications * JIM (SKI) SOKOLOWSKI VP – Comic Book Specialty Sales & Trade Marketing
NANCY SPEARS VP – Mass, Book, Digital Sales & Trade Marketing * MICHELE R. WELLS VP – Content Strategy

BOMBSHELLS: UNITED VOL. 3: TAPS

Published by DC Comics. Compilation and all new material Copyright © 2019 DC Comics. All Rights Reserved.
Originally published in single magazine form in BOMBSHELLS: UNITED 13-19 and online as BOMBSHELLS: UNITED Digital Chapters 25-38.

DC Comics, 2900 West Alameda Ave., Burbank, CA 91505
Printed by LSC Communications, Kendallville, IN, USA. 1/25/19. First Printing.
ISBN: 978-1-4012-8826-6

Library of Congress Cataloging-in-Publication Data is available.

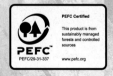

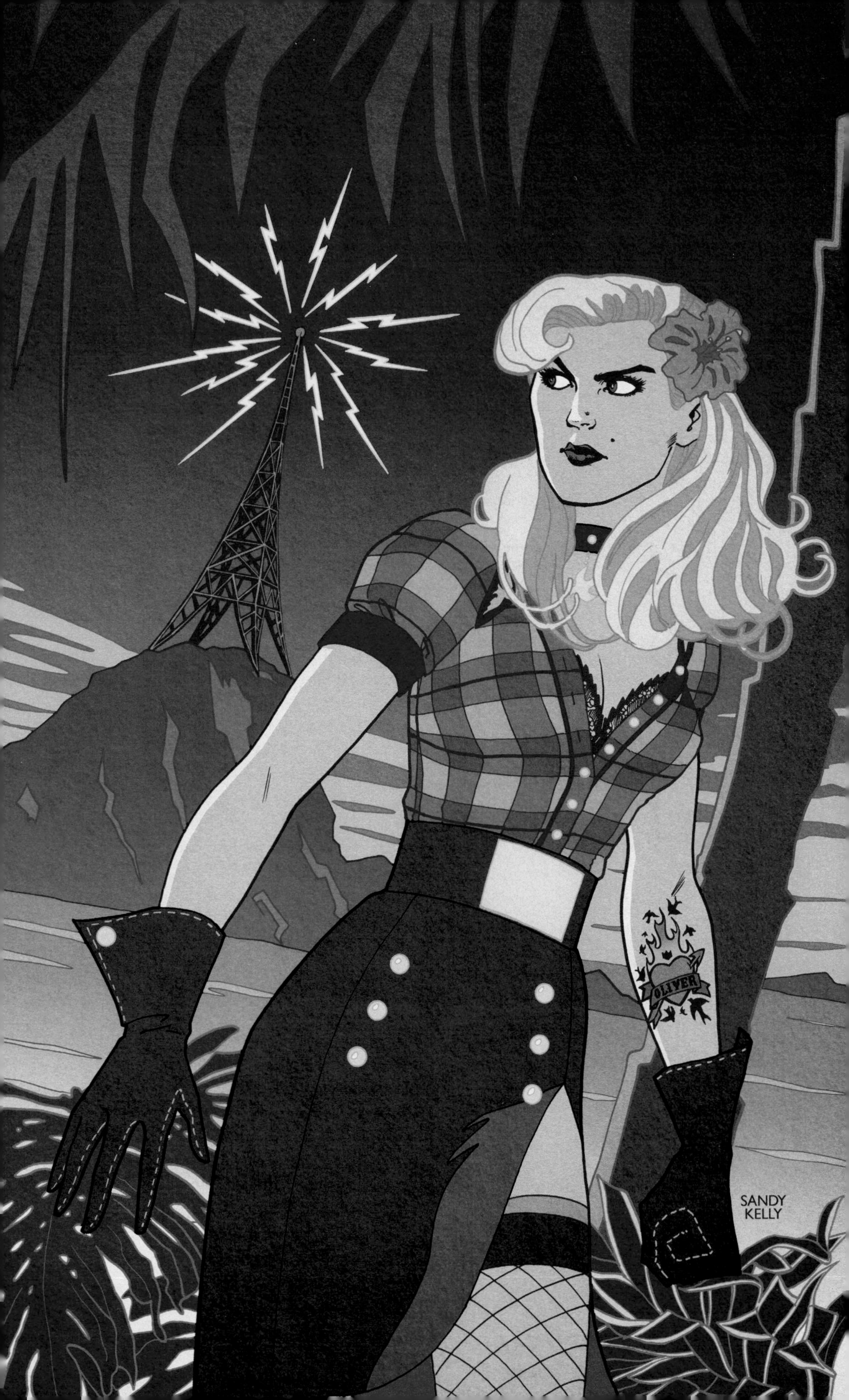
OLIVER
SANDY
KELLY

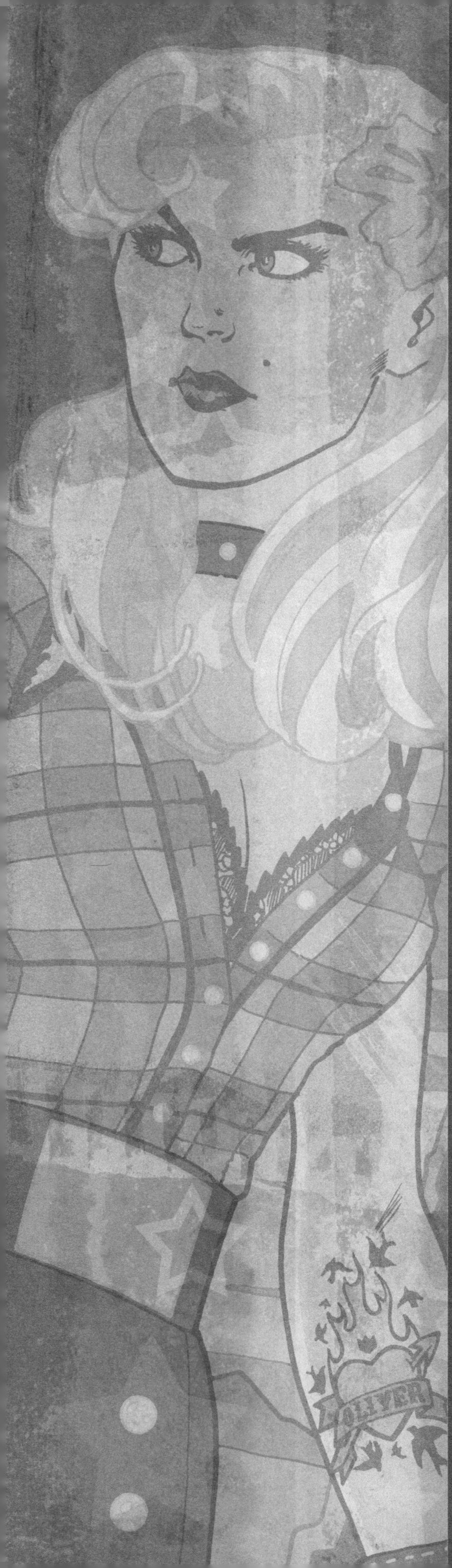
OLIVER

THE BLACK ISLAND

PARTS ONE and TWO

Written by
MARGUERITE BENNETT

Art by
SANDY JARRELL

Colors by
KELLY FITZPATRICK

Letters by
WES ABBOTT

Cover by
SANDY JARRELL *and*
KELLY FITZPATRICK

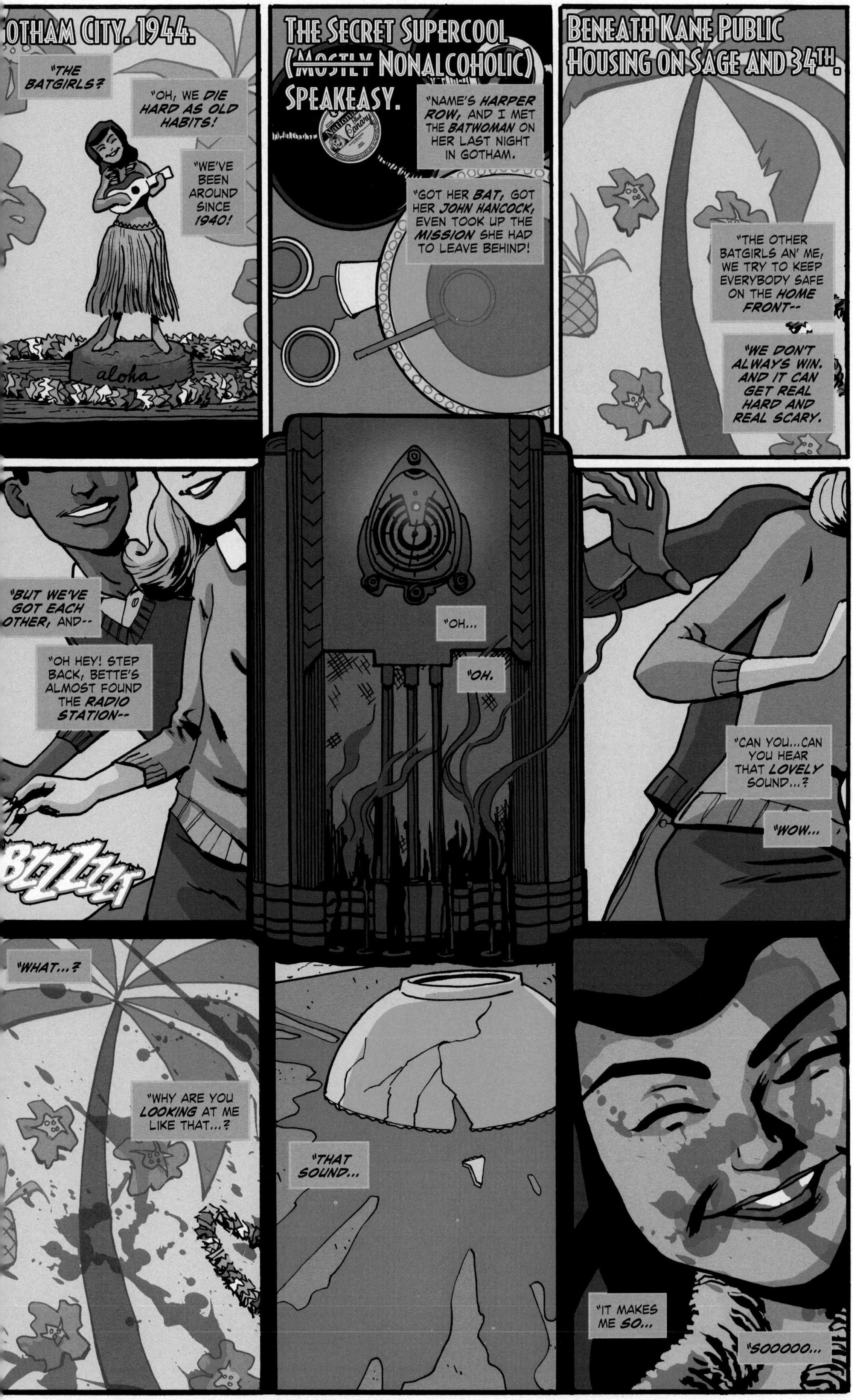

OTHAM CITY. 1944.
"THE BATGIRLS?
"OH, WE DIE HARD AS OLD HABITS!
"WE'VE BEEN AROUND SINCE 1940!
aloha
THE SECRET SUPERCOOL (MOSTLY NONALCOHOLIC) SPEAKEASY.
"NAME'S HARPER ROW, AND I MET THE BATWOMAN ON HER LAST NIGHT IN GOTHAM.
"GOT HER BAT, GOT HER JOHN HANCOCK, EVEN TOOK UP THE MISSION SHE HAD TO LEAVE BEHIND!
BENEATH KANE PUBLIC HOUSING ON SAGE AND 34TH.
"THE OTHER BATGIRLS AN' ME, WE TRY TO KEEP EVERYBODY SAFE ON THE HOME FRONT--
"WE DON'T ALWAYS WIN. AND IT CAN GET REAL HARD AND REAL SCARY.
"BUT WE'VE GOT EACH OTHER, AND--
"OH HEY! STEP BACK, BETTE'S ALMOST FOUND THE RADIO STATION--
BZZZZZT
"OH...
"OH.
"CAN YOU...CAN YOU HEAR THAT LOVELY SOUND...?
"WOW...
"WHAT...?
"WHY ARE YOU LOOKING AT ME LIKE THAT...?
"THAT SOUND...
"IT MAKES ME SO...
"SOOOOO...

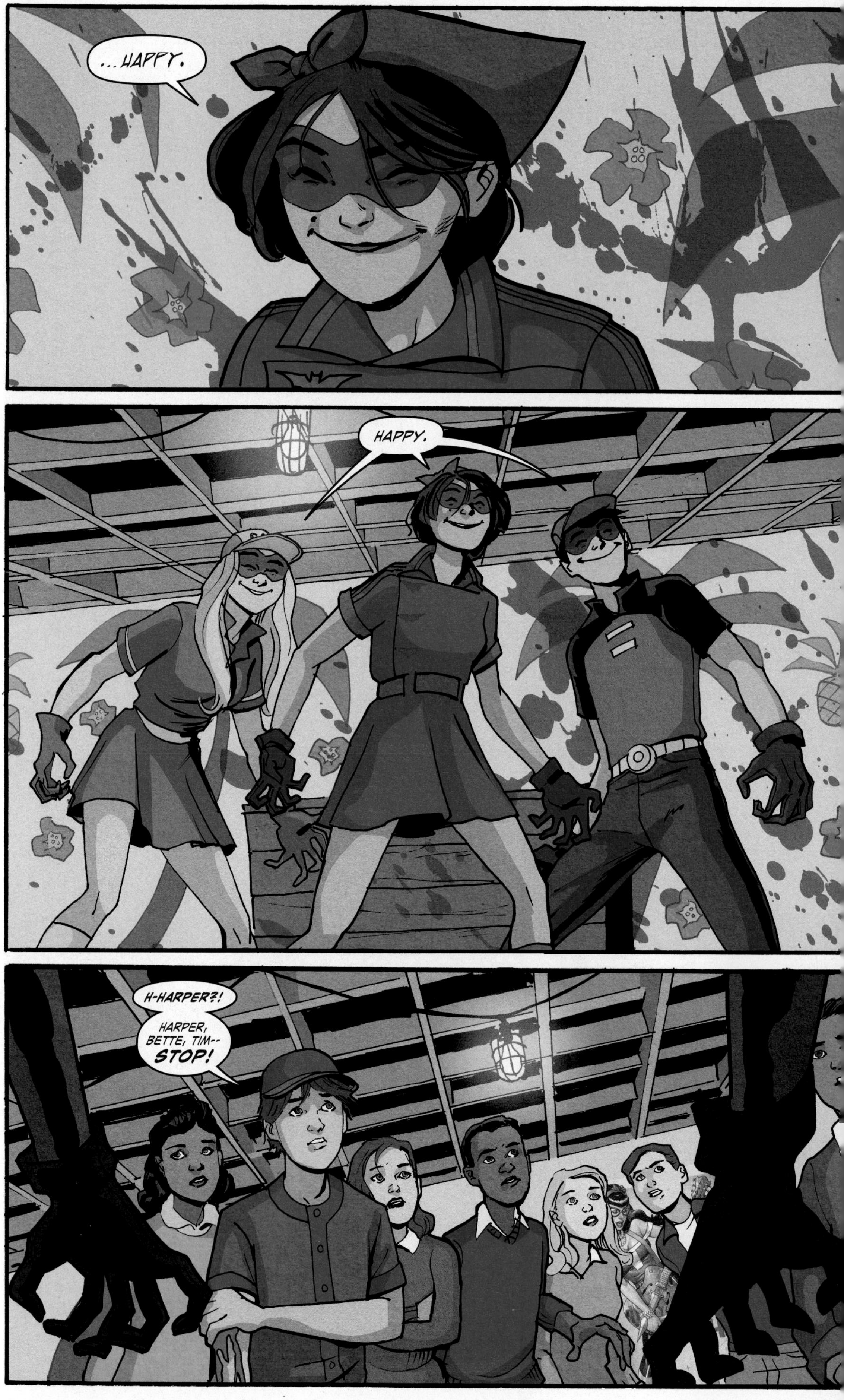
...HAPPY.
HAPPY.
H-HARPER?!
HARPER, BETTE, TIM--
STOP!

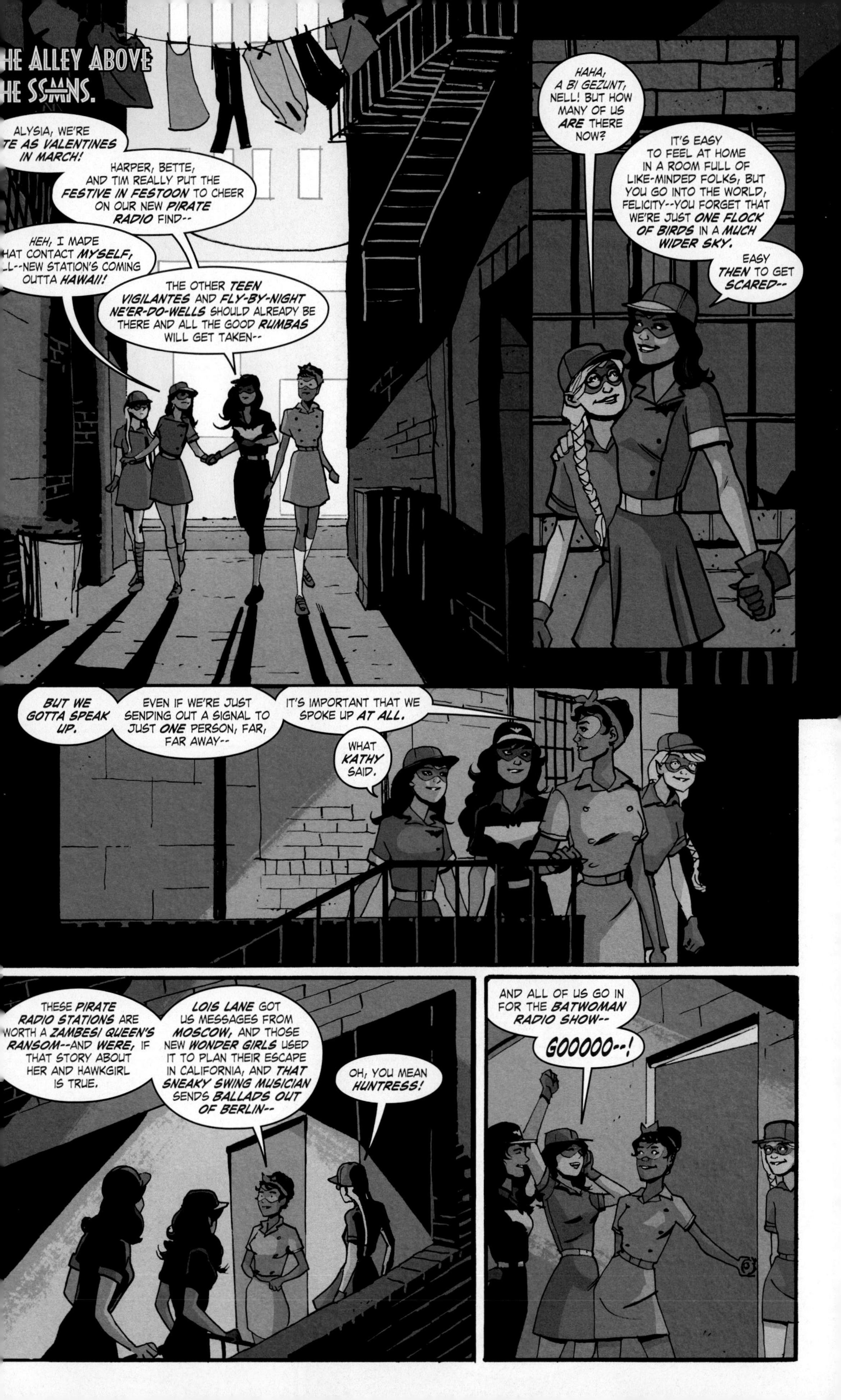

HE ALLEY ABOVE
HE SSMNS.
ALYSIA, WE'RE
TE AS VALENTINES IN MARCH!
HARPER, BETTE, AND TIM REALLY PUT THE FESTIVE IN FESTOON TO CHEER ON OUR NEW PIRATE RADIO FIND--
HEH, I MADE HAT CONTACT MYSELF, L--NEW STATION'S COMING OUTTA HAWAII!
THE OTHER TEEN VIGILANTES AND FLY-BY-NIGHT NE'ER-DO-WELLS SHOULD ALREADY BE THERE AND ALL THE GOOD RUMBAS WILL GET TAKEN--
HAHA, A BI GEZUNT, NELL! BUT HOW MANY OF US ARE THERE NOW?
IT'S EASY TO FEEL AT HOME IN A ROOM FULL OF LIKE-MINDED FOLKS, BUT YOU GO INTO THE WORLD, FELICITY--YOU FORGET THAT WE'RE JUST ONE FLOCK OF BIRDS IN A MUCH WIDER SKY.
EASY THEN TO GET SCARED--
BUT WE GOTTA SPEAK UP.
EVEN IF WE'RE JUST SENDING OUT A SIGNAL TO JUST ONE PERSON, FAR, FAR AWAY--
IT'S IMPORTANT THAT WE SPOKE UP AT ALL.
WHAT KATHY SAID.
THESE PIRATE RADIO STATIONS ARE WORTH A ZAMBESI QUEEN'S RANSOM--AND WERE, IF THAT STORY ABOUT HER AND HAWKGIRL IS TRUE.
LOIS LANE GOT US MESSAGES FROM MOSCOW, AND THOSE NEW WONDER GIRLS USED IT TO PLAN THEIR ESCAPE IN CALIFORNIA, AND THAT SNEAKY SWING MUSICIAN SENDS BALLADS OUT OF BERLIN--
OH, YOU MEAN HUNTRESS!
AND ALL OF US GO IN FOR THE BATWOMAN RADIO SHOW--
GOOOOO--!

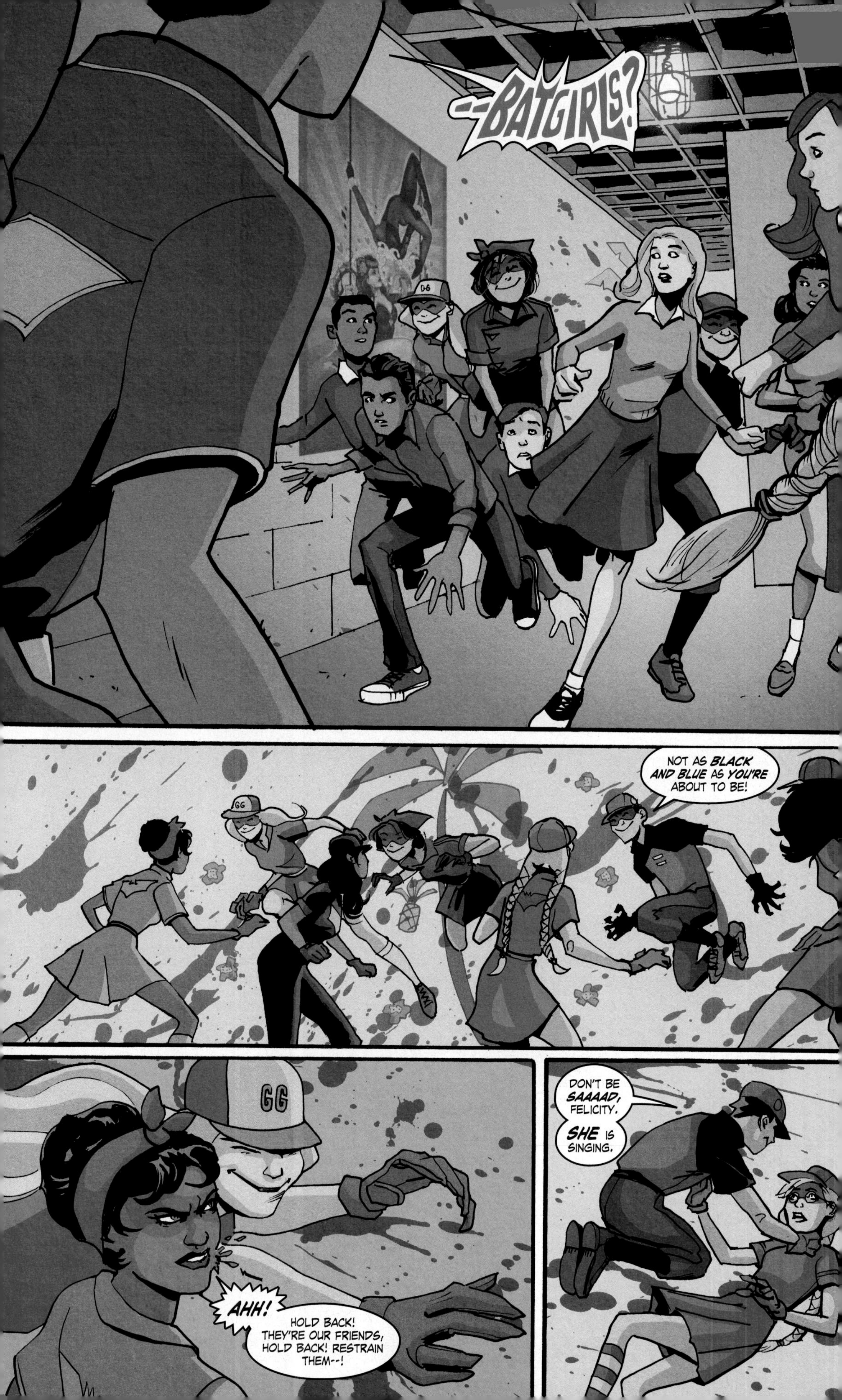
--BATGIRLS?
NOT AS BLACK AND BLUE AS YOU'RE ABOUT TO BE!
AHH!
HOLD BACK! THEY'RE OUR FRIENDS, HOLD BACK! RESTRAIN THEM--!
DON'T BE SAAAAD, FELICITY.
SHE IS SINGING.

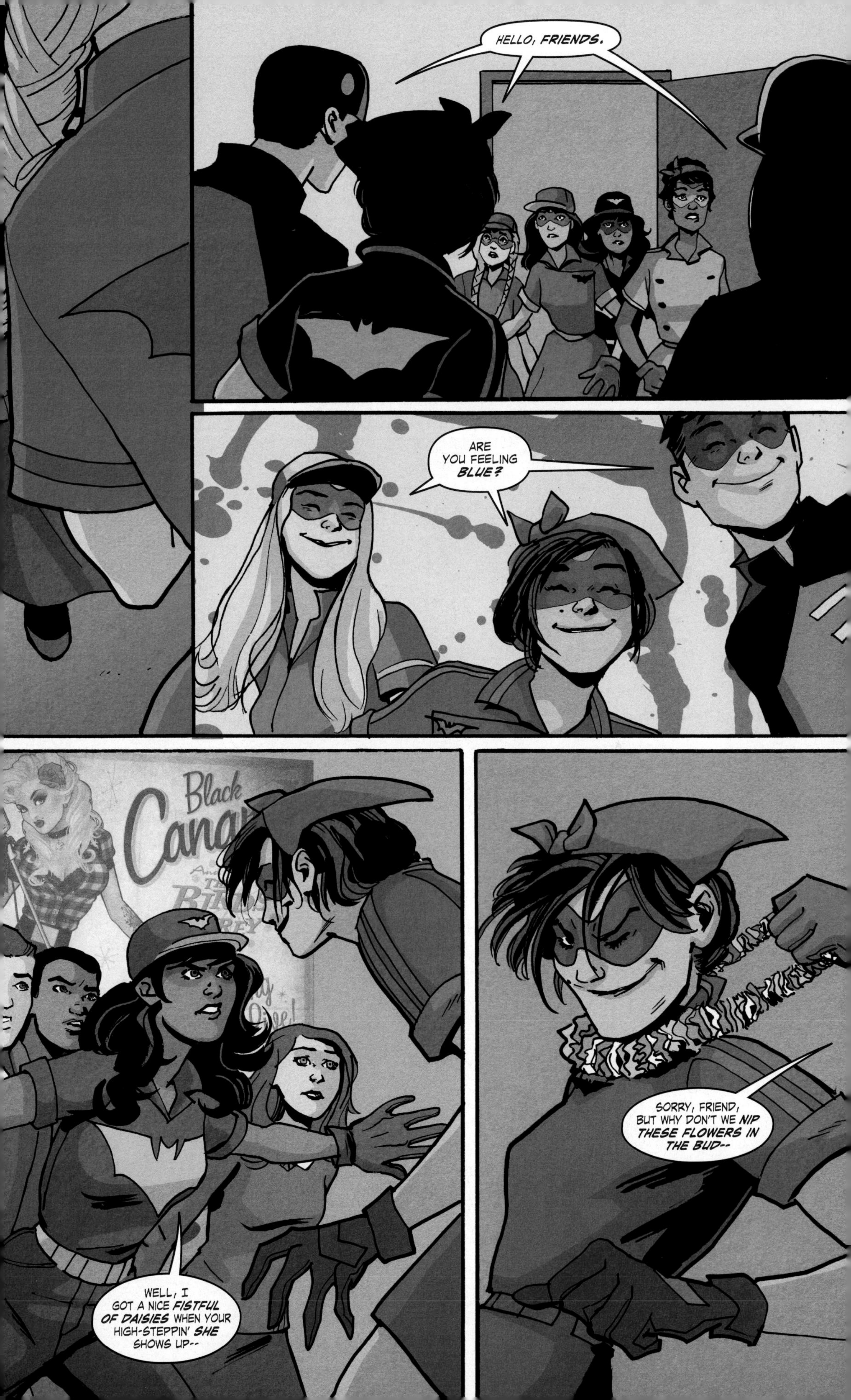
HELLO, FRIENDS.
ARE YOU FEELING BLUE?
Black Canary And The Birds of Prey
WELL, I GOT A NICE FISTFUL OF DAISIES WHEN YOUR HIGH-STEPPIN' SHE SHOWS UP--
SORRY, FRIEND, BUT WHY DON'T WE NIP THESE FLOWERS IN THE BUD--

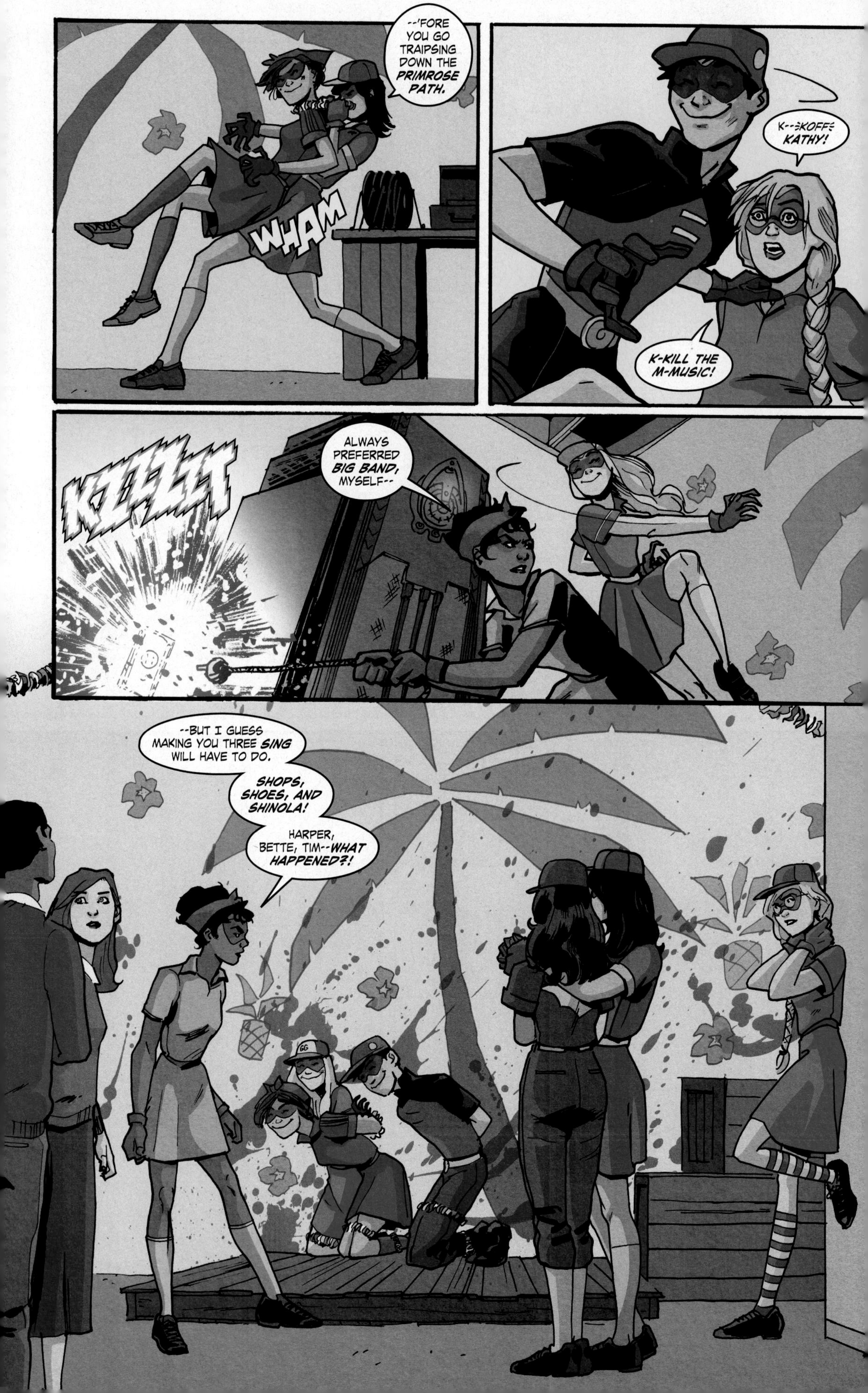
--'FORE YOU GO TRAIPSING DOWN THE PRIMROSE PATH.
WHAM
K--KOFF-- KATHY!
K-KILL THE M-MUSIC!
KZZZZT
ALWAYS PREFERRED BIG BAND, MYSELF--
--BUT I GUESS MAKING YOU THREE SING WILL HAVE TO DO.
SHOPS, SHOES, AND SHINOLA!
HARPER, BETTE, TIM--WHAT HAPPENED?!
GG

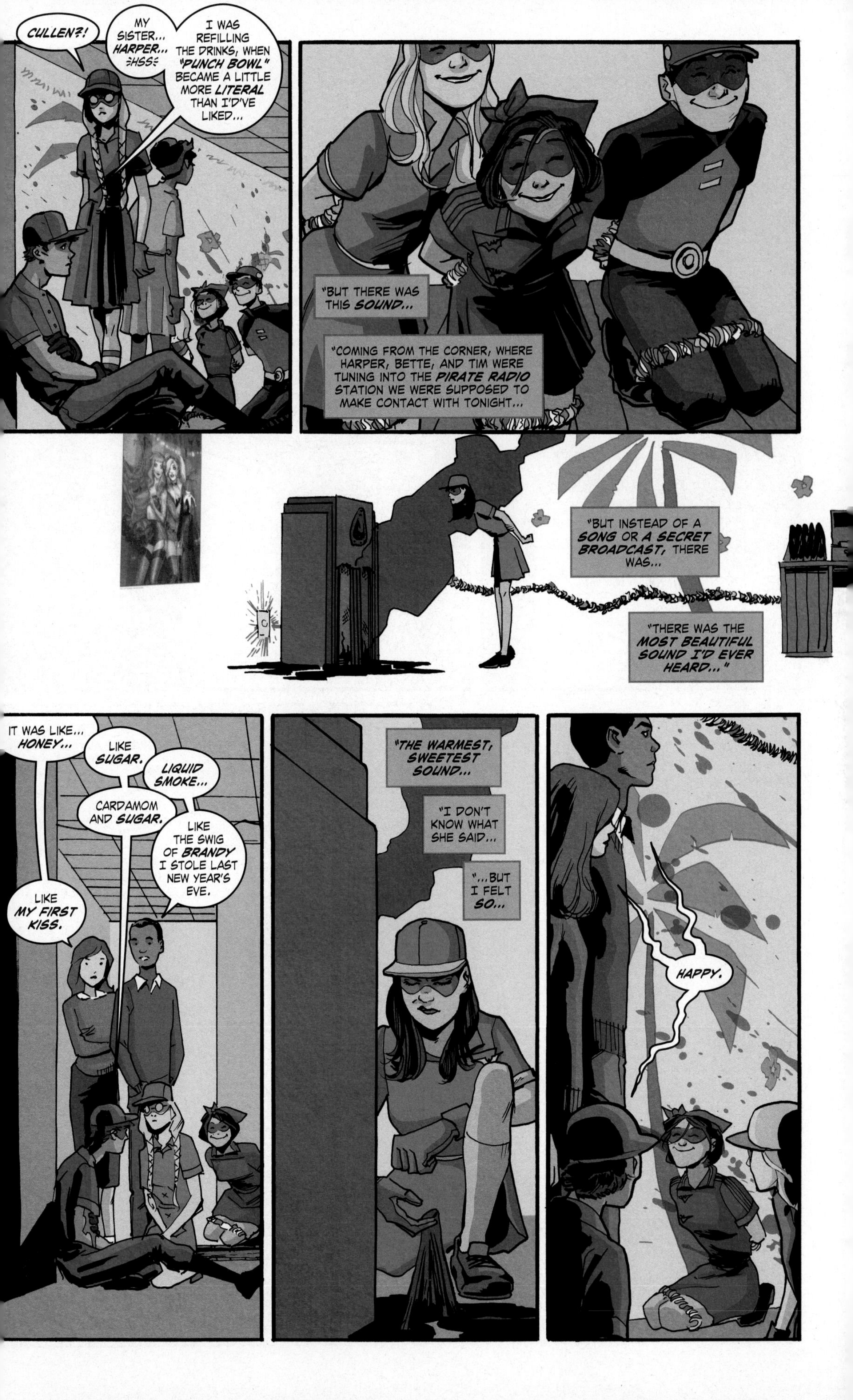
CULLEN?!
MY SISTER... HARPER... ≈HSS≈
I WAS REFILLING THE DRINKS, WHEN "PUNCH BOWL" BECAME A LITTLE MORE LITERAL THAN I'D'VE LIKED...
"BUT THERE WAS THIS SOUND...
"COMING FROM THE CORNER, WHERE HARPER, BETTE, AND TIM WERE TUNING INTO THE PIRATE RADIO STATION WE WERE SUPPOSED TO MAKE CONTACT WITH TONIGHT...
"BUT INSTEAD OF A SONG OR A SECRET BROADCAST, THERE WAS...
"THERE WAS THE MOST BEAUTIFUL SOUND I'D EVER HEARD..."
IT WAS LIKE... HONEY...
LIKE SUGAR.
LIQUID SMOKE...
CARDAMOM AND SUGAR.
LIKE THE SWIG OF BRANDY I STOLE LAST NEW YEAR'S EVE.
LIKE MY FIRST KISS.
"THE WARMEST, SWEETEST SOUND...
"I DON'T KNOW WHAT SHE SAID...
"...BUT I FELT SO...
HAPPY.

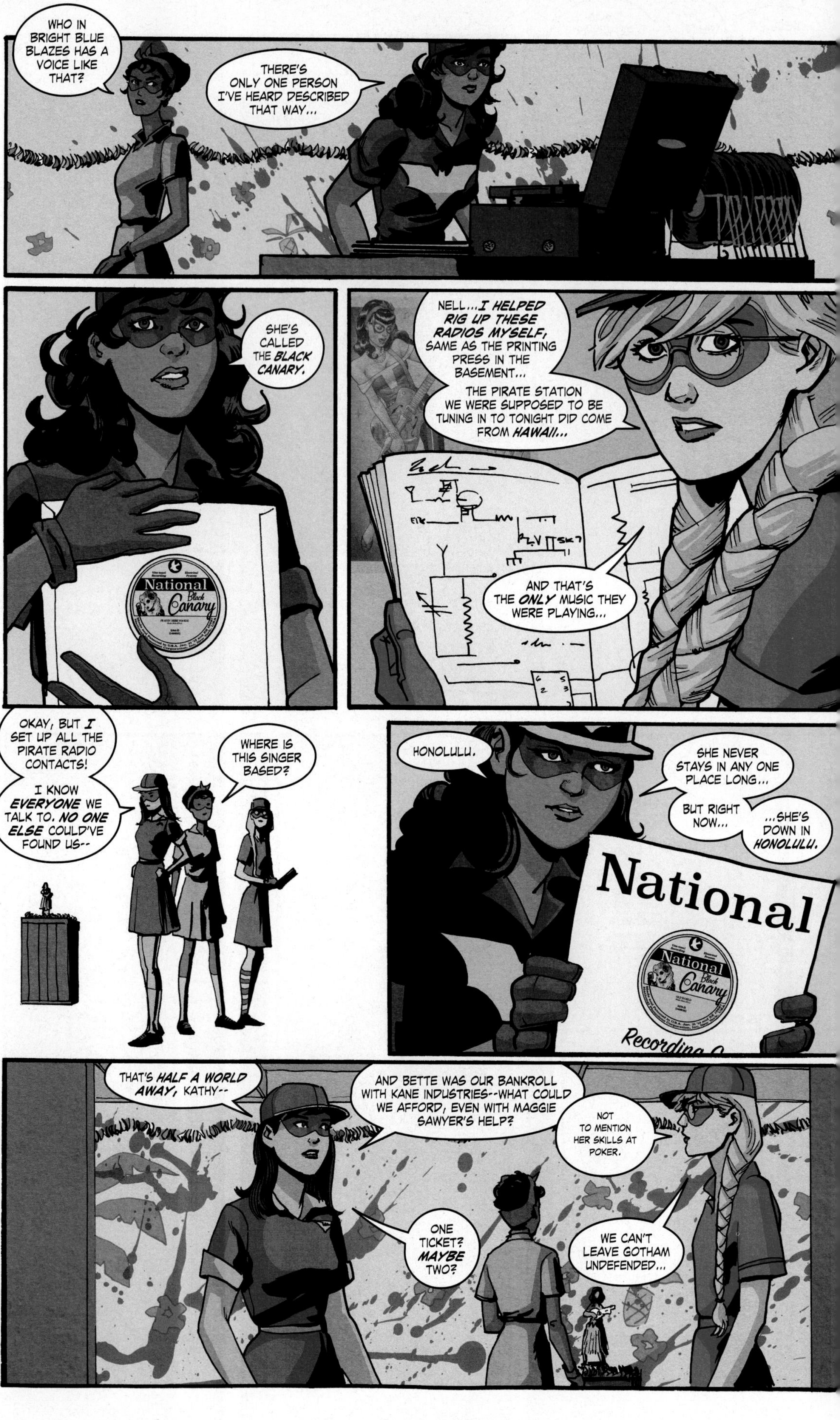
WHO IN BRIGHT BLUE BLAZES HAS A VOICE LIKE THAT?
THERE'S ONLY ONE PERSON I'VE HEARD DESCRIBED THAT WAY...
SHE'S CALLED THE BLACK CANARY.
National
Black Canary
NELL...I HELPED RIG UP THESE RADIOS MYSELF, SAME AS THE PRINTING PRESS IN THE BASEMENT...
THE PIRATE STATION WE WERE SUPPOSED TO BE TUNING IN TO TONIGHT DID COME FROM HAWAII...
AND THAT'S THE ONLY MUSIC THEY WERE PLAYING...
OKAY, BUT I SET UP ALL THE PIRATE RADIO CONTACTS!
I KNOW EVERYONE WE TALK TO. NO ONE ELSE COULD'VE FOUND US--
WHERE IS THIS SINGER BASED?
HONOLULU.
SHE NEVER STAYS IN ANY ONE PLACE LONG...
BUT RIGHT NOW...
...SHE'S DOWN IN HONOLULU.
National
THAT'S HALF A WORLD AWAY, KATHY--
AND BETTE WAS OUR BANKROLL WITH KANE INDUSTRIES--WHAT COULD WE AFFORD, EVEN WITH MAGGIE SAWYER'S HELP?
NOT TO MENTION HER SKILLS AT POKER.
ONE TICKET? MAYBE TWO?
WE CAN'T LEAVE GOTHAM UNDEFENDED...

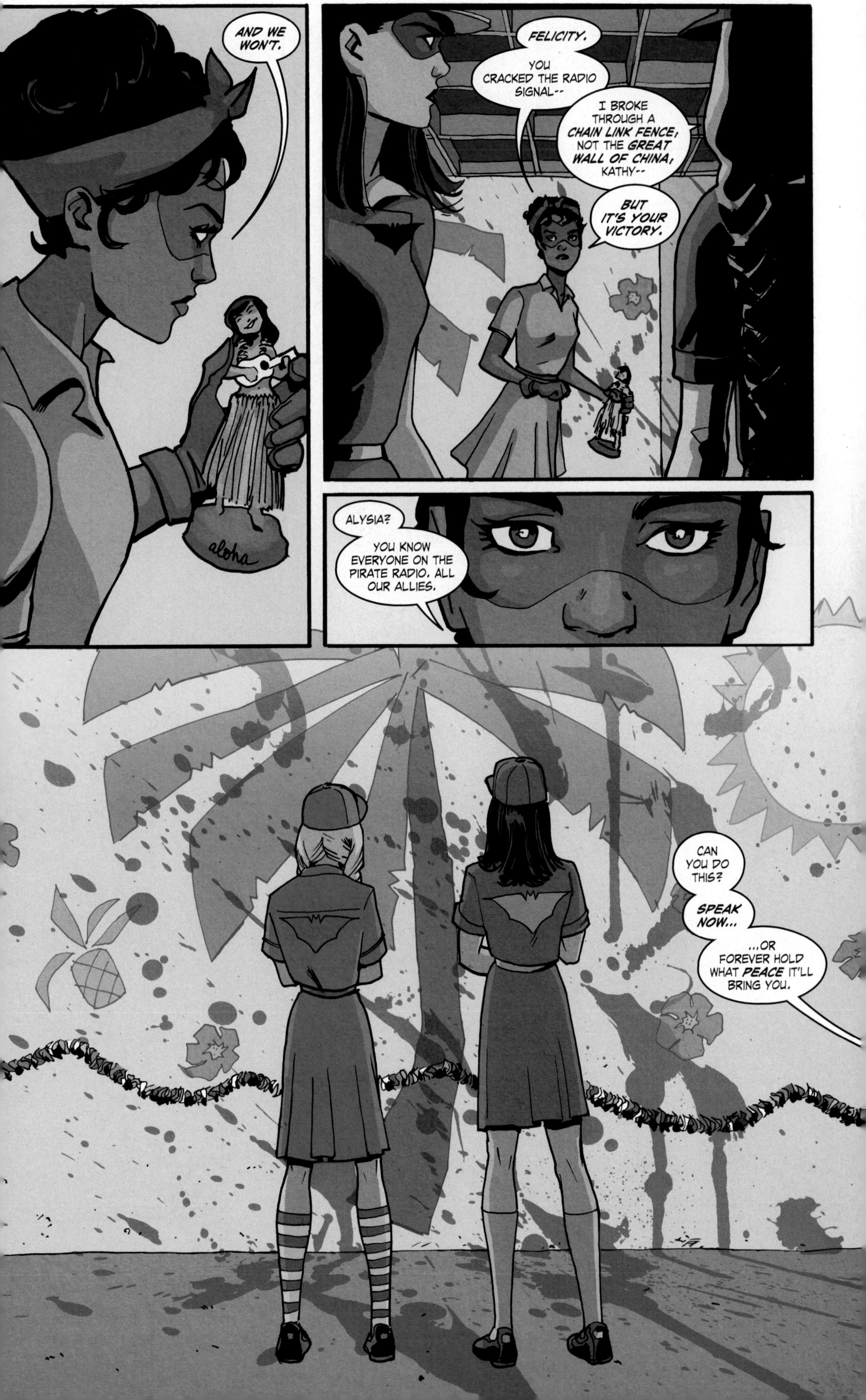
AND WE WON'T.
FELICITY.
YOU CRACKED THE RADIO SIGNAL--
I BROKE THROUGH A CHAIN LINK FENCE, NOT THE GREAT WALL OF CHINA, KATHY--
BUT IT'S YOUR VICTORY.
aloha
ALYSIA?
YOU KNOW EVERYONE ON THE PIRATE RADIO. ALL OUR ALLIES.
CAN YOU DO THIS?
SPEAK NOW...
...OR FOREVER HOLD WHAT PEACE IT'LL BRING YOU.

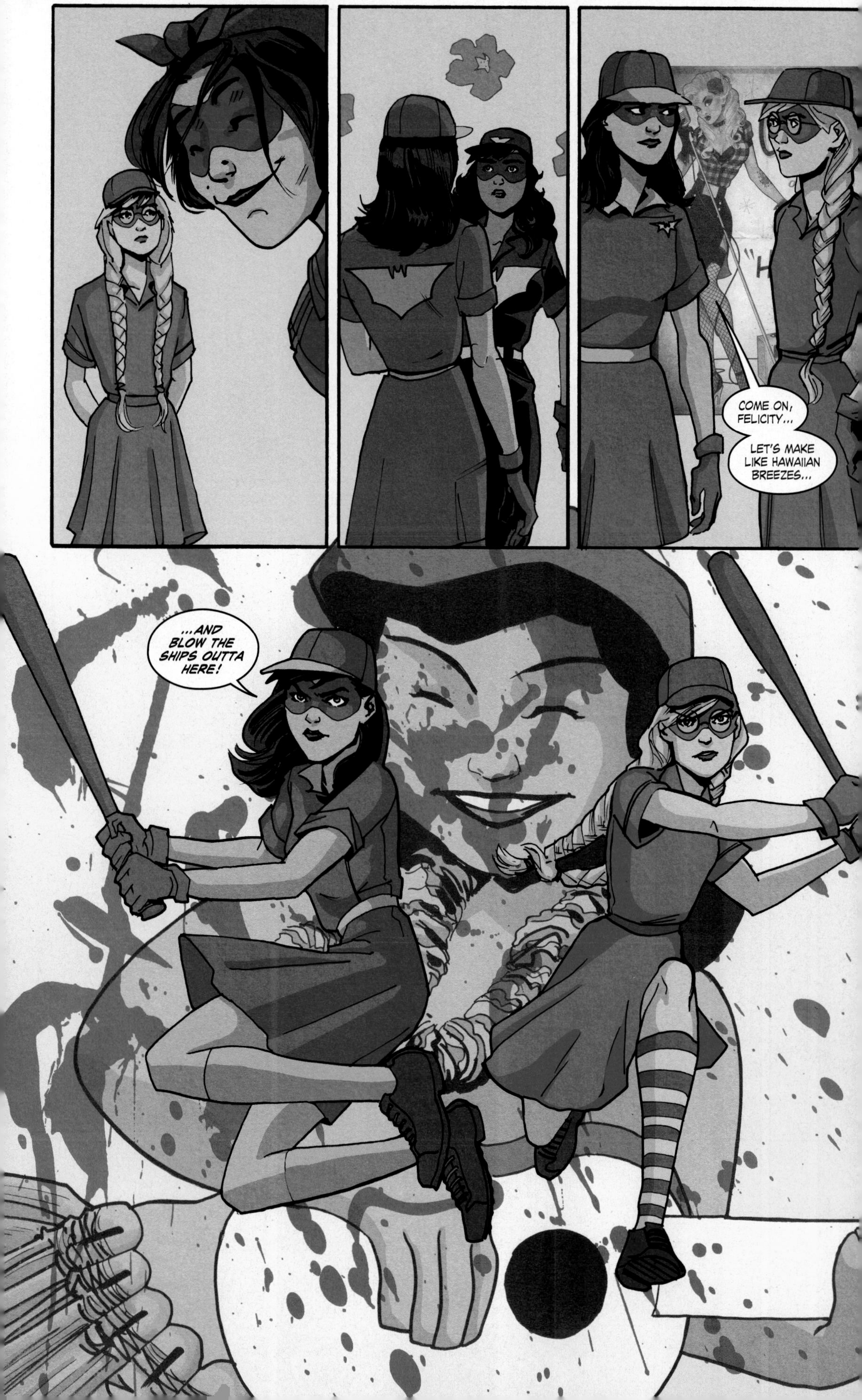
COME ON, FELICITY...
LET'S MAKE LIKE HAWAIIAN BREEZES...
...AND BLOW THE SHIPS OUTTA HERE!

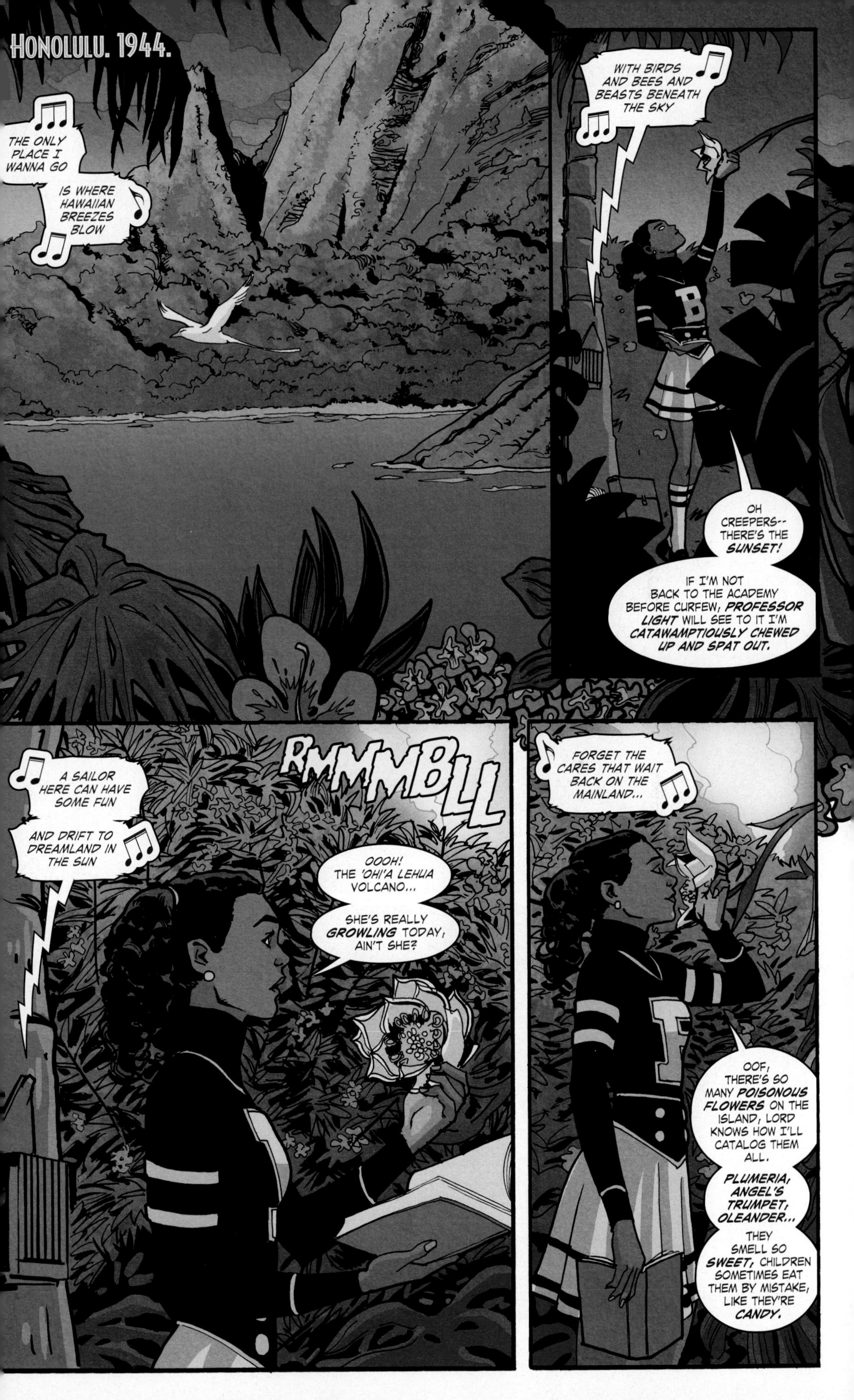
HONOLULU. 1944.
THE ONLY PLACE I WANNA GO
IS WHERE HAWAIIAN BREEZES BLOW
WITH BIRDS AND BEES AND BEASTS BENEATH THE SKY
OH CREEPERS-- THERE'S THE SUNSET!
IF I'M NOT BACK TO THE ACADEMY BEFORE CURFEW, PROFESSOR LIGHT WILL SEE TO IT I'M CATAWAMPTIOUSLY CHEWED UP AND SPAT OUT.
A SAILOR HERE CAN HAVE SOME FUN
AND DRIFT TO DREAMLAND IN THE SUN
RMMMBLL
OOOH! THE 'OHI'A LEHUA VOLCANO...
SHE'S REALLY GROWLING TODAY, AIN'T SHE?
FORGET THE CARES THAT WAIT BACK ON THE MAINLAND...
OOF, THERE'S SO MANY POISONOUS FLOWERS ON THE ISLAND, LORD KNOWS HOW I'LL CATALOG THEM ALL.
PLUMERIA, ANGEL'S TRUMPET, OLEANDER...
THEY SMELL SO SWEET, CHILDREN SOMETIMES EAT THEM BY MISTAKE, LIKE THEY'RE CANDY.

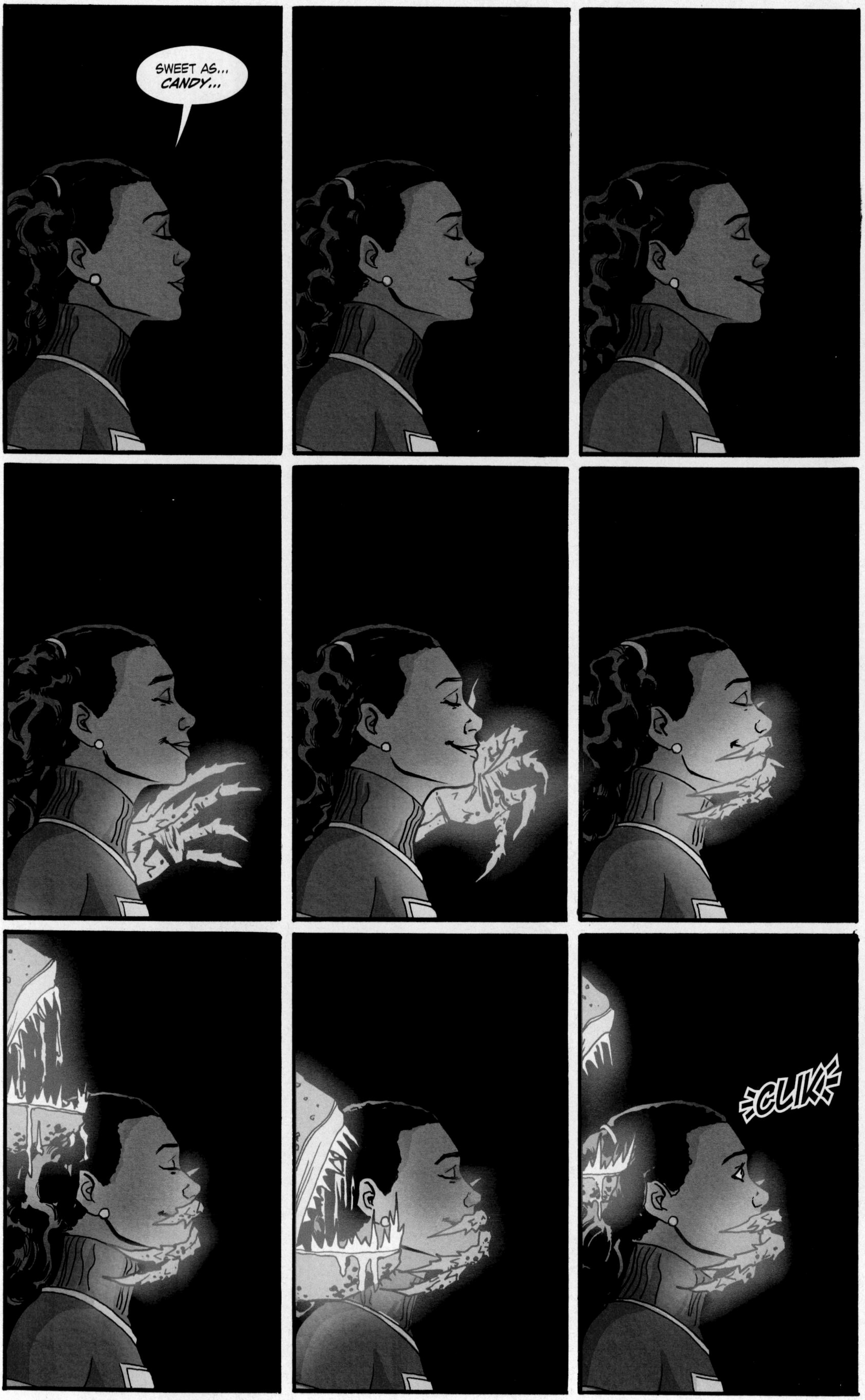
SWEET AS...
CANDY...
CLIK

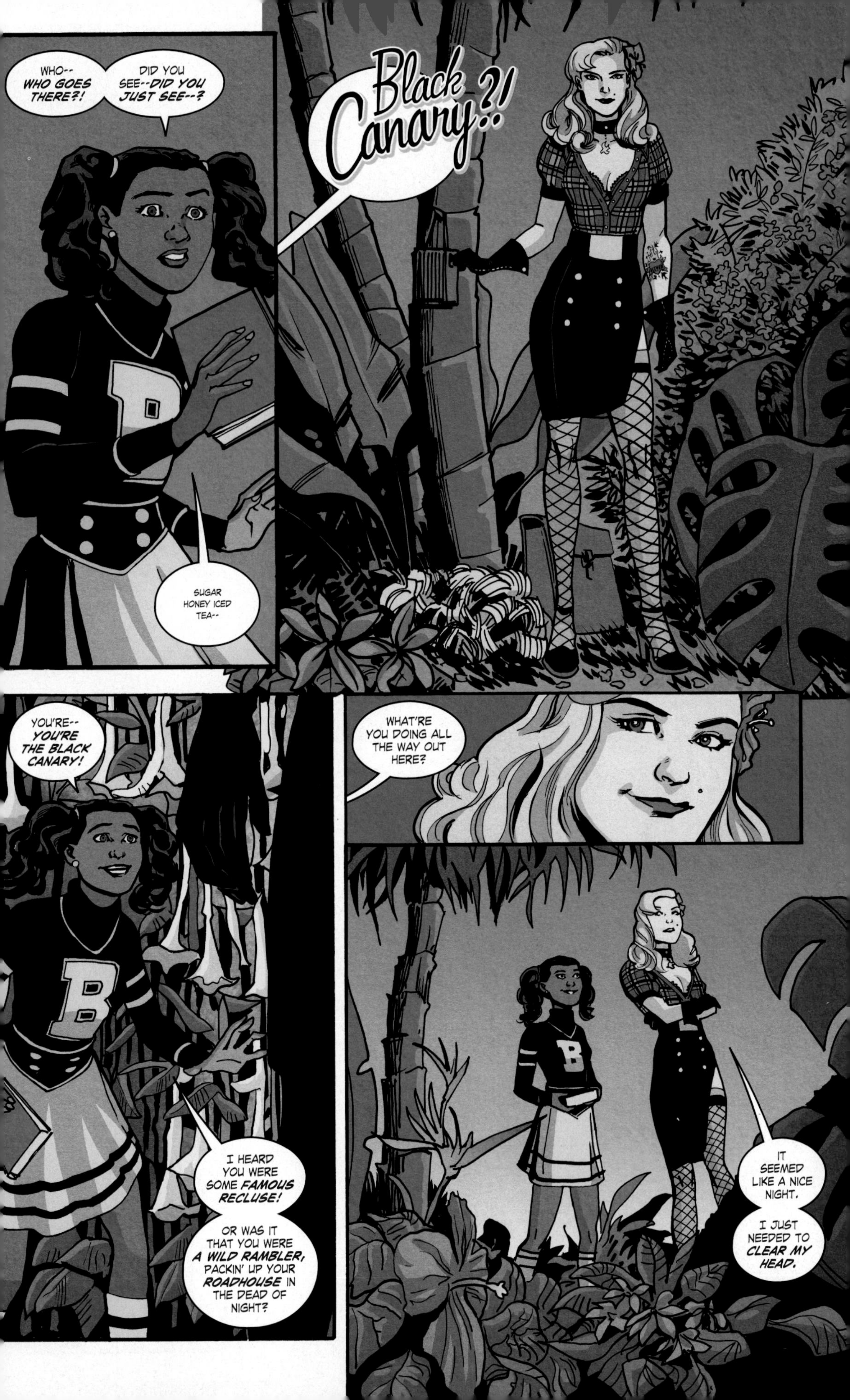
WHO-- WHO GOES THERE?!
DID YOU SEE--DID YOU JUST SEE--?
Black Canary?!
SUGAR HONEY ICED TEA--
YOU'RE-- YOU'RE THE BLACK CANARY!
I HEARD YOU WERE SOME FAMOUS RECLUSE!
OR WAS IT THAT YOU WERE A WILD RAMBLER, PACKIN' UP YOUR ROADHOUSE IN THE DEAD OF NIGHT?
WHAT'RE YOU DOING ALL THE WAY OUT HERE?
IT SEEMED LIKE A NICE NIGHT.
I JUST NEEDED TO CLEAR MY HEAD.

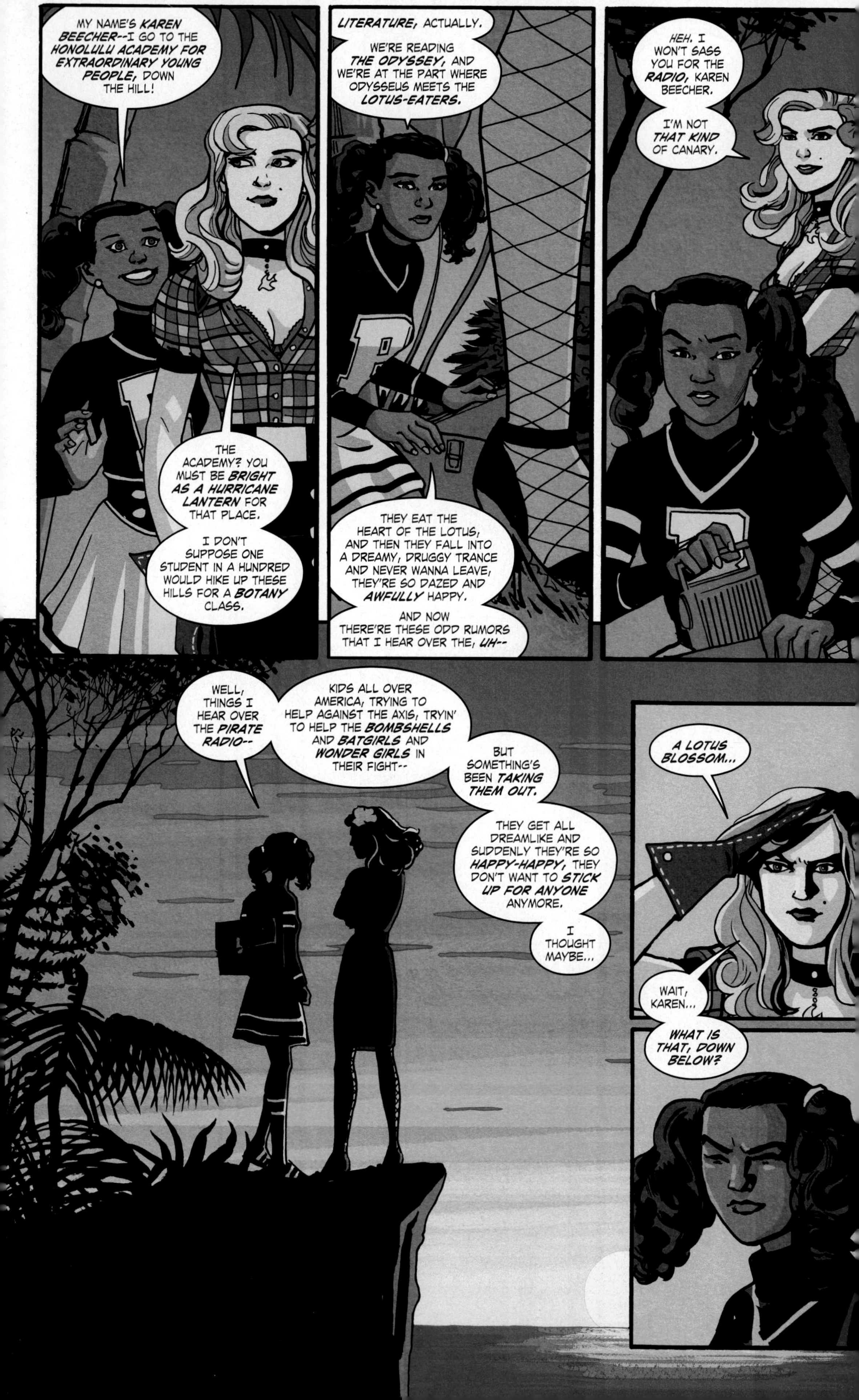
MY NAME'S KAREN BEECHER--I GO TO THE HONOLULU ACADEMY FOR EXTRAORDINARY YOUNG PEOPLE, DOWN THE HILL!
THE ACADEMY? YOU MUST BE BRIGHT AS A HURRICANE LANTERN FOR THAT PLACE.
I DON'T SUPPOSE ONE STUDENT IN A HUNDRED WOULD HIKE UP THESE HILLS FOR A BOTANY CLASS.
LITERATURE, ACTUALLY.
WE'RE READING THE ODYSSEY, AND WE'RE AT THE PART WHERE ODYSSEUS MEETS THE LOTUS-EATERS.
THEY EAT THE HEART OF THE LOTUS, AND THEN THEY FALL INTO A DREAMY, DRUGGY TRANCE AND NEVER WANNA LEAVE, THEY'RE SO DAZED AND AWFULLY HAPPY.
AND NOW THERE'RE THESE ODD RUMORS THAT I HEAR OVER THE, UH--
HEH. I WON'T SASS YOU FOR THE RADIO, KAREN BEECHER.
I'M NOT THAT KIND OF CANARY.
WELL, THINGS I HEAR OVER THE PIRATE RADIO--
KIDS ALL OVER AMERICA, TRYING TO HELP AGAINST THE AXIS, TRYIN' TO HELP THE BOMBSHELLS AND BATGIRLS AND WONDER GIRLS IN THEIR FIGHT--
BUT SOMETHING'S BEEN TAKING THEM OUT.
THEY GET ALL DREAMLIKE AND SUDDENLY THEY'RE SO HAPPY-HAPPY, THEY DON'T WANT TO STICK UP FOR ANYONE ANYMORE.
I THOUGHT MAYBE...
A LOTUS BLOSSOM...
WAIT, KAREN...
WHAT IS THAT, DOWN BELOW?

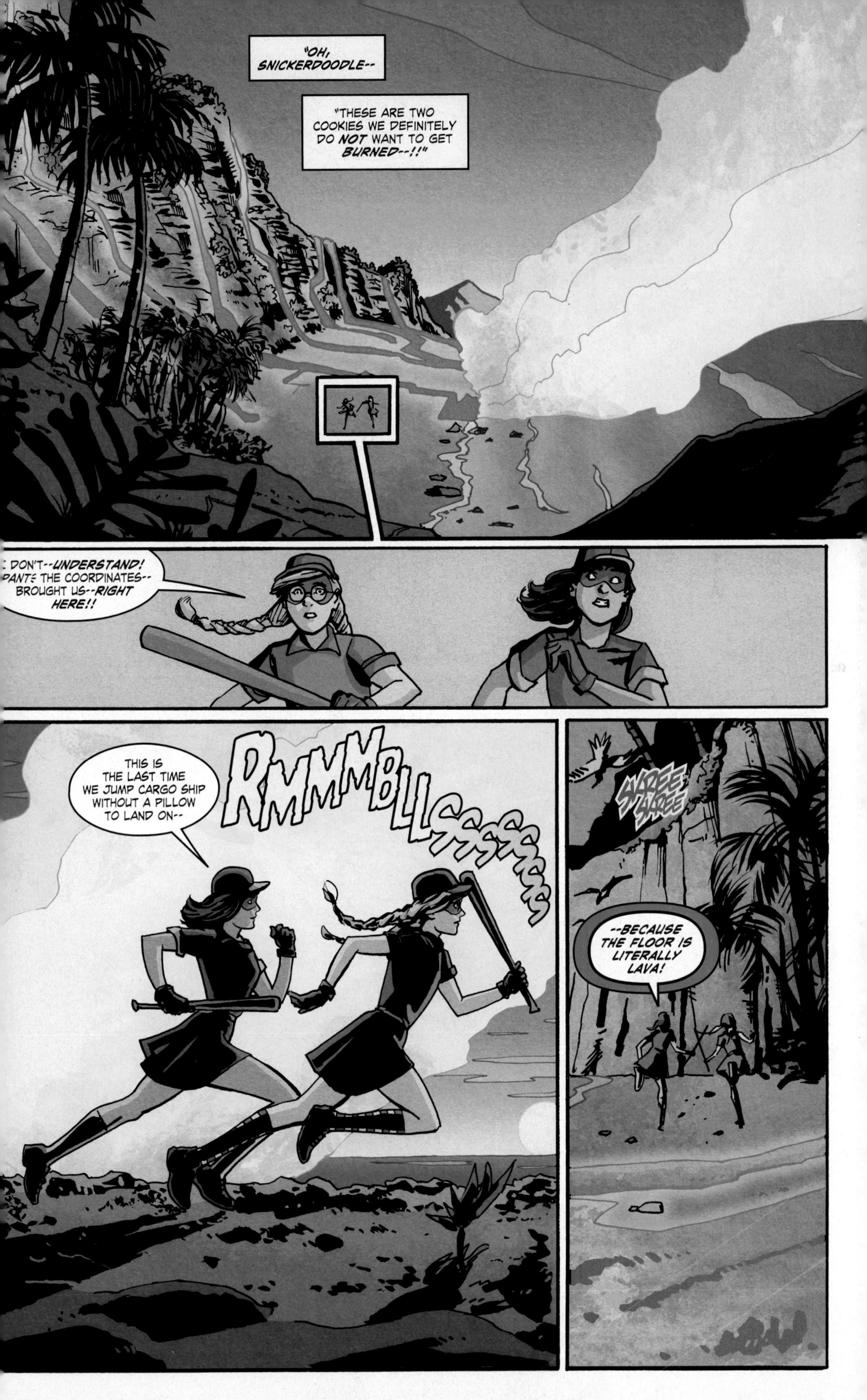
"OH, SNICKERDOODLE--
"THESE ARE TWO COOKIES WE DEFINITELY DO NOT WANT TO GET BURNED--!!"
DON'T--UNDERSTAND! PANT THE COORDINATES-- BROUGHT US--RIGHT HERE!!
THIS IS THE LAST TIME WE JUMP CARGO SHIP WITHOUT A PILLOW TO LAND ON--
SKREE SKREE
--BECAUSE THE FLOOR IS LITERALLY LAVA!

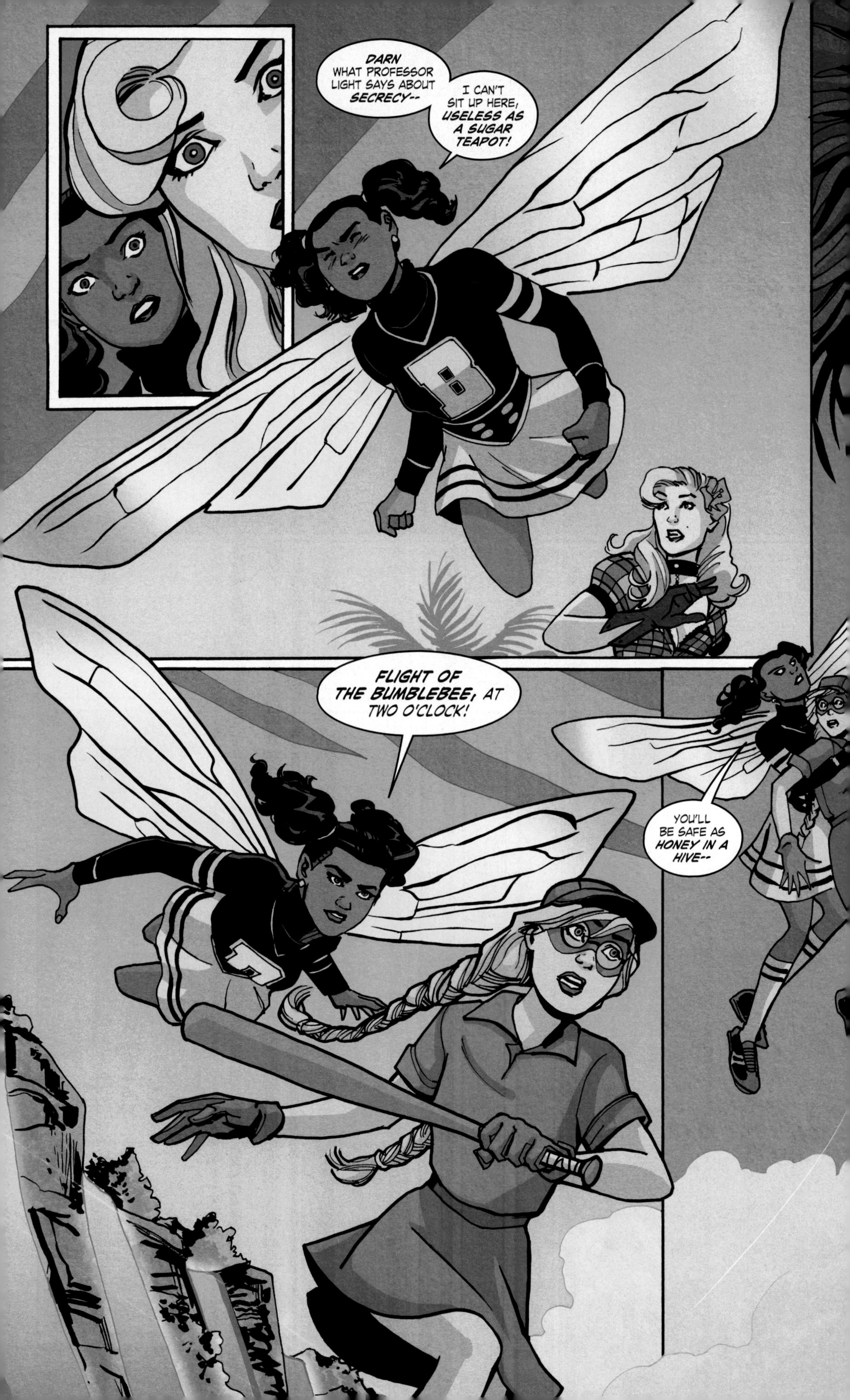
DARN WHAT PROFESSOR LIGHT SAYS ABOUT SECRECY--
I CAN'T SIT UP HERE, USELESS AS A SUGAR TEAPOT!
FLIGHT OF THE BUMBLEBEE, AT TWO O'CLOCK!
YOU'LL BE SAFE AS HONEY IN A HIVE--

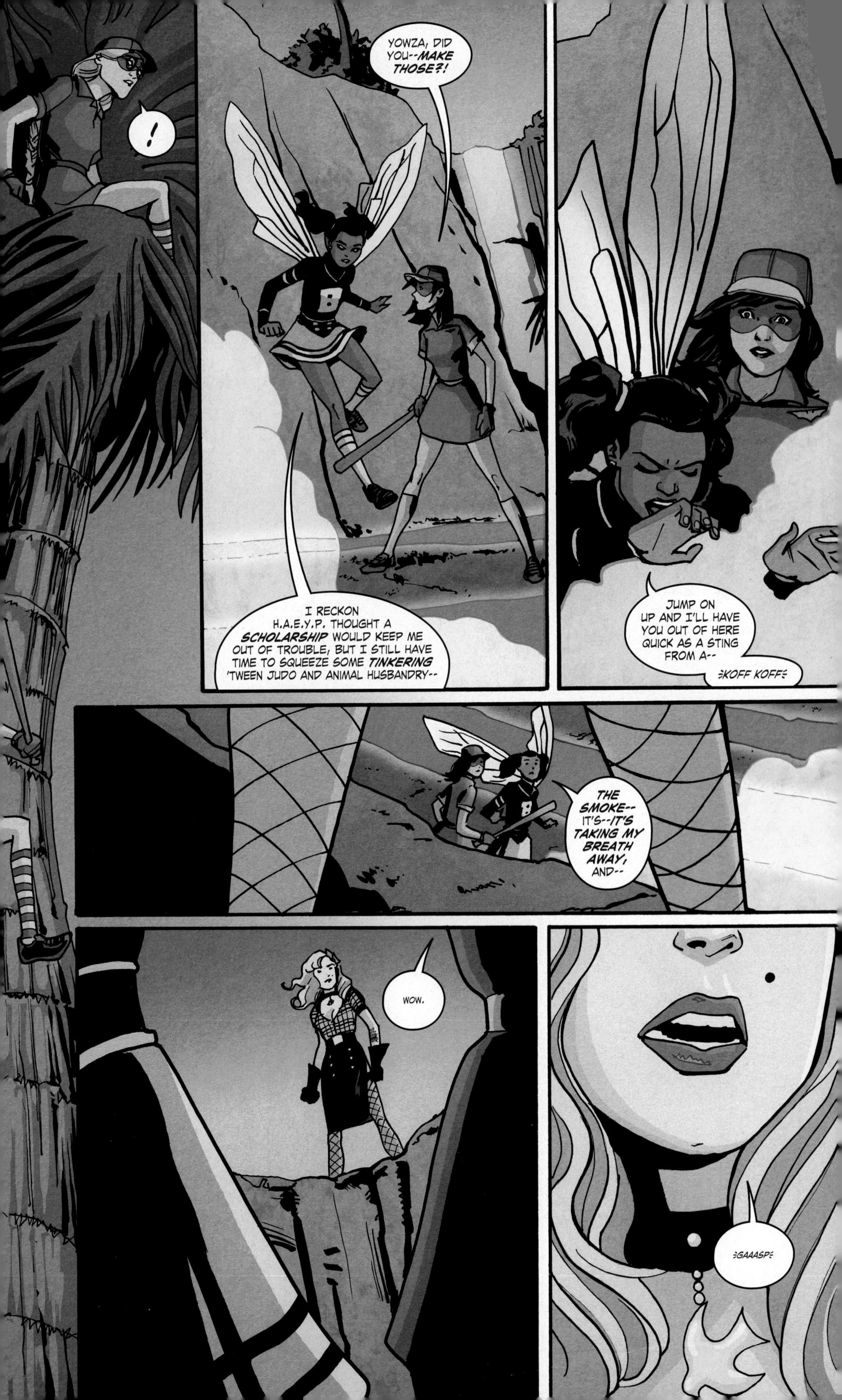
!
YOWZA, DID YOU--MAKE THOSE?!
I RECKON H.A.E.Y.P. THOUGHT A SCHOLARSHIP WOULD KEEP ME OUT OF TROUBLE, BUT I STILL HAVE TIME TO SQUEEZE SOME TINKERING 'TWEEN JUDO AND ANIMAL HUSBANDRY--
JUMP ON UP AND I'LL HAVE YOU OUT OF HERE QUICK AS A STING FROM A--
KOFF KOFF
THE SMOKE-- IT'S--IT'S TAKING MY BREATH AWAY, AND--
WOW.
GAAASP

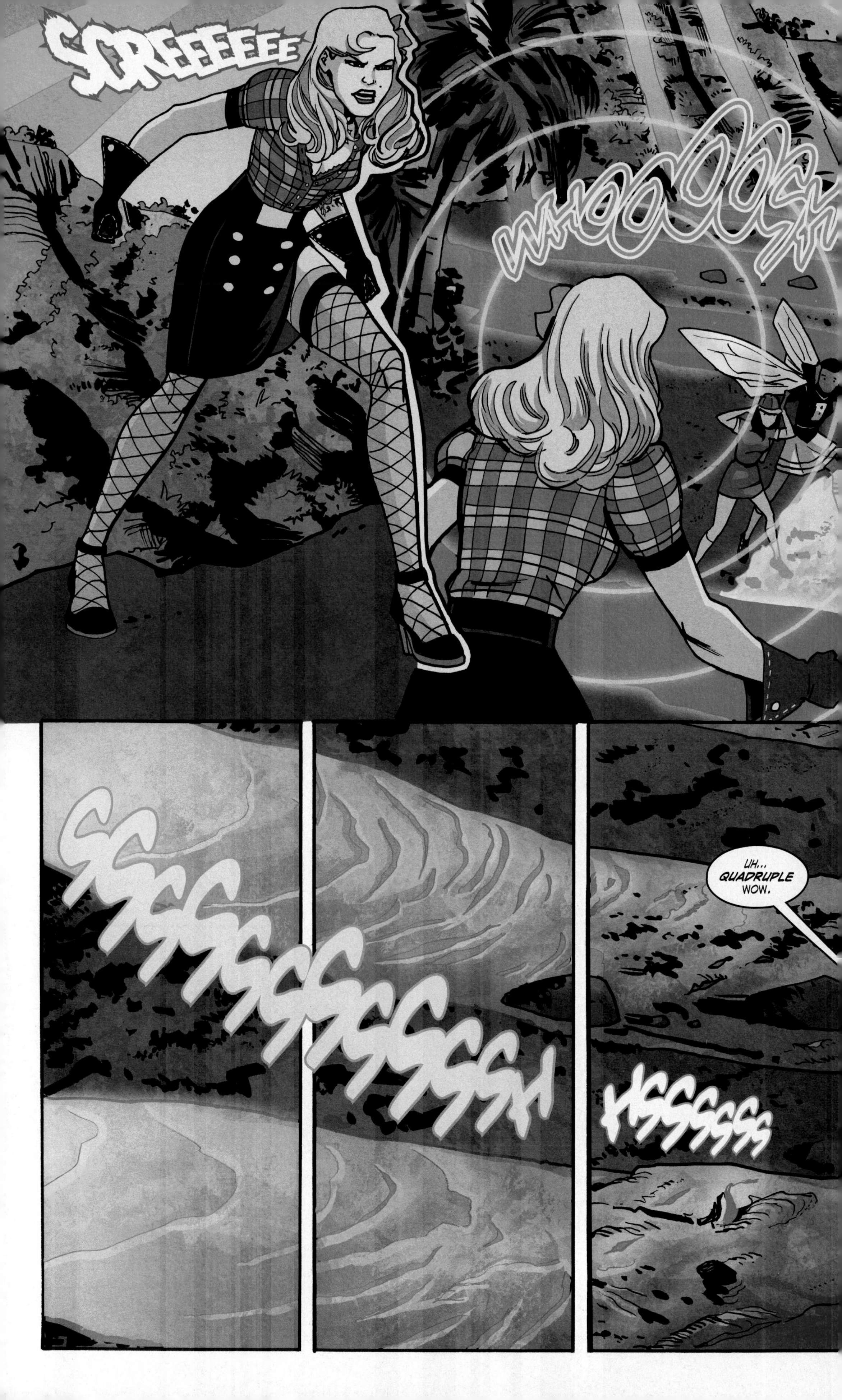
SCREEEEEEE
WHOOOOOOM
SSSSSSSSSSSH
UH... QUADRUPLE WOW.
HSSSSSS

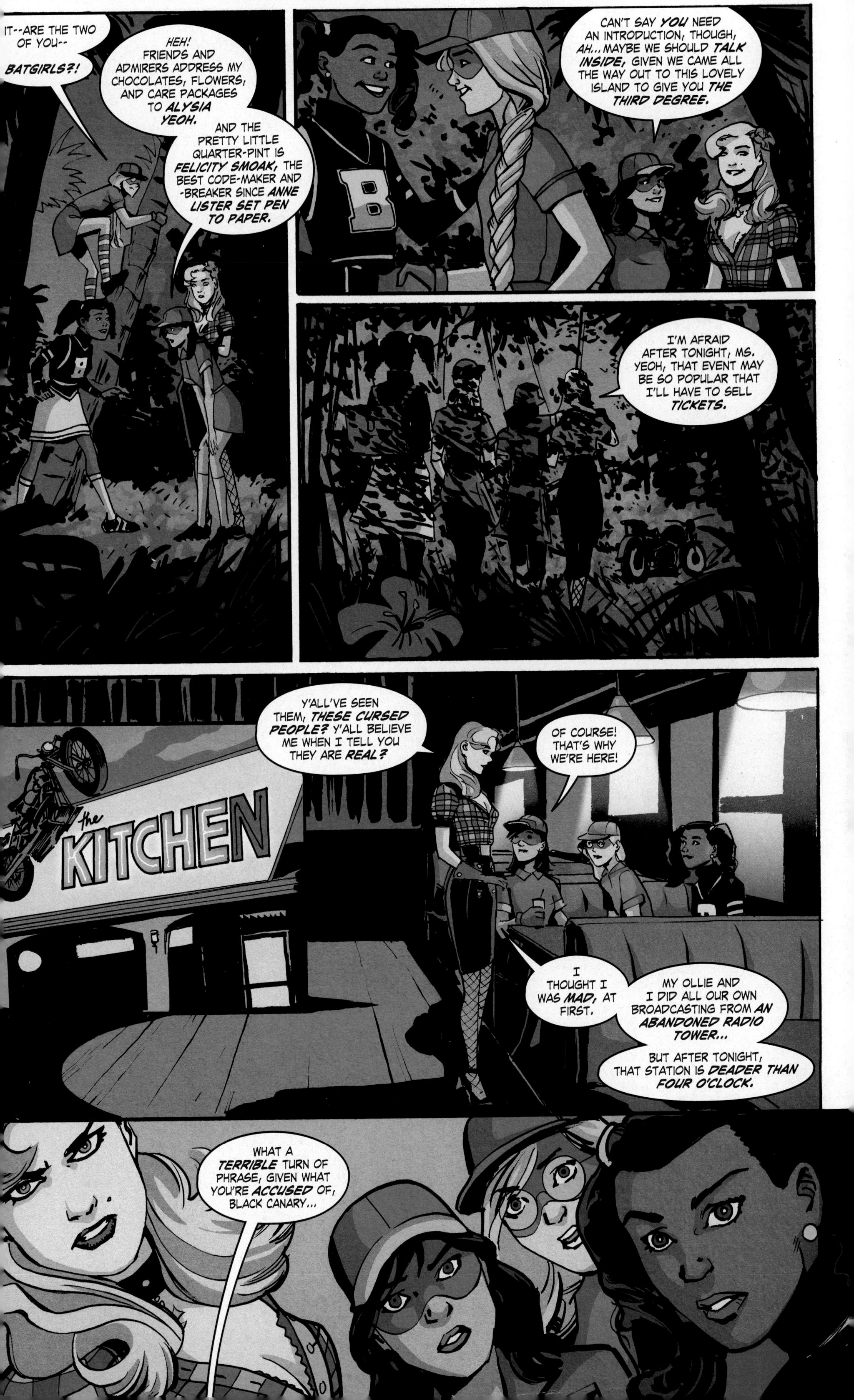
IT--ARE THE TWO OF YOU-- BATGIRLS?!
HEH! FRIENDS AND ADMIRERS ADDRESS MY CHOCOLATES, FLOWERS, AND CARE PACKAGES TO ALYSIA YEOH.
AND THE PRETTY LITTLE QUARTER-PINT IS FELICITY SMOAK, THE BEST CODE-MAKER AND -BREAKER SINCE ANNE LISTER SET PEN TO PAPER.
CAN'T SAY YOU NEED AN INTRODUCTION, THOUGH, AH... MAYBE WE SHOULD TALK INSIDE, GIVEN WE CAME ALL THE WAY OUT TO THIS LOVELY ISLAND TO GIVE YOU THE THIRD DEGREE.
I'M AFRAID AFTER TONIGHT, MS. YEOH, THAT EVENT MAY BE SO POPULAR THAT I'LL HAVE TO SELL TICKETS.
the KITCHEN
Y'ALL'VE SEEN THEM, THESE CURSED PEOPLE? Y'ALL BELIEVE ME WHEN I TELL YOU THEY ARE REAL?
OF COURSE! THAT'S WHY WE'RE HERE!
I THOUGHT I WAS MAD, AT FIRST.
MY OLLIE AND I DID ALL OUR OWN BROADCASTING FROM AN ABANDONED RADIO TOWER...
BUT AFTER TONIGHT, THAT STATION IS DEADER THAN FOUR O'CLOCK.
WHAT A TERRIBLE TURN OF PHRASE, GIVEN WHAT YOU'RE ACCUSED OF, BLACK CANARY...

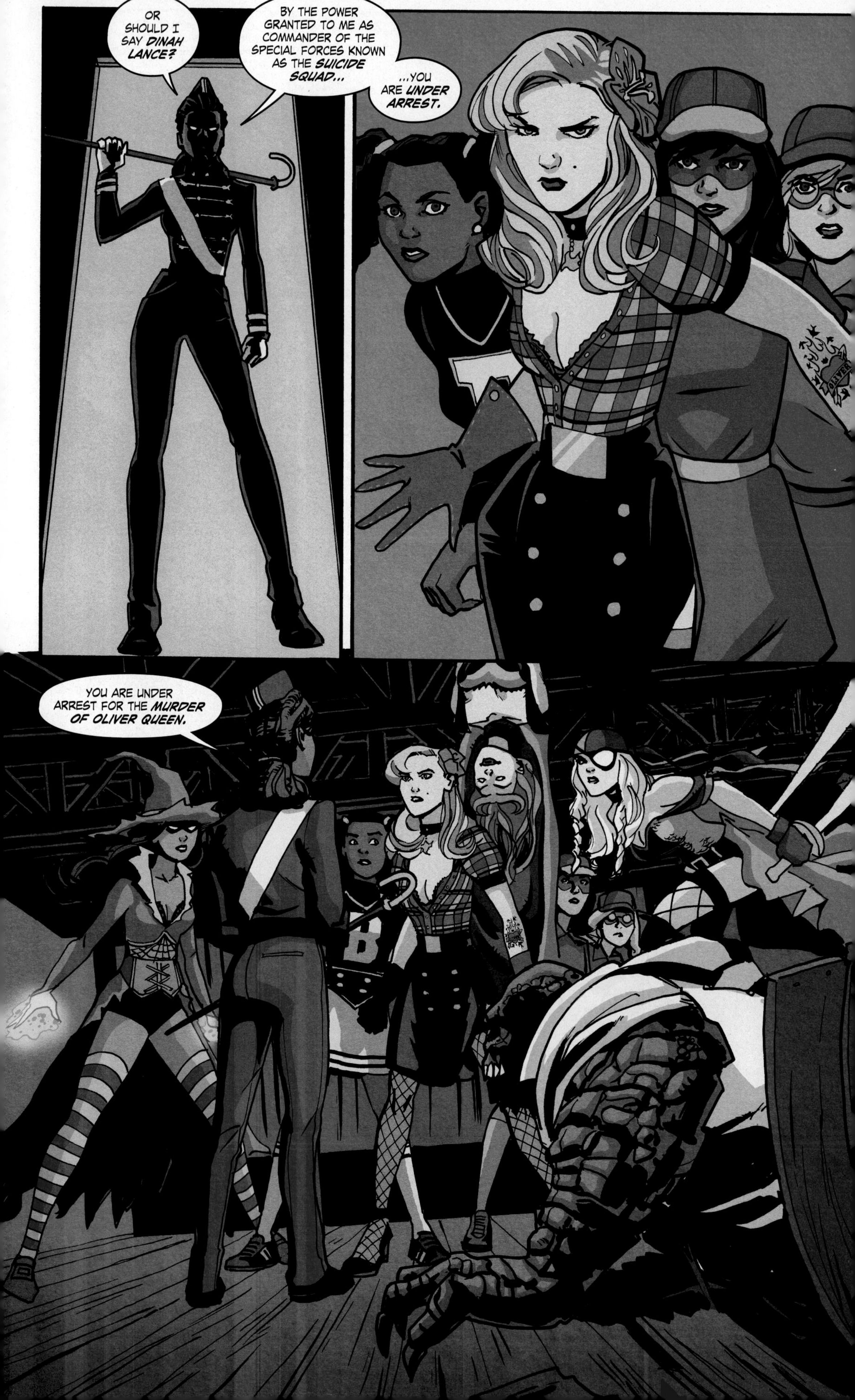
OR SHOULD I SAY DINAH LANCE?
BY THE POWER GRANTED TO ME AS COMMANDER OF THE SPECIAL FORCES KNOWN AS THE SUICIDE SQUAD...
...YOU ARE UNDER ARREST.
OLIVER
YOU ARE UNDER ARREST FOR THE MURDER OF OLIVER QUEEN.
B

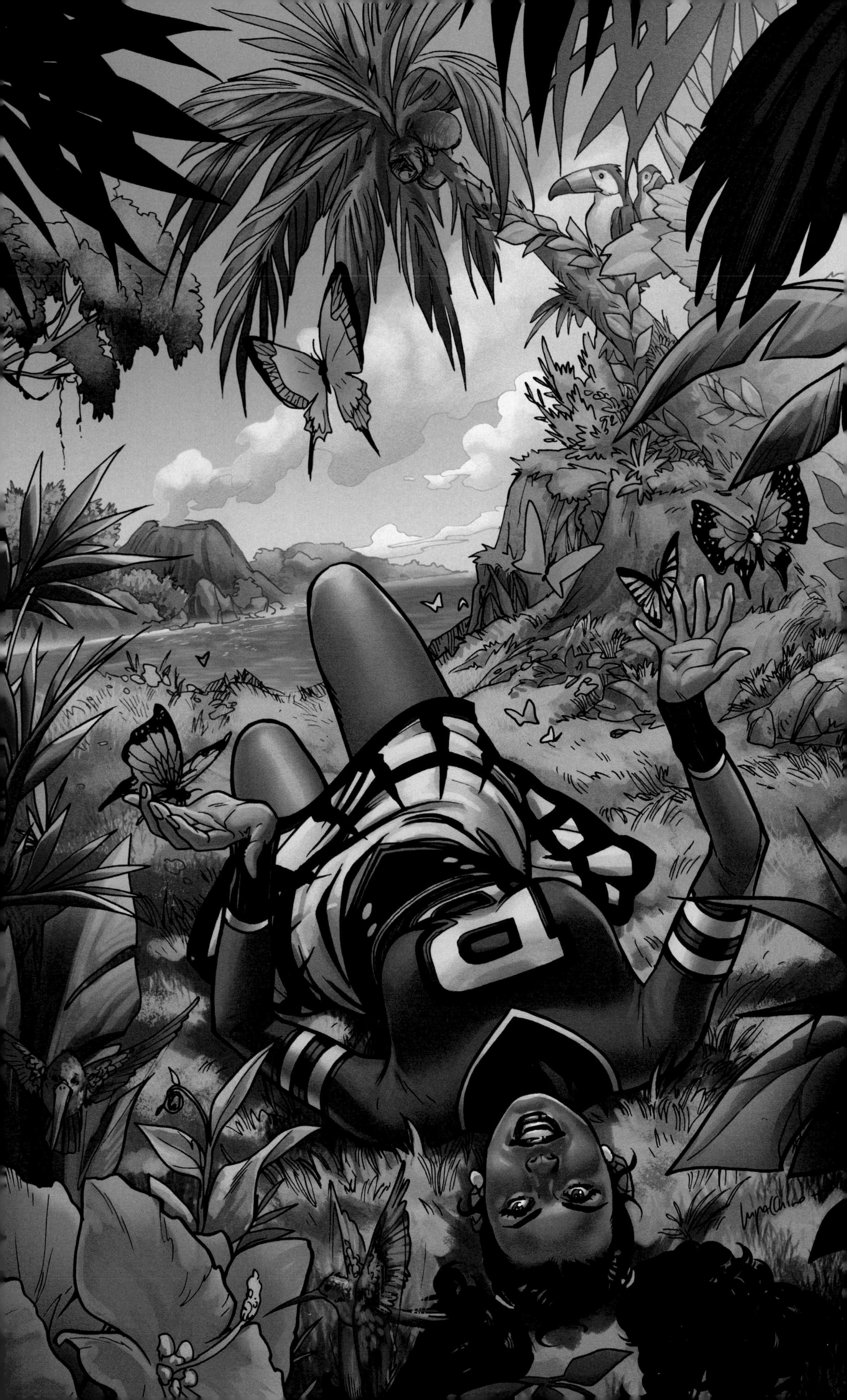

THE BLACK ISLAND

PARTS THREE and FOUR

Written by
MARGUERITE BENNETT

Art by
DAVID HAHN

Colors by
J. NANJAN

Letters by
WES ABBOTT

Cover by
EMANUELA LUPACCHINO *and*
LAURA MARTIN

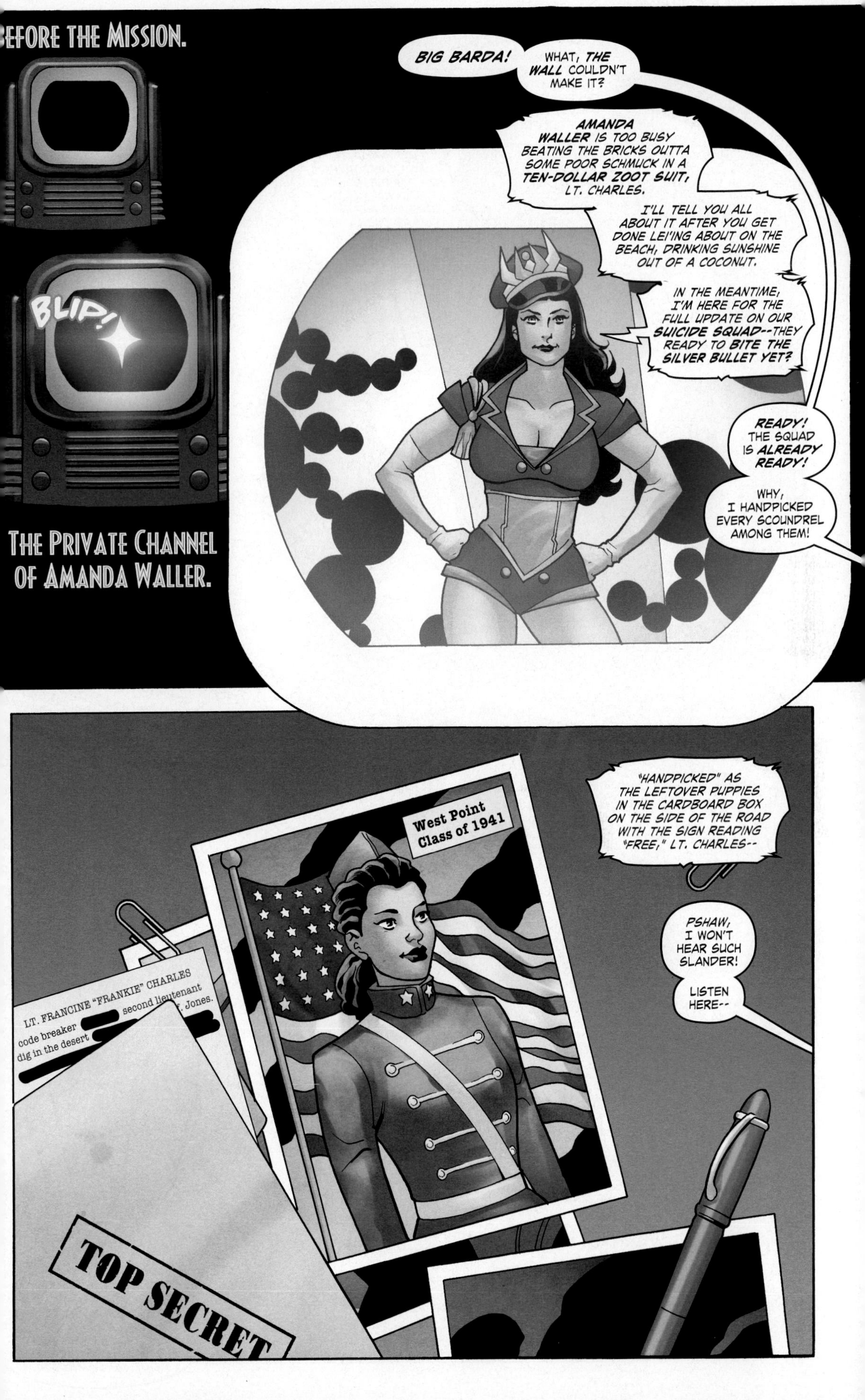

BEFORE THE MISSION.
BLIP!
THE PRIVATE CHANNEL OF AMANDA WALLER.
BIG BARDA!
WHAT, THE WALL COULDN'T MAKE IT?
AMANDA WALLER IS TOO BUSY BEATING THE BRICKS OUTTA SOME POOR SCHMUCK IN A TEN-DOLLAR ZOOT SUIT, LT. CHARLES.
I'LL TELL YOU ALL ABOUT IT AFTER YOU GET DONE LEI'ING ABOUT ON THE BEACH, DRINKING SUNSHINE OUT OF A COCONUT.
IN THE MEANTIME, I'M HERE FOR THE FULL UPDATE ON OUR SUICIDE SQUAD--THEY READY TO BITE THE SILVER BULLET YET?
READY! THE SQUAD IS ALREADY READY!
WHY, I HANDPICKED EVERY SCOUNDREL AMONG THEM!
"HANDPICKED" AS THE LEFTOVER PUPPIES IN THE CARDBOARD BOX ON THE SIDE OF THE ROAD WITH THE SIGN READING "FREE," LT. CHARLES--
West Point Class of 1941
PSHAW, I WON'T HEAR SUCH SLANDER!
LISTEN HERE--
LT. FRANCINE "FRANKIE" CHARLES
[redacted] second lieutenant
code breaker
dig in the desert [redacted] r. Jones.
[redacted]
TOP SECRET

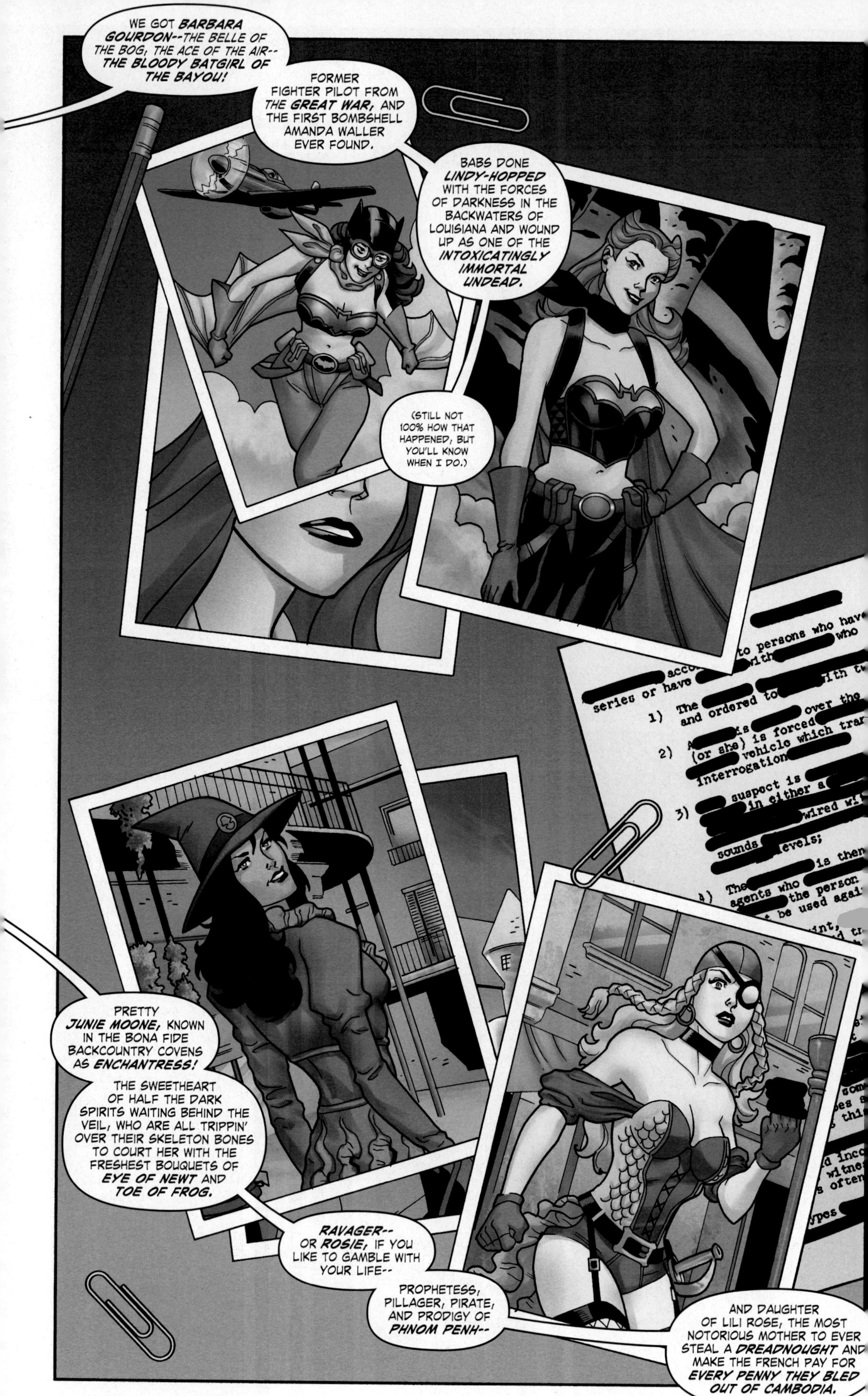

WE GOT BARBARA GOURDON--THE BELLE OF THE BOG, THE ACE OF THE AIR--THE BLOODY BATGIRL OF THE BAYOU!
FORMER FIGHTER PILOT FROM THE GREAT WAR, AND THE FIRST BOMBSHELL AMANDA WALLER EVER FOUND.
BABS DONE LINDY-HOPPED WITH THE FORCES OF DARKNESS IN THE BACKWATERS OF LOUISIANA AND WOUND UP AS ONE OF THE INTOXICATINGLY IMMORTAL UNDEAD.
(STILL NOT 100% HOW THAT HAPPENED, BUT YOU'LL KNOW WHEN I DO.)
PRETTY JUNIE MOONE, KNOWN IN THE BONA FIDE BACKCOUNTRY COVENS AS ENCHANTRESS!
THE SWEETHEART OF HALF THE DARK SPIRITS WAITING BEHIND THE VEIL, WHO ARE ALL TRIPPIN' OVER THEIR SKELETON BONES TO COURT HER WITH THE FRESHEST BOUQUETS OF EYE OF NEWT AND TOE OF FROG.
RAVAGER--OR ROSIE, IF YOU LIKE TO GAMBLE WITH YOUR LIFE--
PROPHETESS, PILLAGER, PIRATE, AND PRODIGY OF PHNOM PENH--
AND DAUGHTER OF LILI ROSE, THE MOST NOTORIOUS MOTHER TO EVER STEAL A DREADNOUGHT AND MAKE THE FRENCH PAY FOR EVERY PENNY THEY BLED OUT OF CAMBODIA.

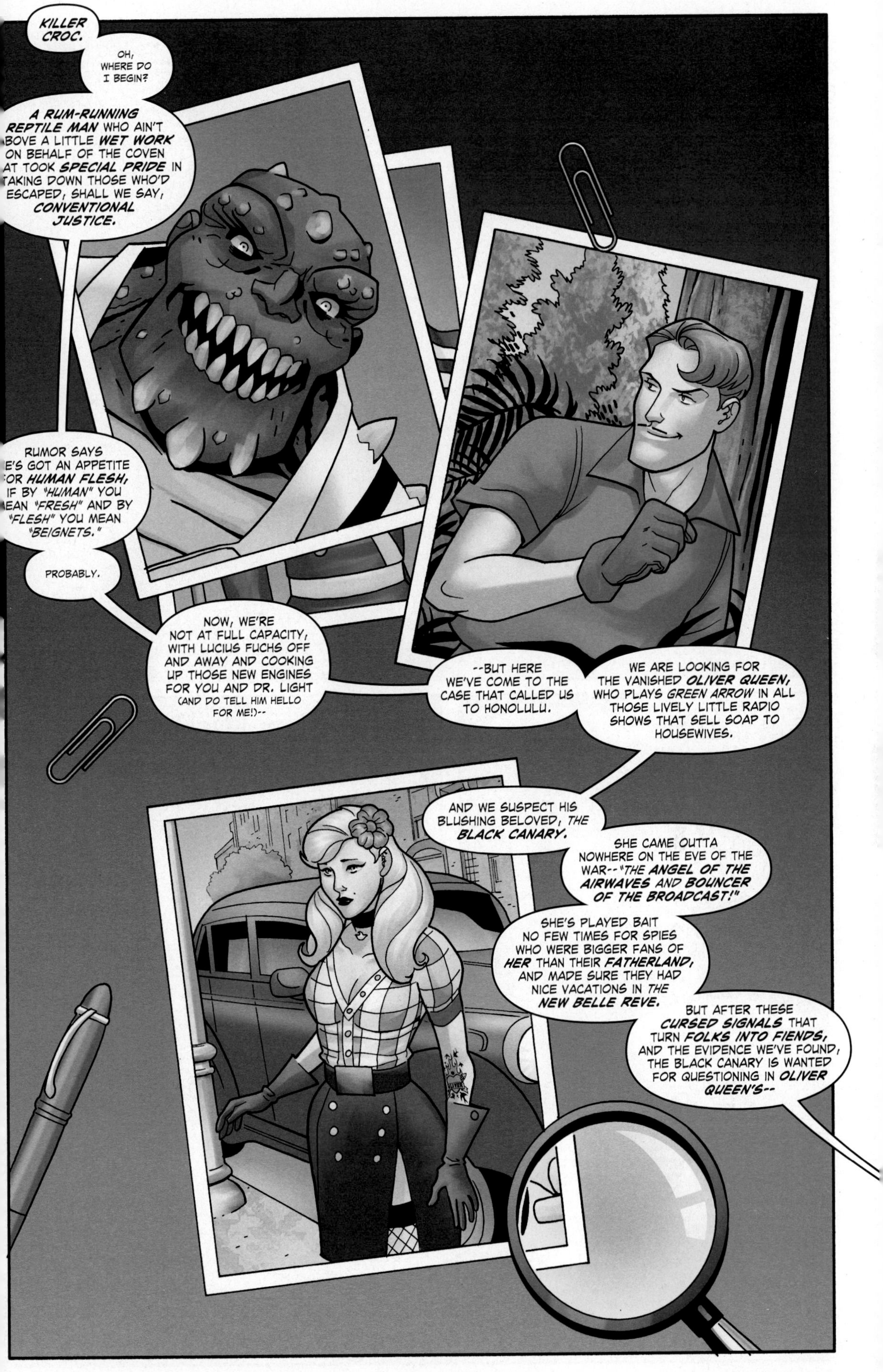

KILLER CROC.
OH, WHERE DO I BEGIN?
A RUM-RUNNING REPTILE MAN WHO AIN'T BOVE A LITTLE WET WORK ON BEHALF OF THE COVEN AT TOOK SPECIAL PRIDE IN TAKING DOWN THOSE WHO'D ESCAPED, SHALL WE SAY, CONVENTIONAL JUSTICE.
RUMOR SAYS E'S GOT AN APPETITE FOR HUMAN FLESH, IF BY "HUMAN" YOU EAN "FRESH" AND BY "FLESH" YOU MEAN "BEIGNETS."
PROBABLY.
NOW, WE'RE NOT AT FULL CAPACITY, WITH LUCIUS FUCHS OFF AND AWAY AND COOKING UP THOSE NEW ENGINES FOR YOU AND DR. LIGHT (AND DO TELL HIM HELLO FOR ME!)--
--BUT HERE WE'VE COME TO THE CASE THAT CALLED US TO HONOLULU.
WE ARE LOOKING FOR THE VANISHED OLIVER QUEEN, WHO PLAYS GREEN ARROW IN ALL THOSE LIVELY LITTLE RADIO SHOWS THAT SELL SOAP TO HOUSEWIVES.
AND WE SUSPECT HIS BLUSHING BELOVED, THE BLACK CANARY.
SHE CAME OUTTA NOWHERE ON THE EVE OF THE WAR--"THE ANGEL OF THE AIRWAVES AND BOUNCER OF THE BROADCAST!"
SHE'S PLAYED BAIT NO FEW TIMES FOR SPIES WHO WERE BIGGER FANS OF HER THAN THEIR FATHERLAND, AND MADE SURE THEY HAD NICE VACATIONS IN THE NEW BELLE REVE.
BUT AFTER THESE CURSED SIGNALS THAT TURN FOLKS INTO FIENDS, AND THE EVIDENCE WE'VE FOUND, THE BLACK CANARY IS WANTED FOR QUESTIONING IN OLIVER QUEEN'S--

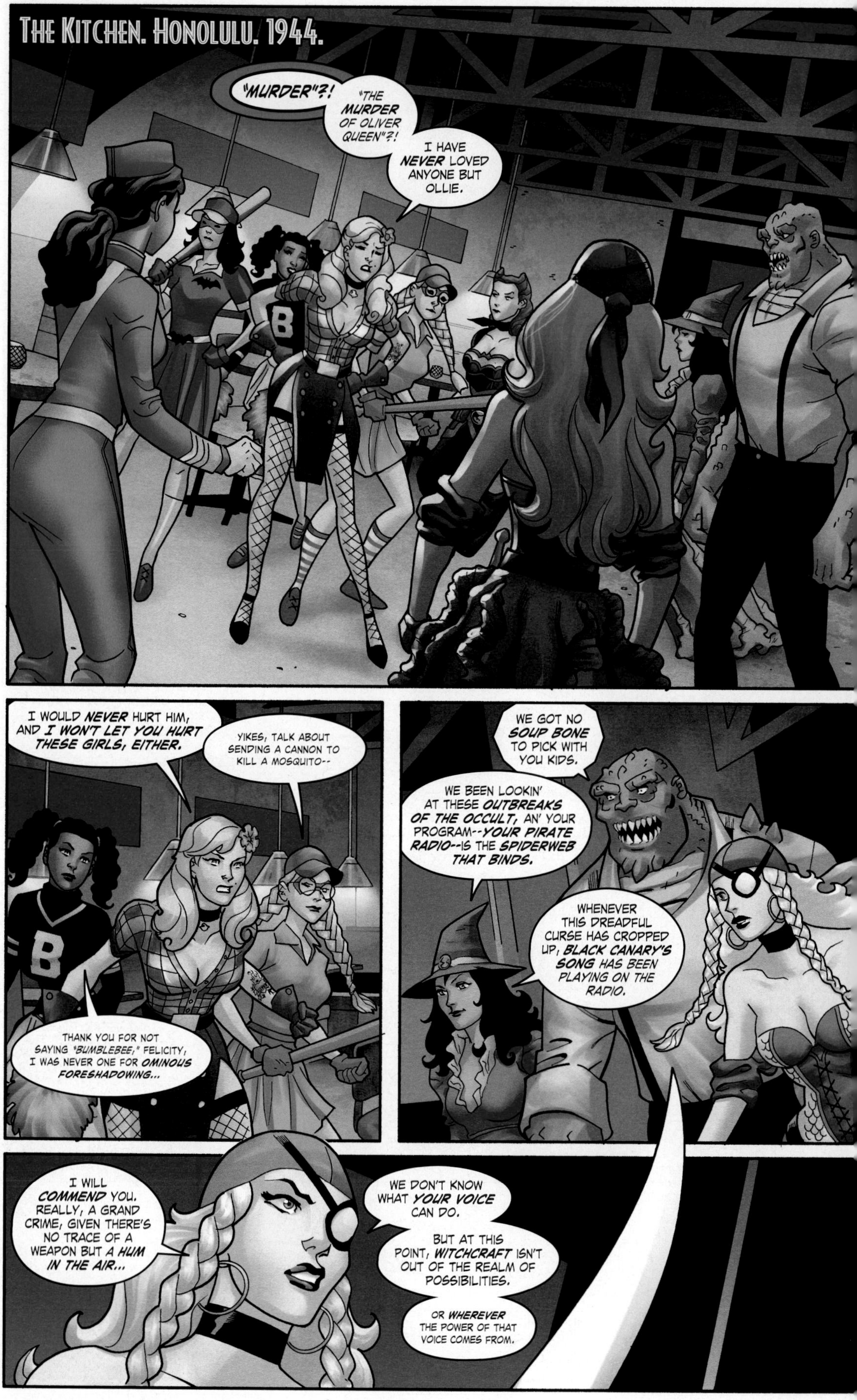

THE KITCHEN. HONOLULU. 1944.
"MURDER"?!
"THE MURDER OF OLIVER QUEEN"?!
I HAVE NEVER LOVED ANYONE BUT OLLIE.
I WOULD NEVER HURT HIM, AND I WON'T LET YOU HURT THESE GIRLS, EITHER.
YIKES, TALK ABOUT SENDING A CANNON TO KILL A MOSQUITO--
THANK YOU FOR NOT SAYING "BUMBLEBEE," FELICITY, I WAS NEVER ONE FOR OMINOUS FORESHADOWING...
WE GOT NO SOUP BONE TO PICK WITH YOU KIDS.
WE BEEN LOOKIN' AT THESE OUTBREAKS OF THE OCCULT, AN' YOUR PROGRAM--YOUR PIRATE RADIO--IS THE SPIDERWEB THAT BINDS.
WHENEVER THIS DREADFUL CURSE HAS CROPPED UP, BLACK CANARY'S SONG HAS BEEN PLAYING ON THE RADIO.
I WILL COMMEND YOU. REALLY, A GRAND CRIME, GIVEN THERE'S NO TRACE OF A WEAPON BUT A HUM IN THE AIR...
WE DON'T KNOW WHAT YOUR VOICE CAN DO.
BUT AT THIS POINT, WITCHCRAFT ISN'T OUT OF THE REALM OF POSSIBILITIES.
OR WHEREVER THE POWER OF THAT VOICE COMES FROM.

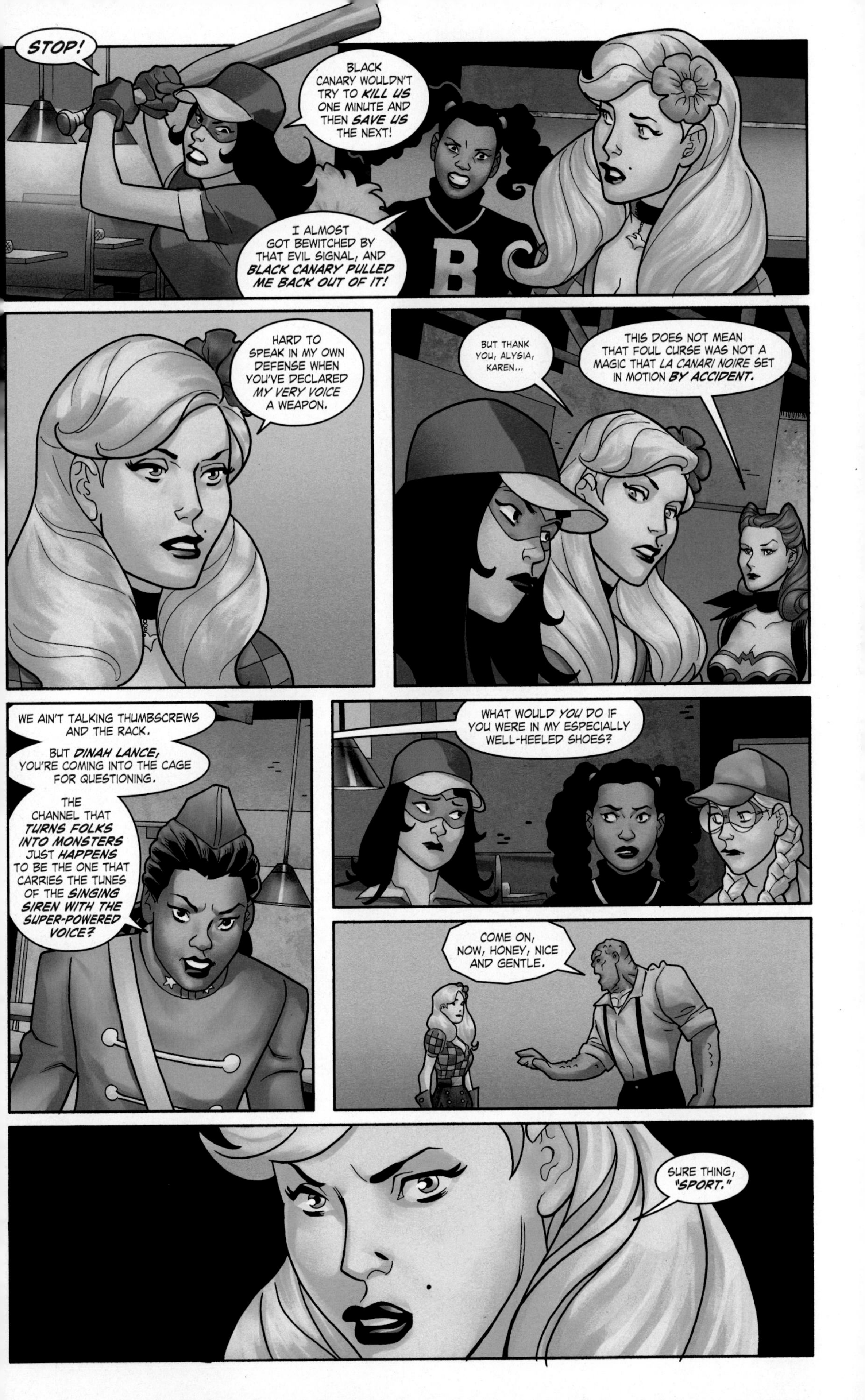
STOP!
BLACK CANARY WOULDN'T TRY TO KILL US ONE MINUTE AND THEN SAVE US THE NEXT!
I ALMOST GOT BEWITCHED BY THAT EVIL SIGNAL, AND BLACK CANARY PULLED ME BACK OUT OF IT!
HARD TO SPEAK IN MY OWN DEFENSE WHEN YOU'VE DECLARED MY VERY VOICE A WEAPON.
BUT THANK YOU, ALYSIA, KAREN...
THIS DOES NOT MEAN THAT FOUL CURSE WAS NOT A MAGIC THAT LA CANARI NOIRE SET IN MOTION BY ACCIDENT.
WE AIN'T TALKING THUMBSCREWS AND THE RACK.
BUT DINAH LANCE, YOU'RE COMING INTO THE CAGE FOR QUESTIONING.
THE CHANNEL THAT TURNS FOLKS INTO MONSTERS JUST HAPPENS TO BE THE ONE THAT CARRIES THE TUNES OF THE SINGING SIREN WITH THE SUPER-POWERED VOICE?
WHAT WOULD YOU DO IF YOU WERE IN MY ESPECIALLY WELL-HEELED SHOES?
COME ON, NOW, HONEY, NICE AND GENTLE.
SURE THING, "SPORT."

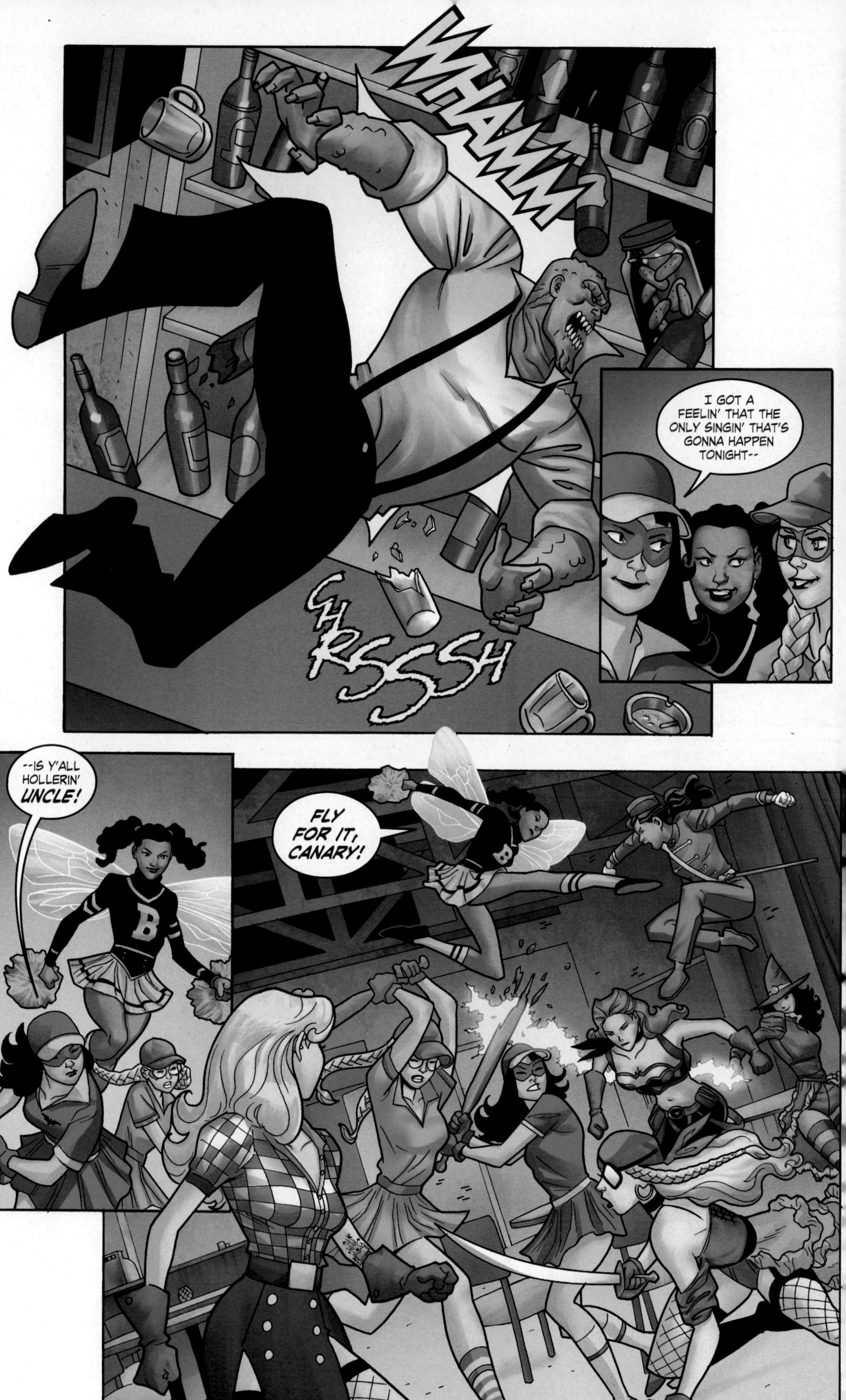
WHAMM
CHRSSSH
I GOT A FEELIN' THAT THE ONLY SINGIN' THAT'S GONNA HAPPEN TONIGHT--
--IS Y'ALL HOLLERIN' UNCLE!
FLY FOR IT, CANARY!

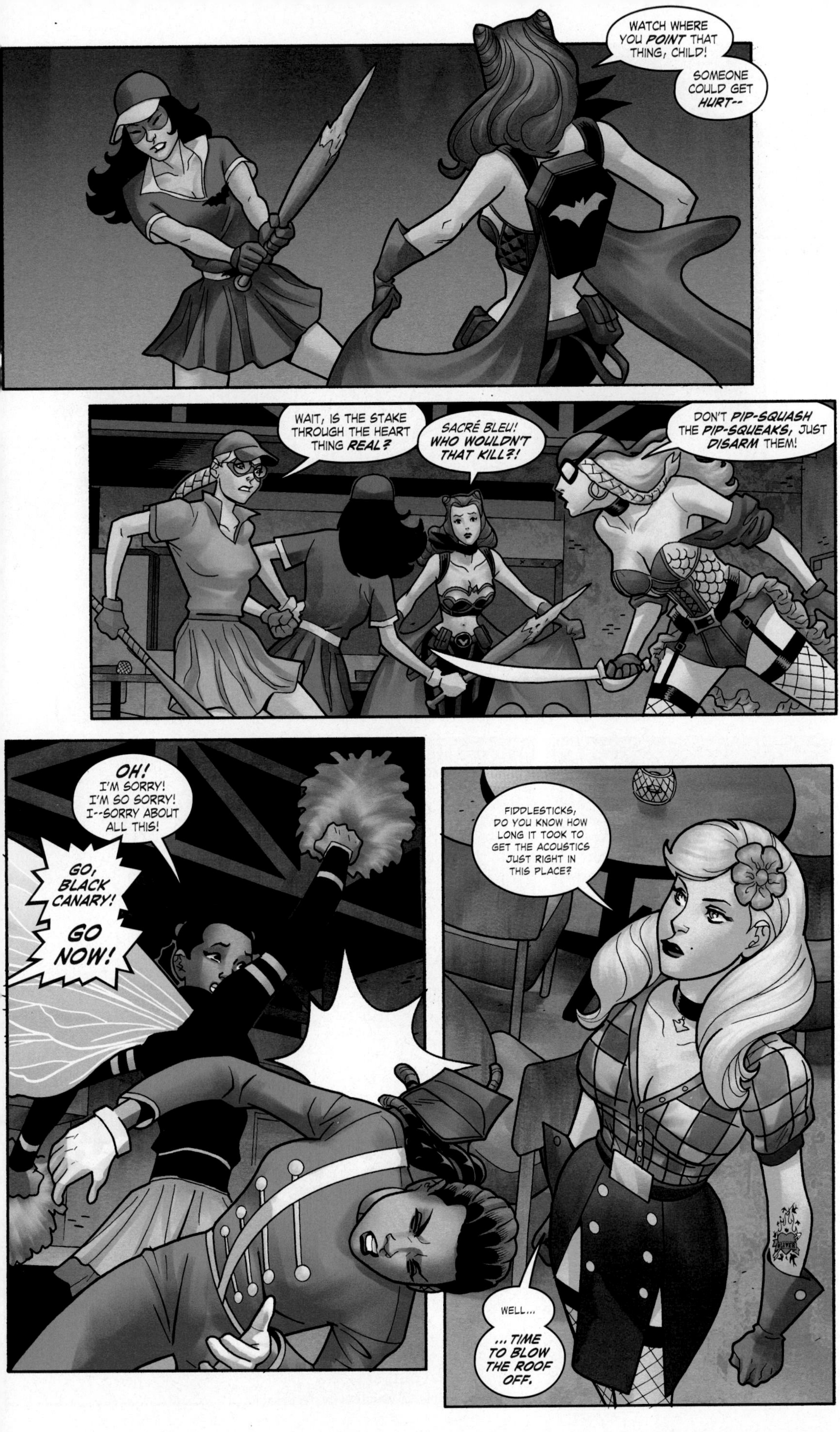
WATCH WHERE YOU POINT THAT THING, CHILD!
SOMEONE COULD GET HURT--
WAIT, IS THE STAKE THROUGH THE HEART THING REAL?
SACRÉ BLEU! WHO WOULDN'T THAT KILL?!
DON'T PIP-SQUASH THE PIP-SQUEAKS, JUST DISARM THEM!
OH! I'M SORRY! I'M SO SORRY! I--SORRY ABOUT ALL THIS!
GO, BLACK CANARY! GO NOW!
FIDDLESTICKS, DO YOU KNOW HOW LONG IT TOOK TO GET THE ACOUSTICS JUST RIGHT IN THIS PLACE?
WELL...
...TIME TO BLOW THE ROOF OFF.

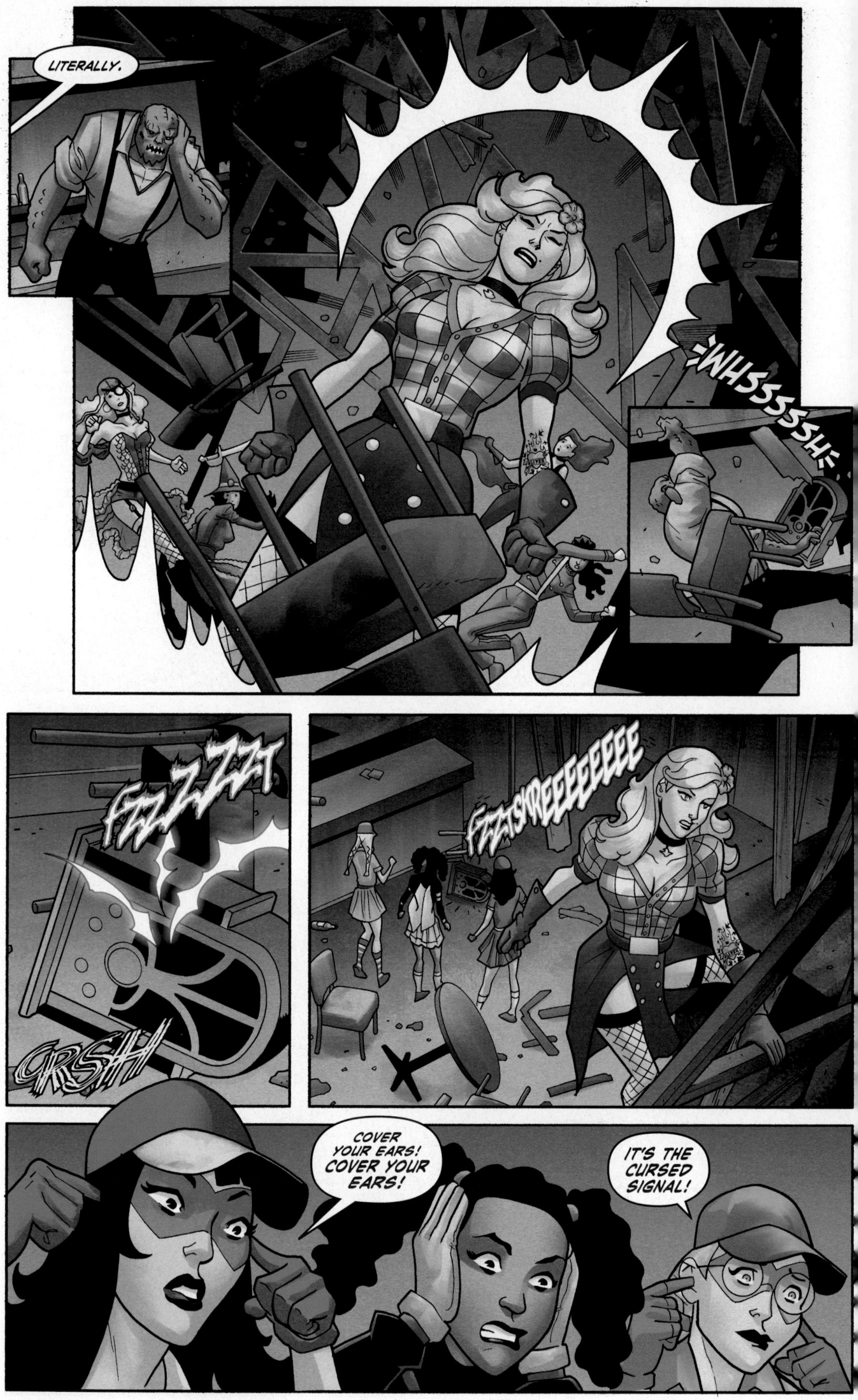
LITERALLY.
-WHSSSSSSH-
FZZZZZT
GRSH
FZZTSHREEEEEEEEE
COVER YOUR EARS! COVER YOUR EARS!
IT'S THE CURSED SIGNAL!

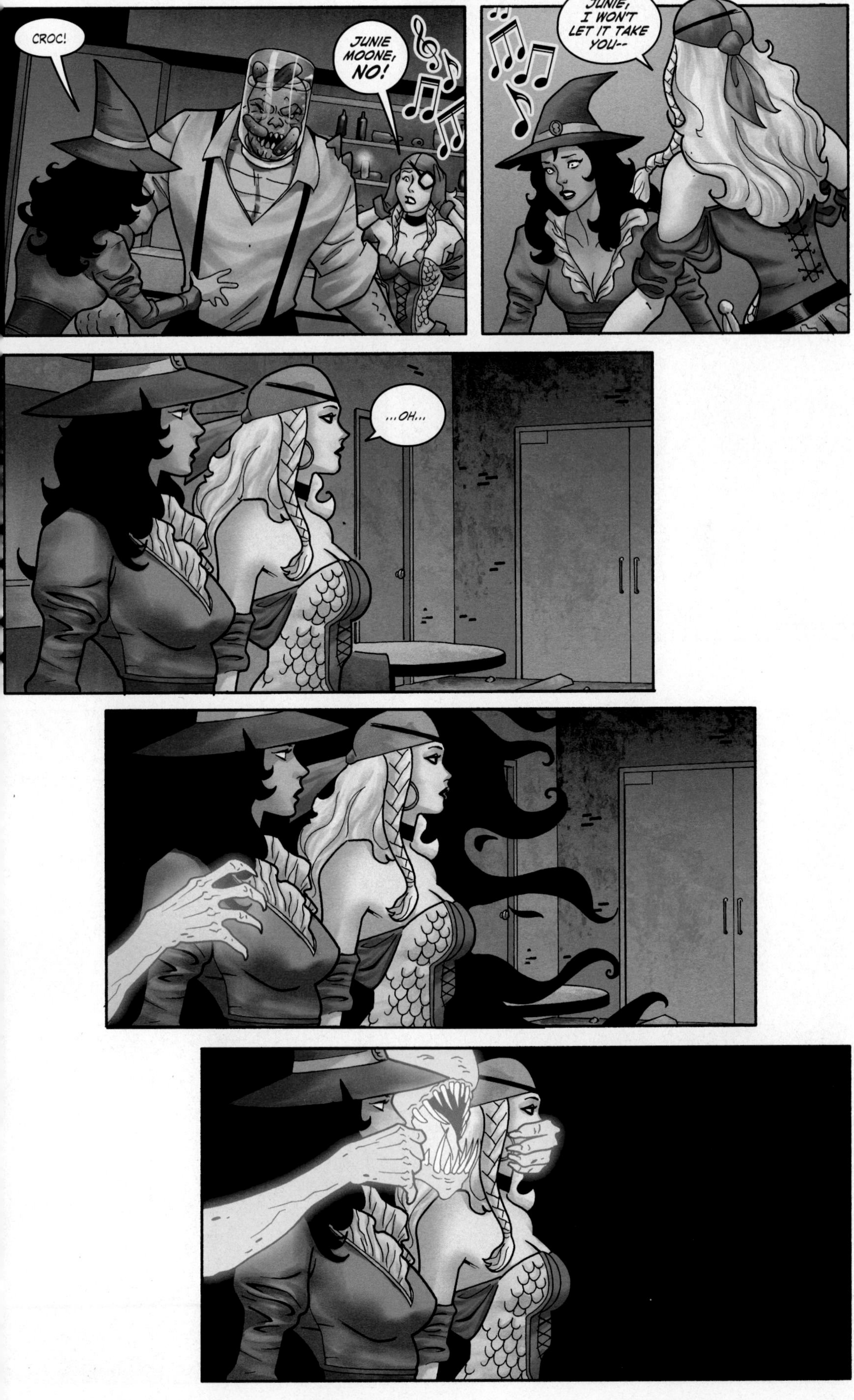
CROC!
JUNIE MOONE, NO!
JUNIE, I WON'T LET IT TAKE YOU--
...OH...

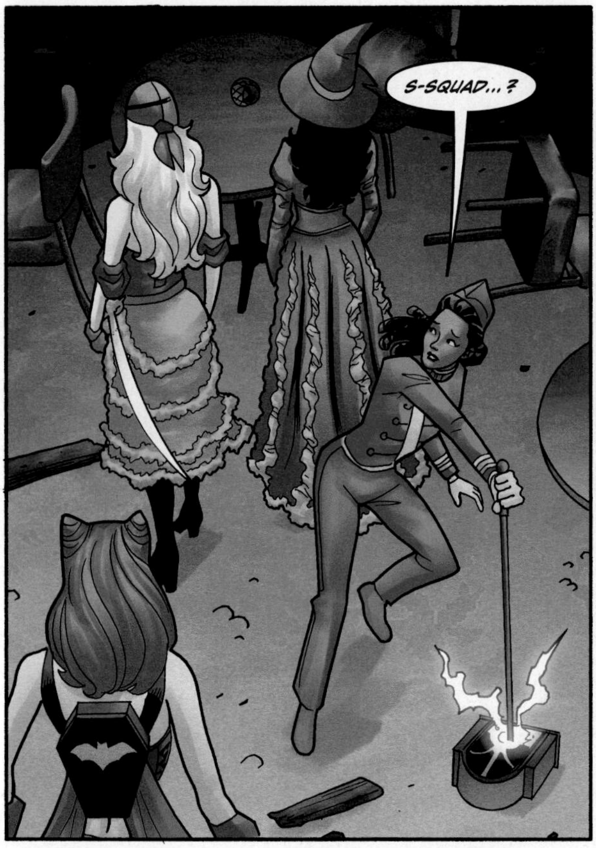
S-SQUAD...?

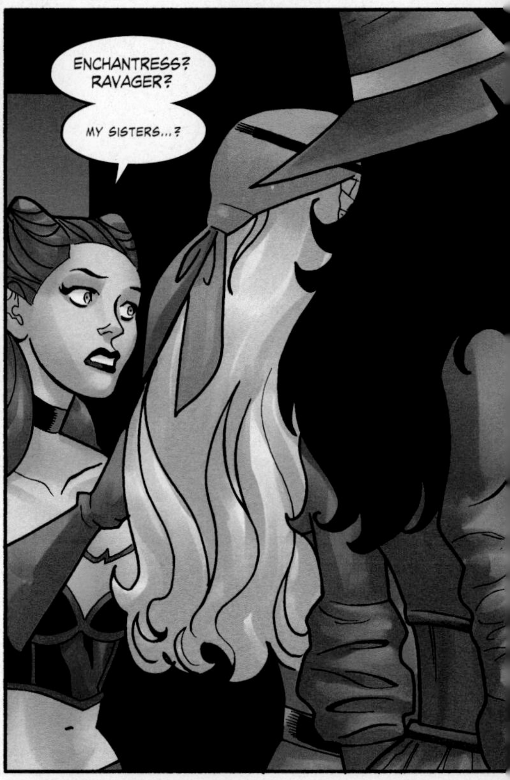
ENCHANTRESS? RAVAGER?
MY SISTERS...?

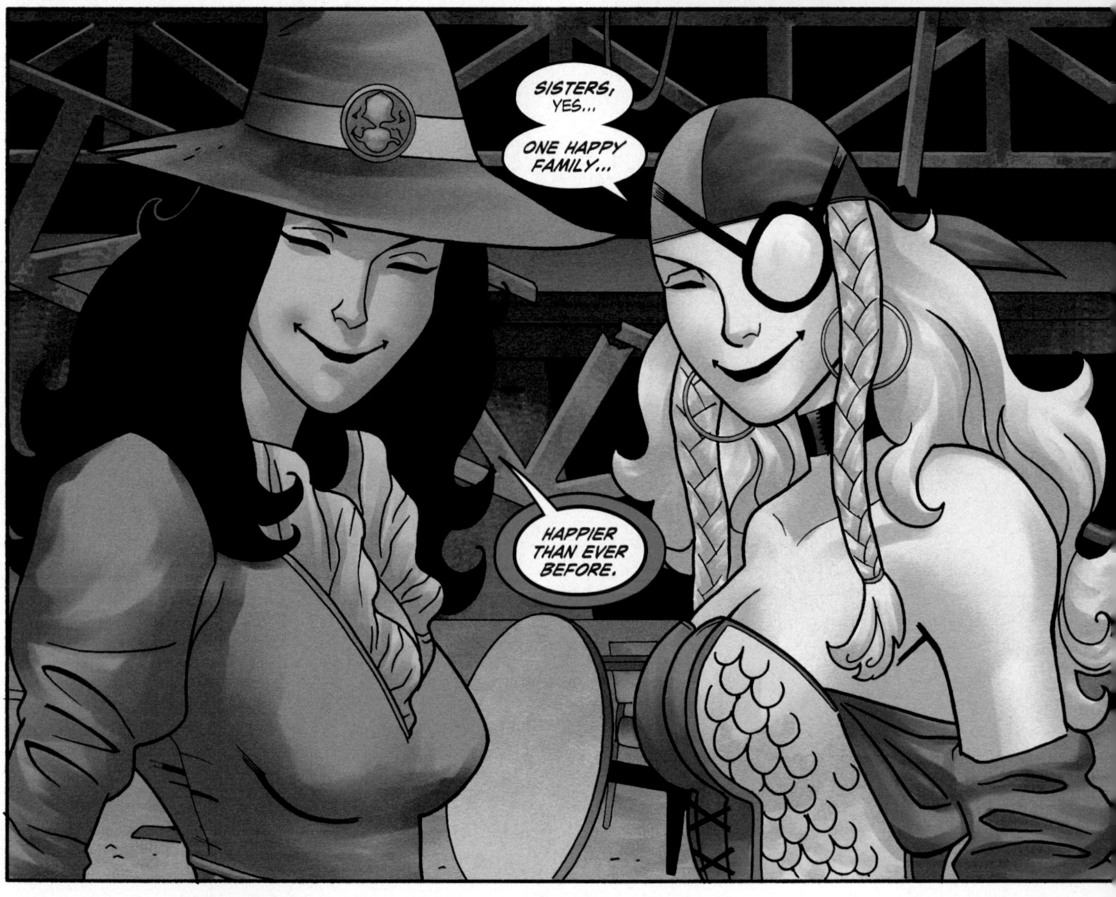
SISTERS, YES...
ONE HAPPY FAMILY...
HAPPIER THAN EVER BEFORE.

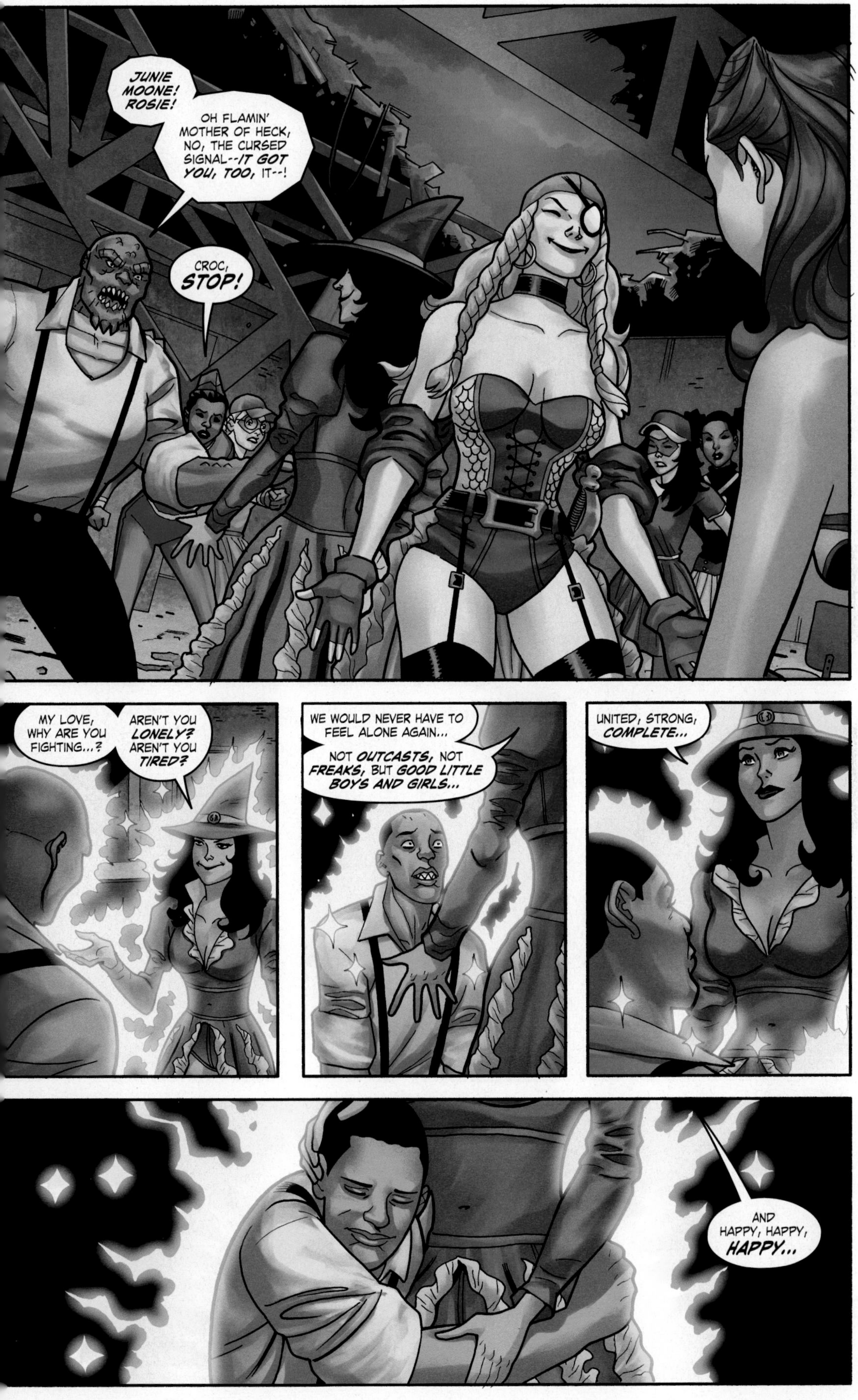
JUNIE MOONE! ROSIE!
OH FLAMIN' MOTHER OF HECK, NO, THE CURSED SIGNAL--IT GOT YOU, TOO, IT--!
CROC, STOP!
MY LOVE, WHY ARE YOU FIGHTING...?
AREN'T YOU LONELY? AREN'T YOU TIRED?
WE WOULD NEVER HAVE TO FEEL ALONE AGAIN...
NOT OUTCASTS, NOT FREAKS, BUT GOOD LITTLE BOYS AND GIRLS...
UNITED, STRONG, COMPLETE...
AND HAPPY, HAPPY, HAPPY...

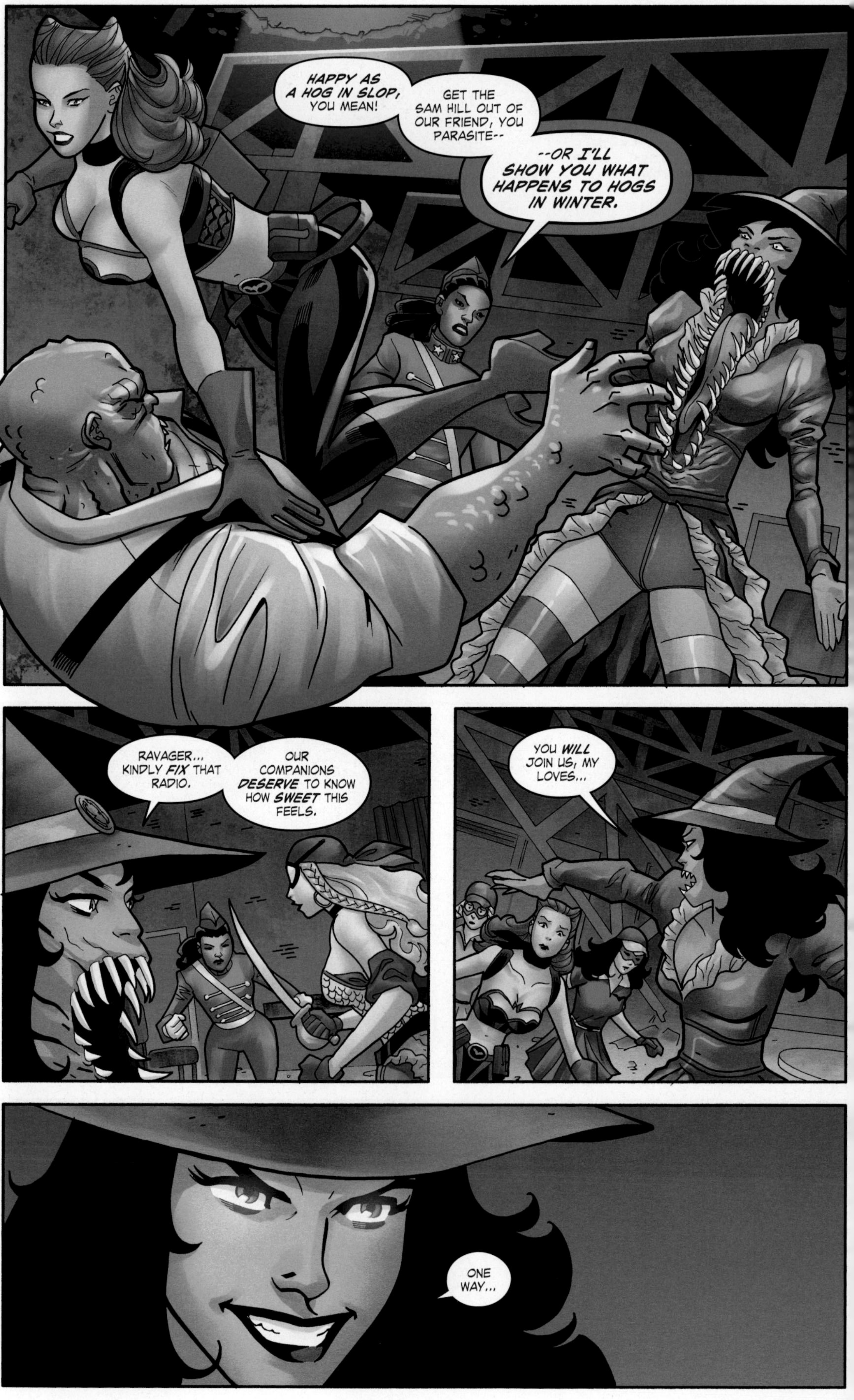
HAPPY AS A HOG IN SLOP, YOU MEAN!
GET THE SAM HILL OUT OF OUR FRIEND, YOU PARASITE--
--OR I'LL SHOW YOU WHAT HAPPENS TO HOGS IN WINTER.
RAVAGER... KINDLY FIX THAT RADIO.
OUR COMPANIONS DESERVE TO KNOW HOW SWEET THIS FEELS.
YOU WILL JOIN US, MY LOVES...
ONE WAY...

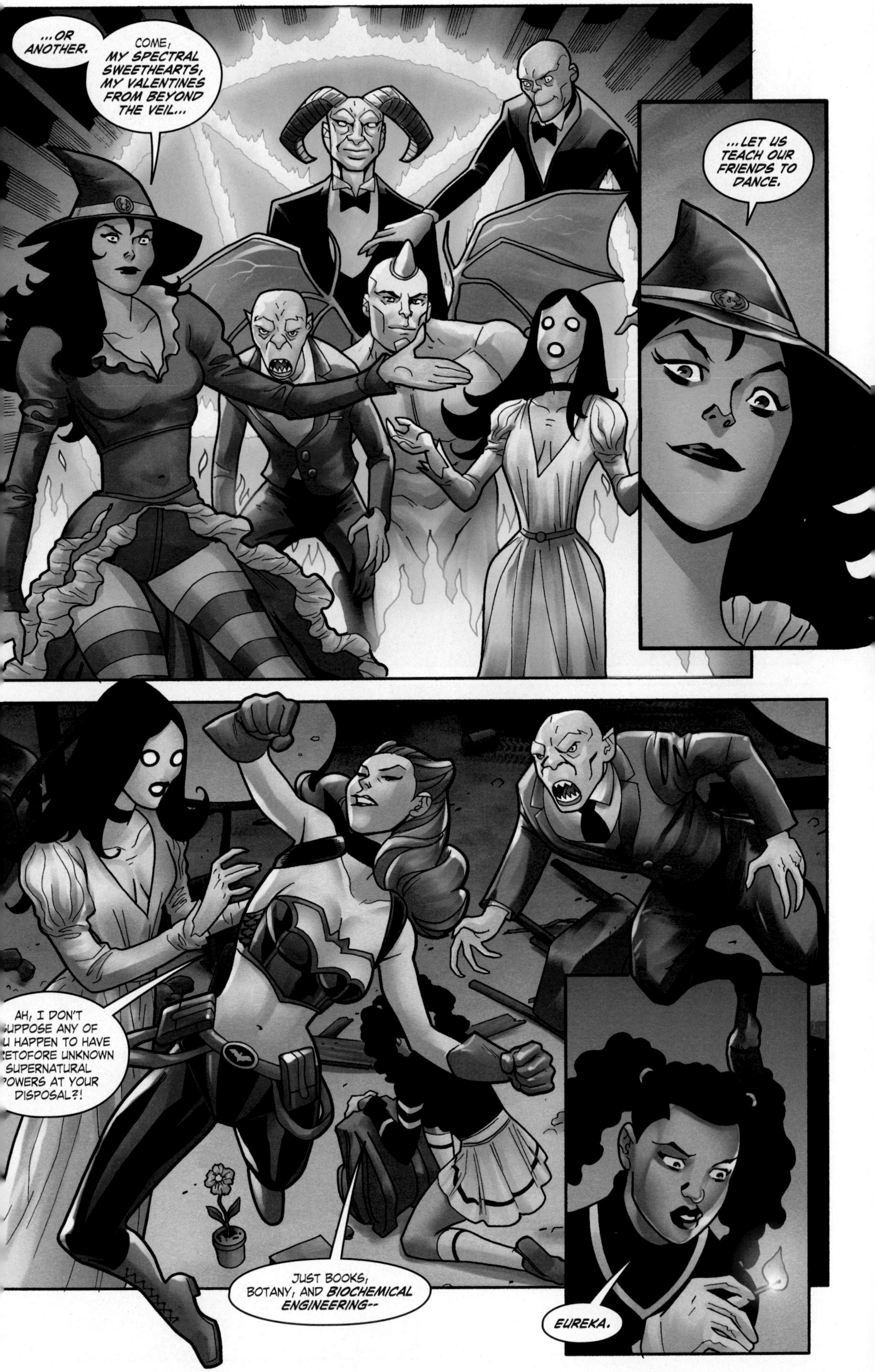
...OR ANOTHER.
COME, MY SPECTRAL SWEETHEARTS, MY VALENTINES FROM BEYOND THE VEIL...
...LET US TEACH OUR FRIENDS TO DANCE.
AH, I DON'T UPPOSE ANY OF U HAPPEN TO HAVE RETOFORE UNKNOWN SUPERNATURAL POWERS AT YOUR DISPOSAL?!
JUST BOOKS, BOTANY, AND BIOCHEMICAL ENGINEERING--
EUREKA.

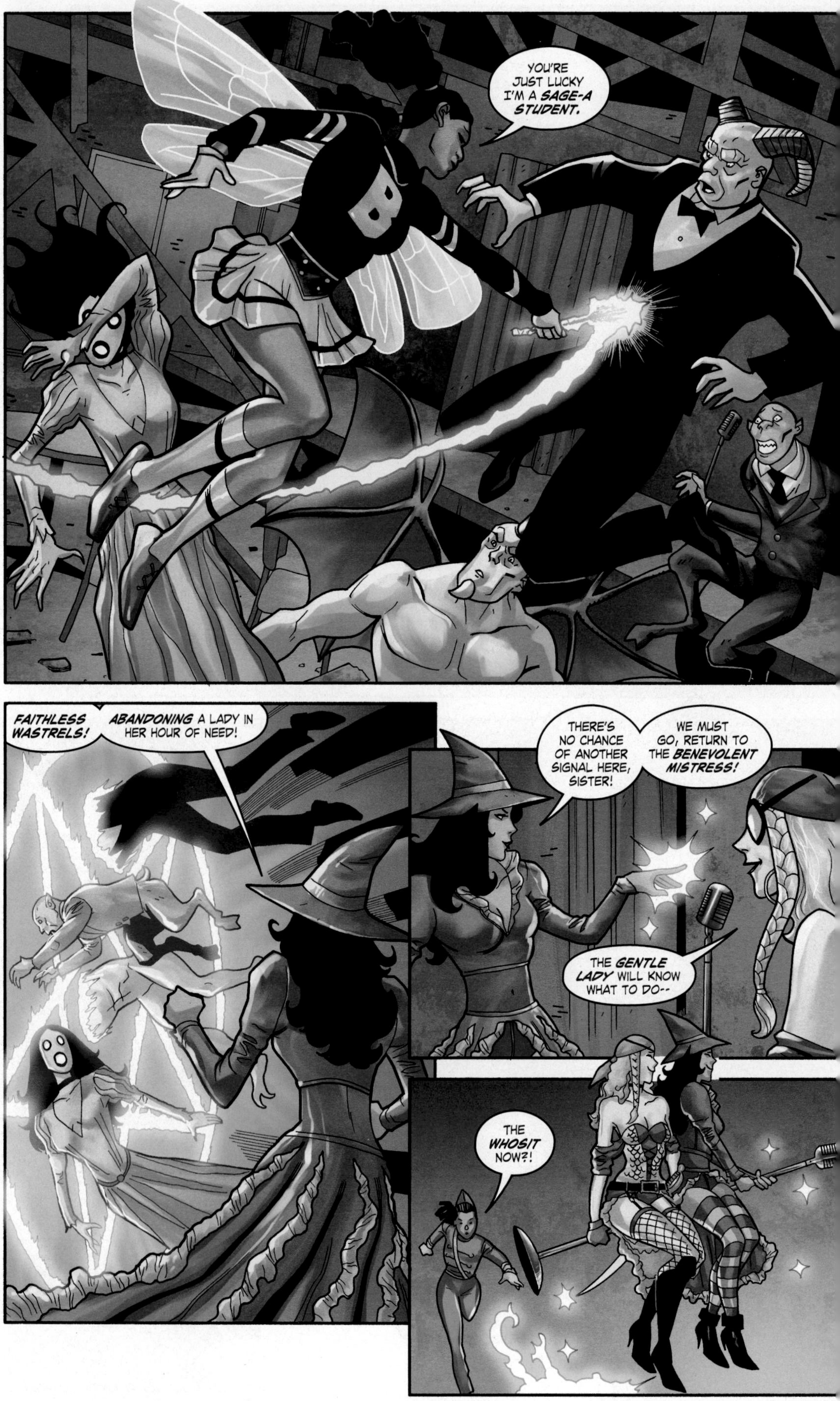

YOU'RE JUST LUCKY I'M A SAGE-A STUDENT.
FAITHLESS WASTRELS!
ABANDONING A LADY IN HER HOUR OF NEED!
THERE'S NO CHANCE OF ANOTHER SIGNAL HERE, SISTER!
WE MUST GO, RETURN TO THE BENEVOLENT MISTRESS!
THE GENTLE LADY WILL KNOW WHAT TO DO--
THE WHOSIT NOW?!

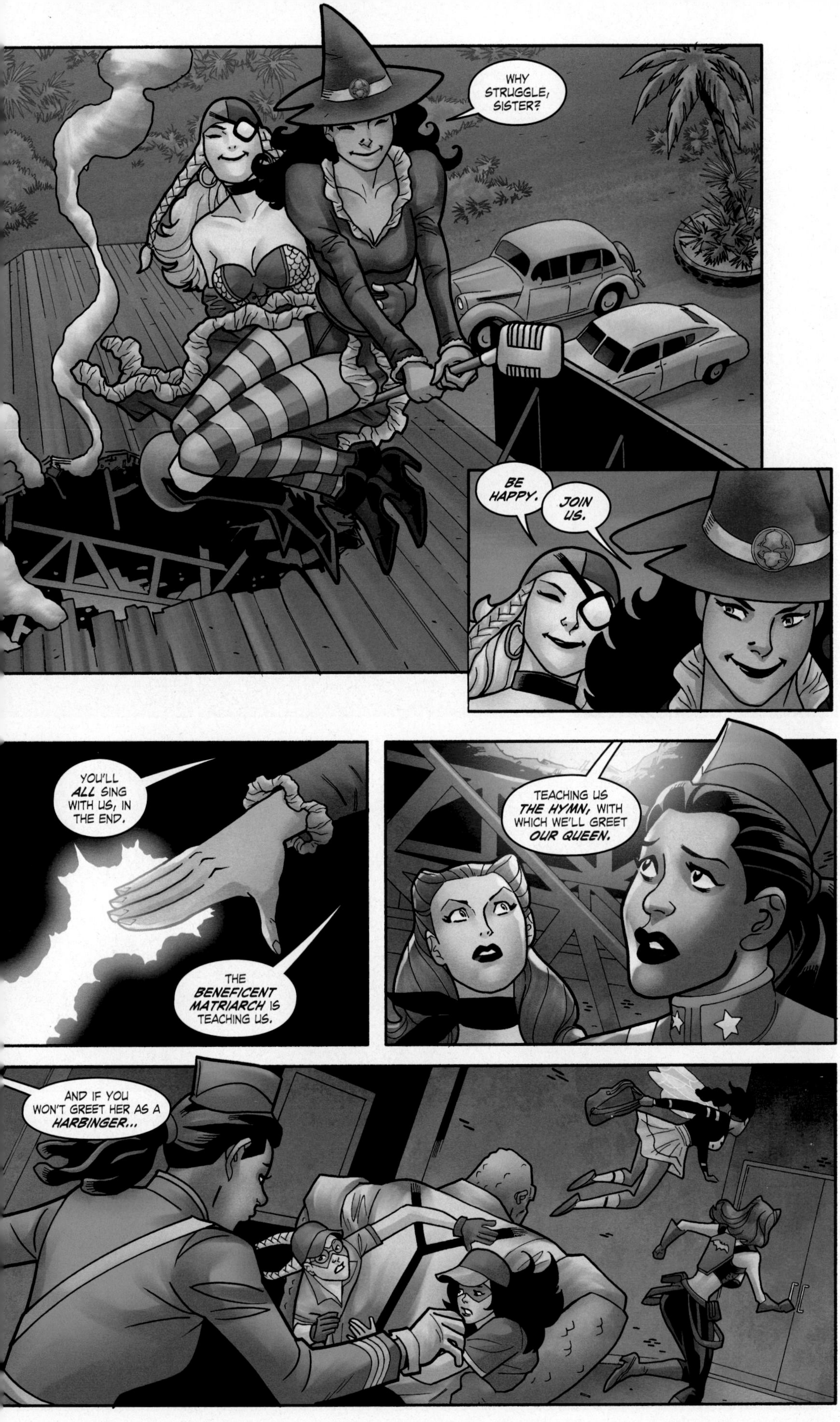
WHY STRUGGLE, SISTER?
BE HAPPY.
JOIN US.
YOU'LL ALL SING WITH US, IN THE END.
THE BENEFICENT MATRIARCH IS TEACHING US.
TEACHING US THE HYMN, WITH WHICH WE'LL GREET OUR QUEEN.
AND IF YOU WON'T GREET HER AS A HARBINGER...

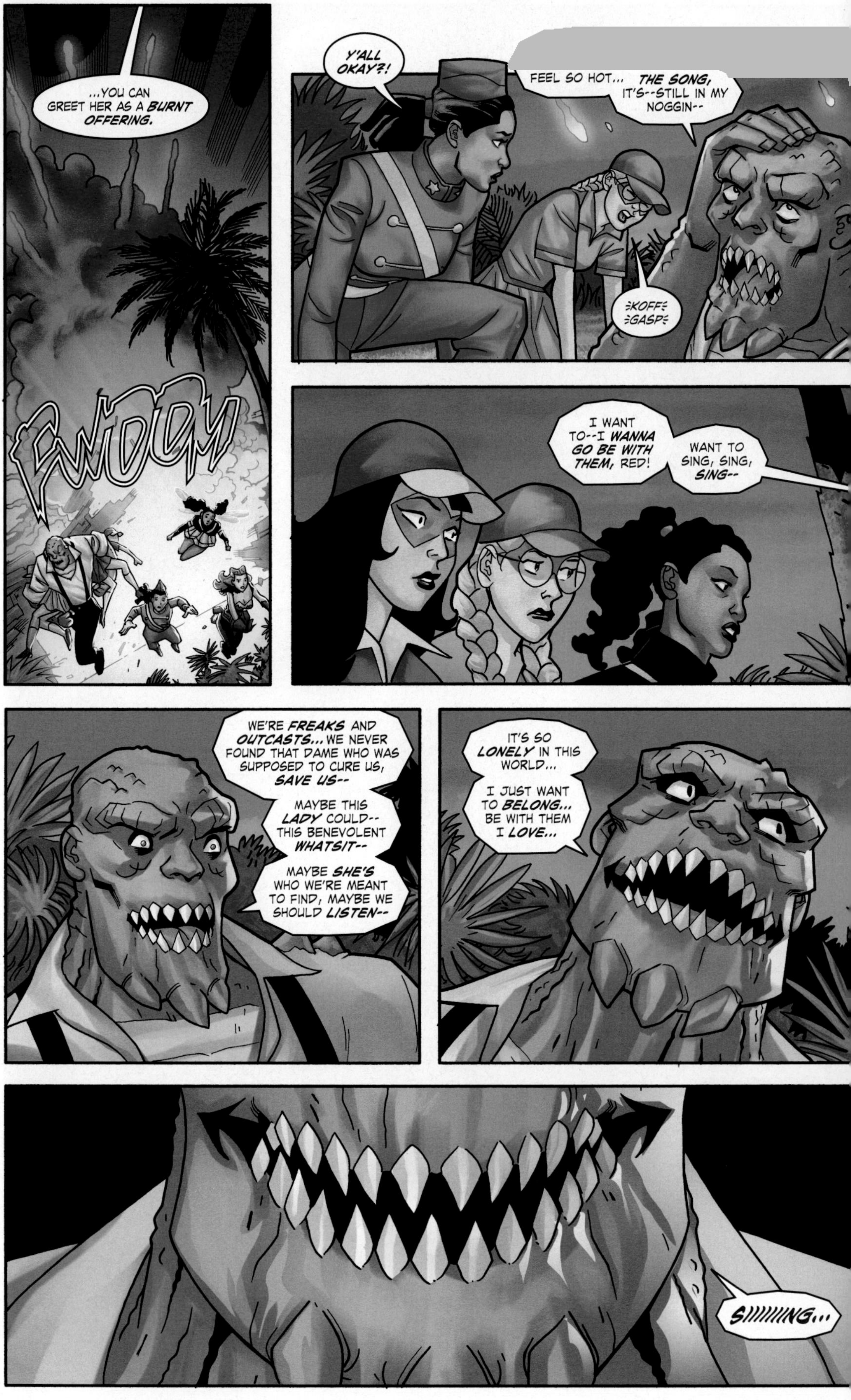

...YOU CAN GREET HER AS A BURNT OFFERING.
PWOOM
Y'ALL OKAY?!
FEEL SO HOT... THE SONG, IT'S--STILL IN MY NOGGIN--
KOFF GASP
I WANT TO--I WANNA GO BE WITH THEM, RED!
WANT TO SING, SING, SING--
WE'RE FREAKS AND OUTCASTS... WE NEVER FOUND THAT DAME WHO WAS SUPPOSED TO CURE US, SAVE US--
MAYBE THIS LADY COULD--THIS BENEVOLENT WHATSIT--
MAYBE SHE'S WHO WE'RE MEANT TO FIND, MAYBE WE SHOULD LISTEN--
IT'S SO LONELY IN THIS WORLD...
I JUST WANT TO BELONG... BE WITH THEM I LOVE...
SIIIIIIING...

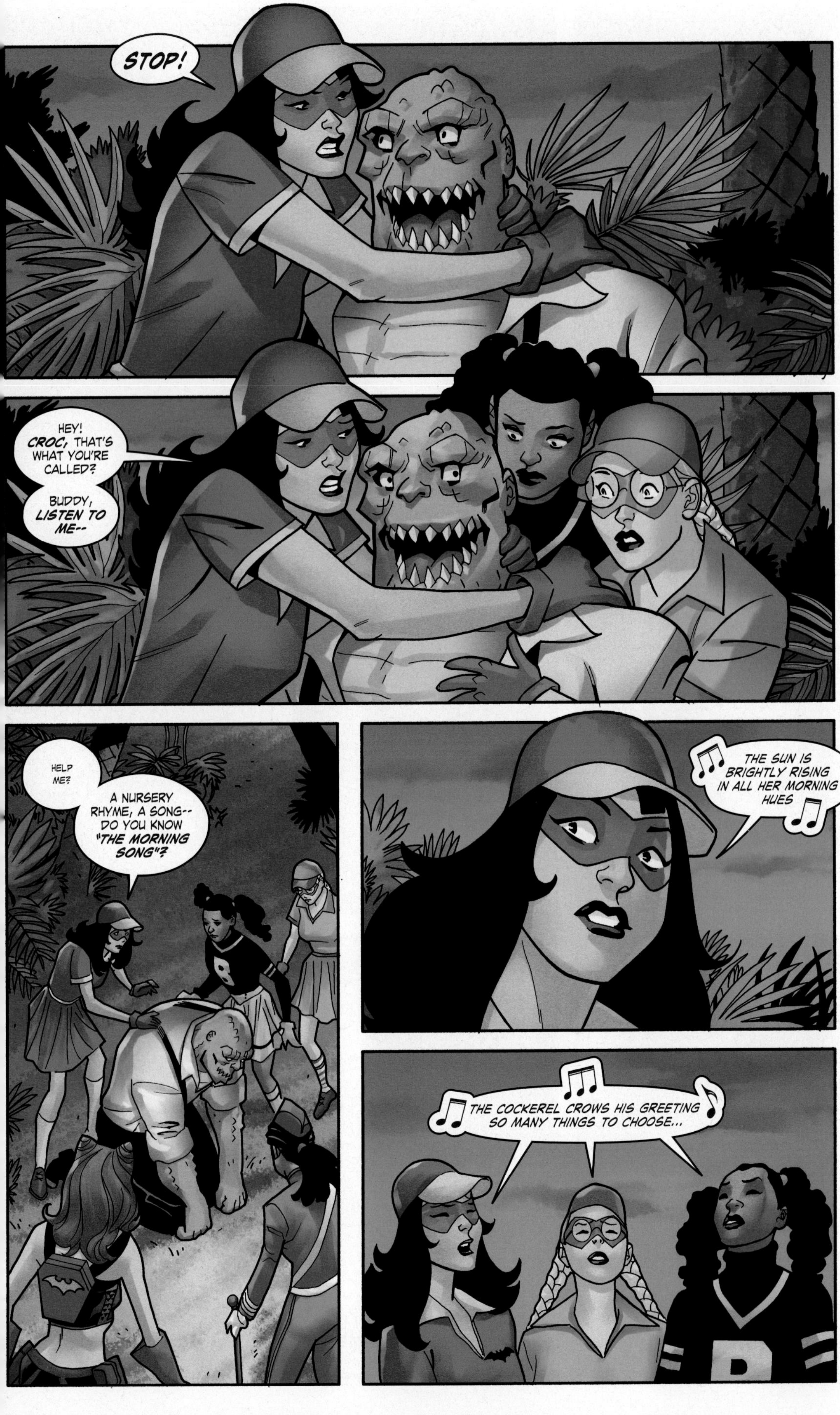
STOP!
HEY! CROC, THAT'S WHAT YOU'RE CALLED?
BUDDY, LISTEN TO ME--
HELP ME?
A NURSERY RHYME, A SONG-- DO YOU KNOW "THE MORNING SONG"?
THE SUN IS BRIGHTLY RISING IN ALL HER MORNING HUES
THE COCKEREL CROWS HIS GREETING SO MANY THINGS TO CHOOSE...

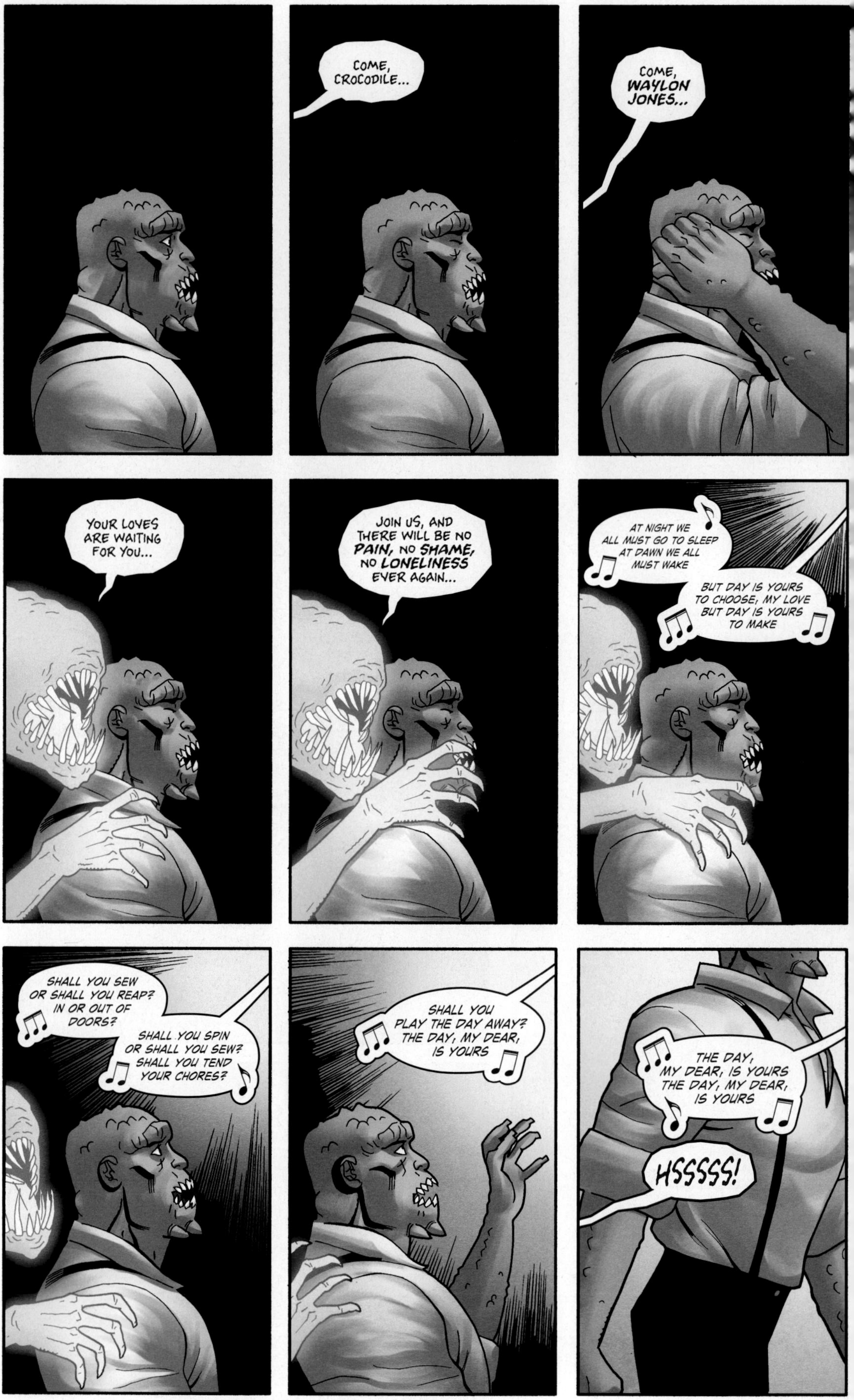
COME, CROCODILE...
COME, WAYLON JONES...
YOUR LOVES ARE WAITING FOR YOU...
JOIN US, AND THERE WILL BE NO PAIN, NO SHAME, NO LONELINESS EVER AGAIN...
AT NIGHT WE ALL MUST GO TO SLEEP AT DAWN WE ALL MUST WAKE
BUT DAY IS YOURS TO CHOOSE, MY LOVE BUT DAY IS YOURS TO MAKE
SHALL YOU SEW OR SHALL YOU REAP? IN OR OUT OF DOORS?
SHALL YOU SPIN OR SHALL YOU SEW? SHALL YOU TEND YOUR CHORES?
SHALL YOU PLAY THE DAY AWAY? THE DAY, MY DEAR, IS YOURS
THE DAY, MY DEAR, IS YOURS THE DAY, MY DEAR, IS YOURS
HSSSSS!

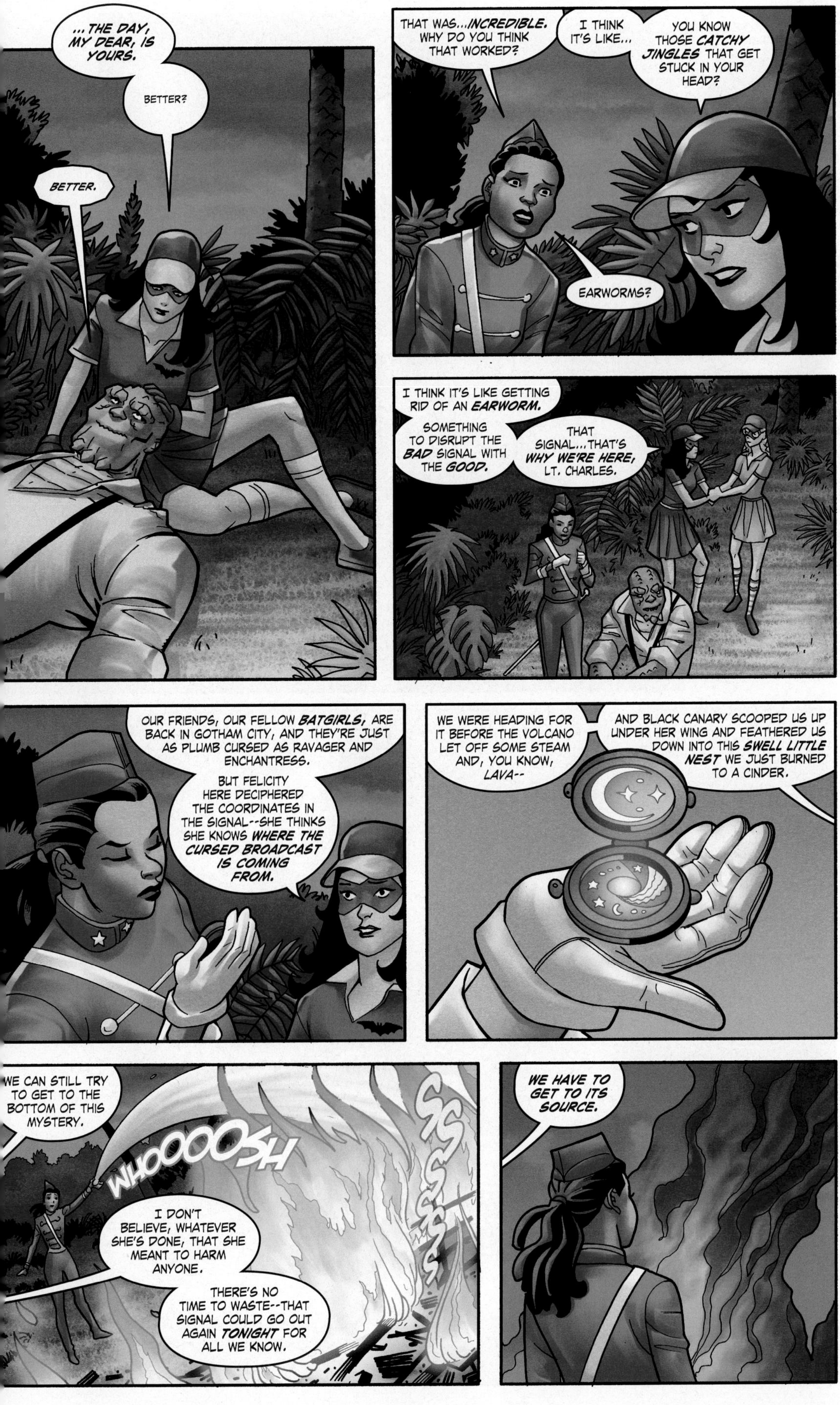
...THE DAY, MY DEAR, IS YOURS.
BETTER?
BETTER.
THAT WAS...INCREDIBLE. WHY DO YOU THINK THAT WORKED?
I THINK IT'S LIKE...
YOU KNOW THOSE CATCHY JINGLES THAT GET STUCK IN YOUR HEAD?
EARWORMS?
I THINK IT'S LIKE GETTING RID OF AN EARWORM.
SOMETHING TO DISRUPT THE BAD SIGNAL WITH THE GOOD.
THAT SIGNAL...THAT'S WHY WE'RE HERE, LT. CHARLES.
OUR FRIENDS, OUR FELLOW BATGIRLS, ARE BACK IN GOTHAM CITY, AND THEY'RE JUST AS PLUMB CURSED AS RAVAGER AND ENCHANTRESS.
BUT FELICITY HERE DECIPHERED THE COORDINATES IN THE SIGNAL--SHE THINKS SHE KNOWS WHERE THE CURSED BROADCAST IS COMING FROM.
WE WERE HEADING FOR IT BEFORE THE VOLCANO LET OFF SOME STEAM AND, YOU KNOW, LAVA--
AND BLACK CANARY SCOOPED US UP UNDER HER WING AND FEATHERED US DOWN INTO THIS SWELL LITTLE NEST WE JUST BURNED TO A CINDER.
WE CAN STILL TRY TO GET TO THE BOTTOM OF THIS MYSTERY.
WHOOOOSH
SSSSSSS
I DON'T BELIEVE, WHATEVER SHE'S DONE, THAT SHE MEANT TO HARM ANYONE.
THERE'S NO TIME TO WASTE--THAT SIGNAL COULD GO OUT AGAIN TONIGHT FOR ALL WE KNOW.
WE HAVE TO GET TO ITS SOURCE.

SO, MA CHÈRE FRANKIE--

SHALL WE HUNT DOWN BLACK CANARY, CHASE AFTER ENCHANTRESS AND RAVAGER OR FOLLOW THESE BAT-BABIES TO THEIR *HAUNTED ISLAND?*

ALL WE MANAGED TO DO WAS *F-U* THIS SITUATION SOMETHIN' *-BAR.*

MAYBE IT'S TIME WE SWITCH TO A *DIFFERENT STATION.*

YOU GOT THE COORDINATES, FELICITY?

YOU KNOW WHAT THEY SAY--

TIME, TIDE, AND *HORRIFYING SUPERNATURAL RADIO SIGNALS* WAIT FOR NO MAN.

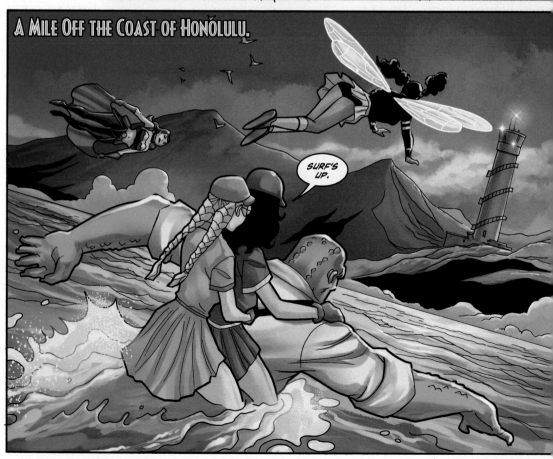

A MILE OFF THE COAST OF HONOLULU.

SURF'S UP.

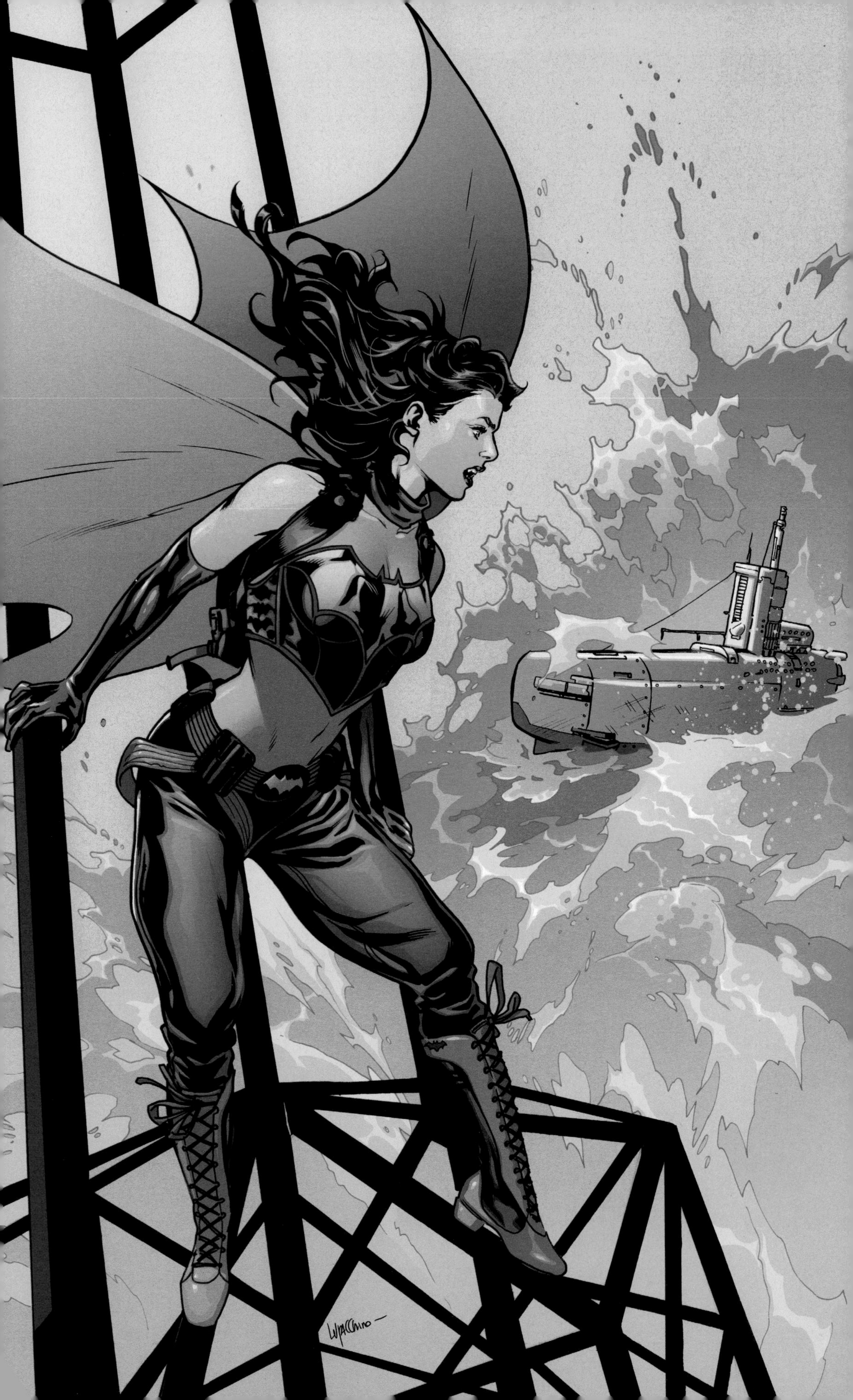

THE BLACK ISLAND

PARTS FIVE and SIX

Written by
MARGUERITE BENNETT

Art by
ANEKE

Colors by
J. NANJAN

Letters by
WES ABBOTT

Cover by
EMANUELA LUPACCHINO *with*
DAVE McCAIG

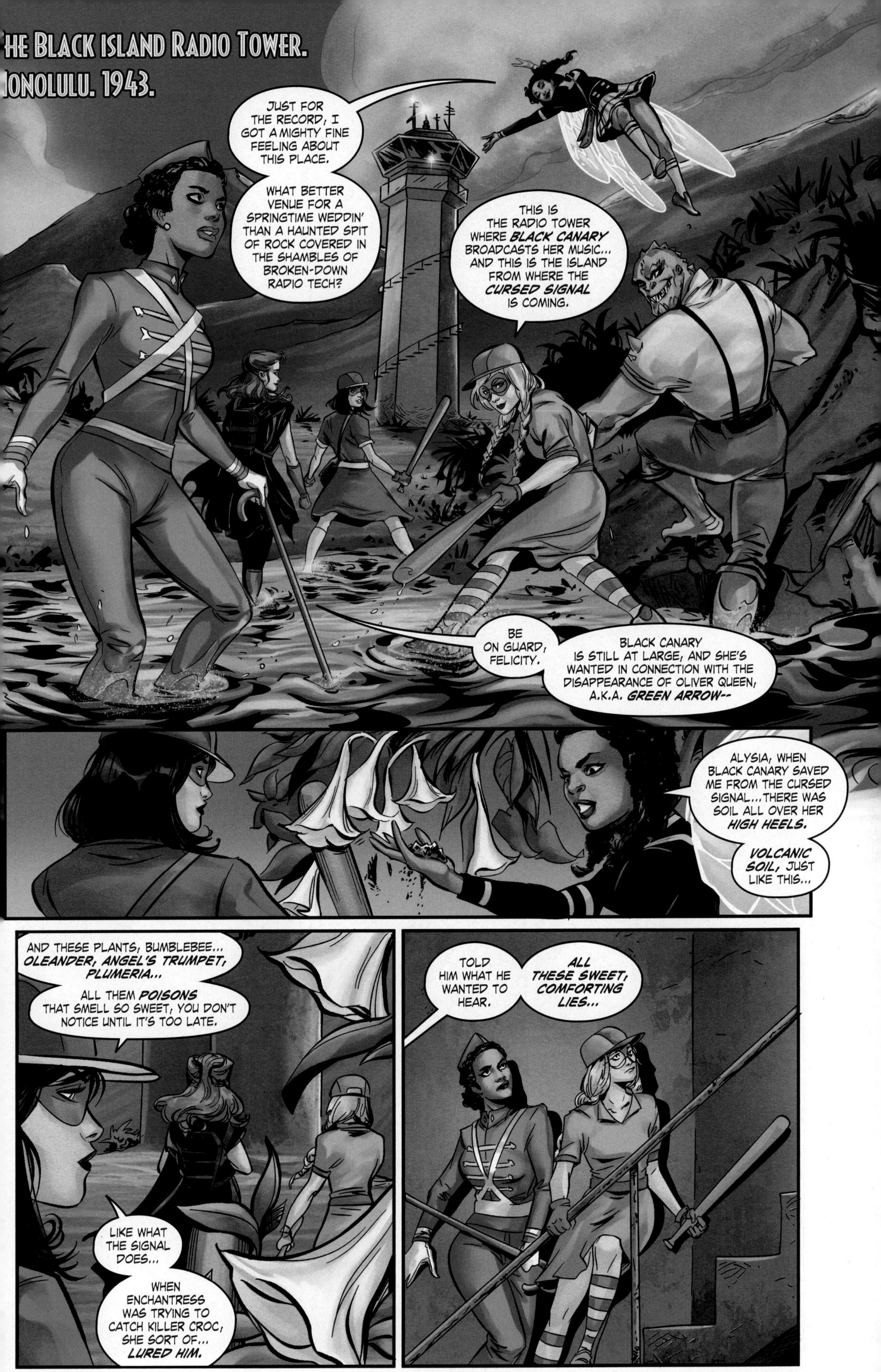

HE BLACK ISLAND RADIO TOWER.
ONOLULU. 1943.
JUST FOR THE RECORD, I GOT A MIGHTY FINE FEELING ABOUT THIS PLACE.
WHAT BETTER VENUE FOR A SPRINGTIME WEDDIN' THAN A HAUNTED SPIT OF ROCK COVERED IN THE SHAMBLES OF BROKEN-DOWN RADIO TECH?
THIS IS THE RADIO TOWER WHERE BLACK CANARY BROADCASTS HER MUSIC... AND THIS IS THE ISLAND FROM WHERE THE CURSED SIGNAL IS COMING.
BE ON GUARD, FELICITY.
BLACK CANARY IS STILL AT LARGE, AND SHE'S WANTED IN CONNECTION WITH THE DISAPPEARANCE OF OLIVER QUEEN, A.K.A. GREEN ARROW--
ALYSIA, WHEN BLACK CANARY SAVED ME FROM THE CURSED SIGNAL... THERE WAS SOIL ALL OVER HER HIGH HEELS.
VOLCANIC SOIL, JUST LIKE THIS...
AND THESE PLANTS, BUMBLEBEE... OLEANDER, ANGEL'S TRUMPET, PLUMERIA...
ALL THEM POISONS THAT SMELL SO SWEET, YOU DON'T NOTICE UNTIL IT'S TOO LATE.
LIKE WHAT THE SIGNAL DOES...
WHEN ENCHANTRESS WAS TRYING TO CATCH KILLER CROC, SHE SORT OF... LURED HIM.
TOLD HIM WHAT HE WANTED TO HEAR.
ALL THESE SWEET, COMFORTING LIES...

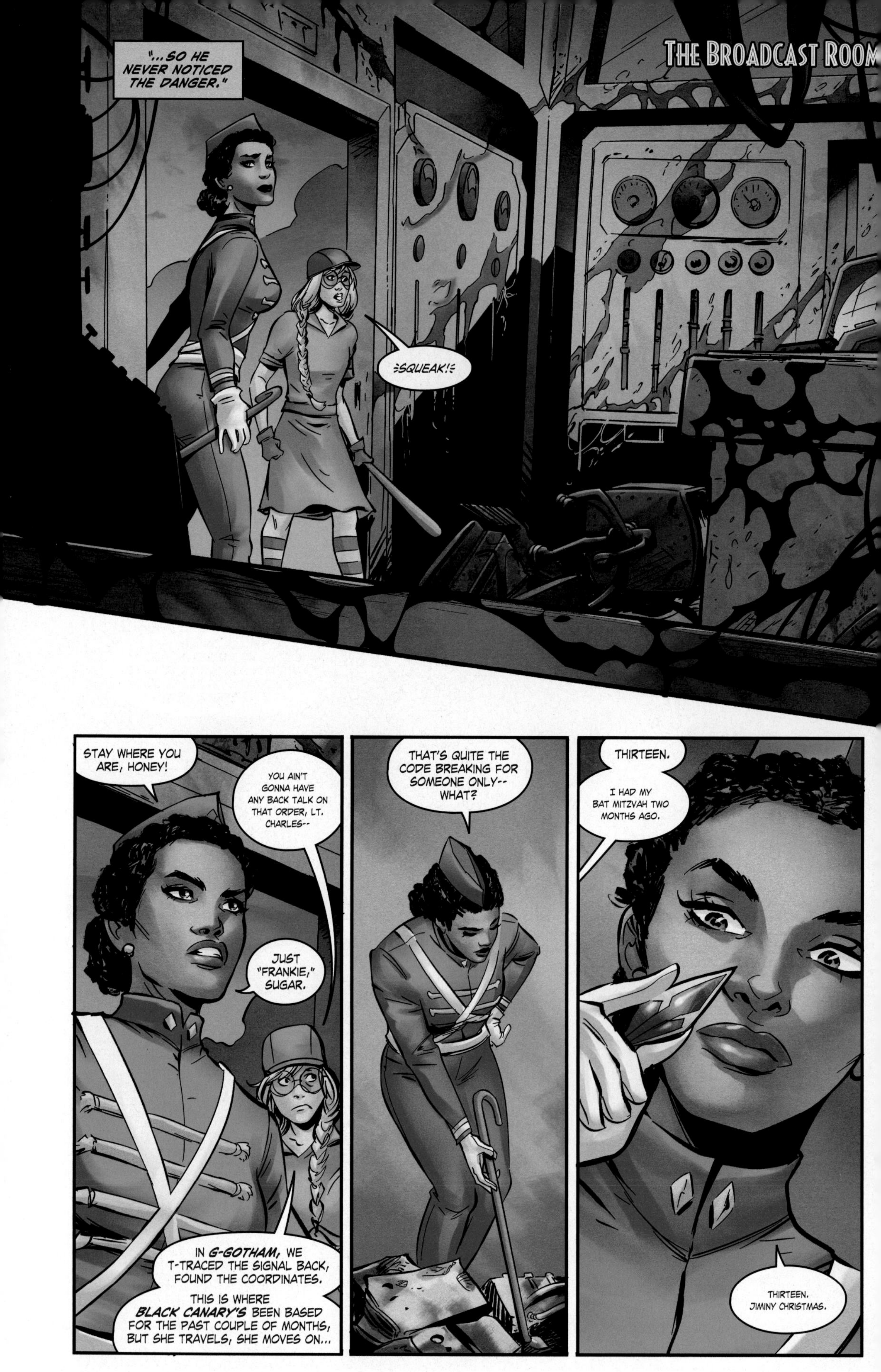
"...SO HE NEVER NOTICED THE DANGER."
THE BROADCAST ROOM
SQUEAK!
STAY WHERE YOU ARE, HONEY!
YOU AIN'T GONNA HAVE ANY BACK TALK ON THAT ORDER, LT. CHARLES--
JUST "FRANKIE," SUGAR.
IN G-GOTHAM, WE T-TRACED THE SIGNAL BACK, FOUND THE COORDINATES.
THIS IS WHERE BLACK CANARY'S BEEN BASED FOR THE PAST COUPLE OF MONTHS, BUT SHE TRAVELS, SHE MOVES ON...
THAT'S QUITE THE CODE BREAKING FOR SOMEONE ONLY-- WHAT?
THIRTEEN.
I HAD MY BAT MITZVAH TWO MONTHS AGO.
THIRTEEN. JIMINY CHRISTMAS.

FELICITY... I HATE TO ASK THIS OF YOU.

YOU'RE NOT MEANT TO BE MIXED IN ANY OF THIS. *THIS SHOULDN'T HAVE TO FALL TO YOU.*

BUT WILL YOU HELP ME LOOK AT THESE CODES? THIS TECH?

WEST POINT AND AMANDA WALLER'S BOMBSHELLS HAVE ME PREPPED FOR A LOT...*BUT NOT EVERYTHING.*

THIS SETUP... THIS IS A LOT MORE THAN A RADIO TOWER. THERE'S *RADAR, MILITARY CODES,* THINGS TO *SCRAMBLE FREQUENCIES*--

THE BATGIRLS, THE WONDER GIRLS, AND ALL THE OTHER *KID VIGILANTES*-- WE TRADE MESSAGES. SECRET LETTERS AND STUFF.

WE TRADE TECH, WHEN WE CAPTURE IT--*NAZI ROBOTS, KILLER BEES,* THE USUAL.

THIS. HERE.

THIS HAS A *SONAR* CAPACITY, FOR--

--GEOLOGICAL EXCAVATION.

I'VE DONE MY SHARE OF DIGGIN' IN THE DESERT.

IS THERE SOME STRANGE FEATURE ON THE ISLAND?

THERE'S SOMETHING *HOLLOW* NEARBY, DISTORTING THE FREQUENCY...

A NATURAL CONCAVITY.

COULD A CORRUPTED FREQUENCY CAUSE THIS?

FREQUENCY AND SOUND DO ALL KINDS OF STUFF TO *THE HUMAN BRAIN.*

THEY CAN CAUSE *ANXIETY* AND *PANIC,* OR INTENSE PAIN IN THE EARDRUMS, OR EVEN PUT PRESSURE ON YOUR LUNGS SO STRONG THAT YOU CAN SUFFER *ORGAN FAILURE.*

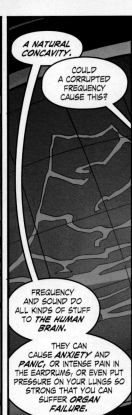

BUT WHAT HAPPENED HERE...? THE BLOOD, OR THE SIGNAL...IT COULD'VE--≶GASP≷

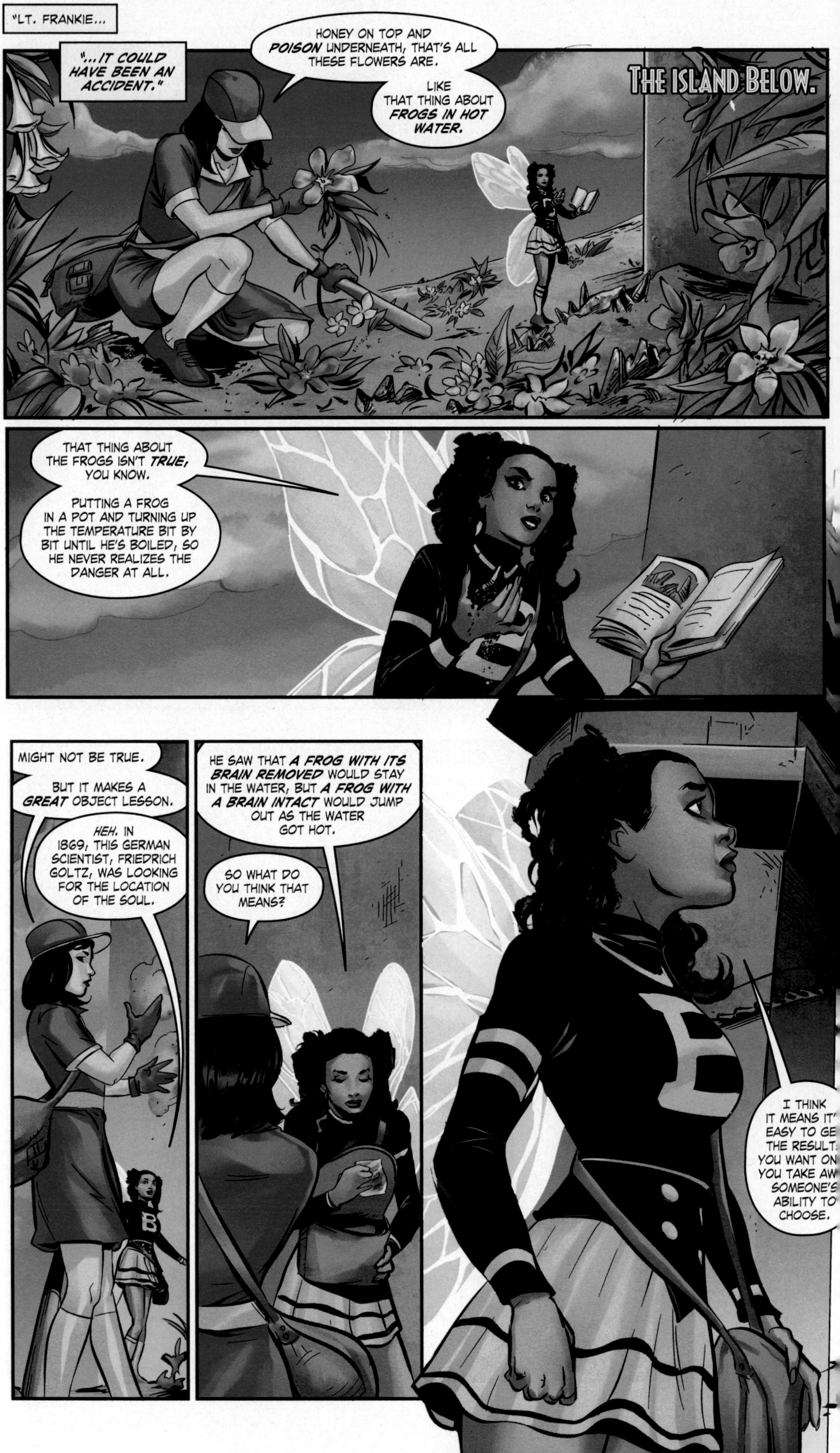

"LT. FRANKIE...
"...IT COULD HAVE BEEN AN ACCIDENT."
HONEY ON TOP AND POISON UNDERNEATH, THAT'S ALL THESE FLOWERS ARE.
LIKE THAT THING ABOUT FROGS IN HOT WATER.
THE ISLAND BELOW.
THAT THING ABOUT THE FROGS ISN'T TRUE, YOU KNOW.
PUTTING A FROG IN A POT AND TURNING UP THE TEMPERATURE BIT BY BIT UNTIL HE'S BOILED, SO HE NEVER REALIZES THE DANGER AT ALL.
MIGHT NOT BE TRUE.
BUT IT MAKES A GREAT OBJECT LESSON.
HEH. IN 1869, THIS GERMAN SCIENTIST, FRIEDRICH GOLTZ, WAS LOOKING FOR THE LOCATION OF THE SOUL.
HE SAW THAT A FROG WITH ITS BRAIN REMOVED WOULD STAY IN THE WATER, BUT A FROG WITH A BRAIN INTACT WOULD JUMP OUT AS THE WATER GOT HOT.
SO WHAT DO YOU THINK THAT MEANS?
I THINK IT MEANS IT' EASY TO GE THE RESULT YOU WANT ON YOU TAKE AW SOMEONE'S ABILITY TO CHOOSE.

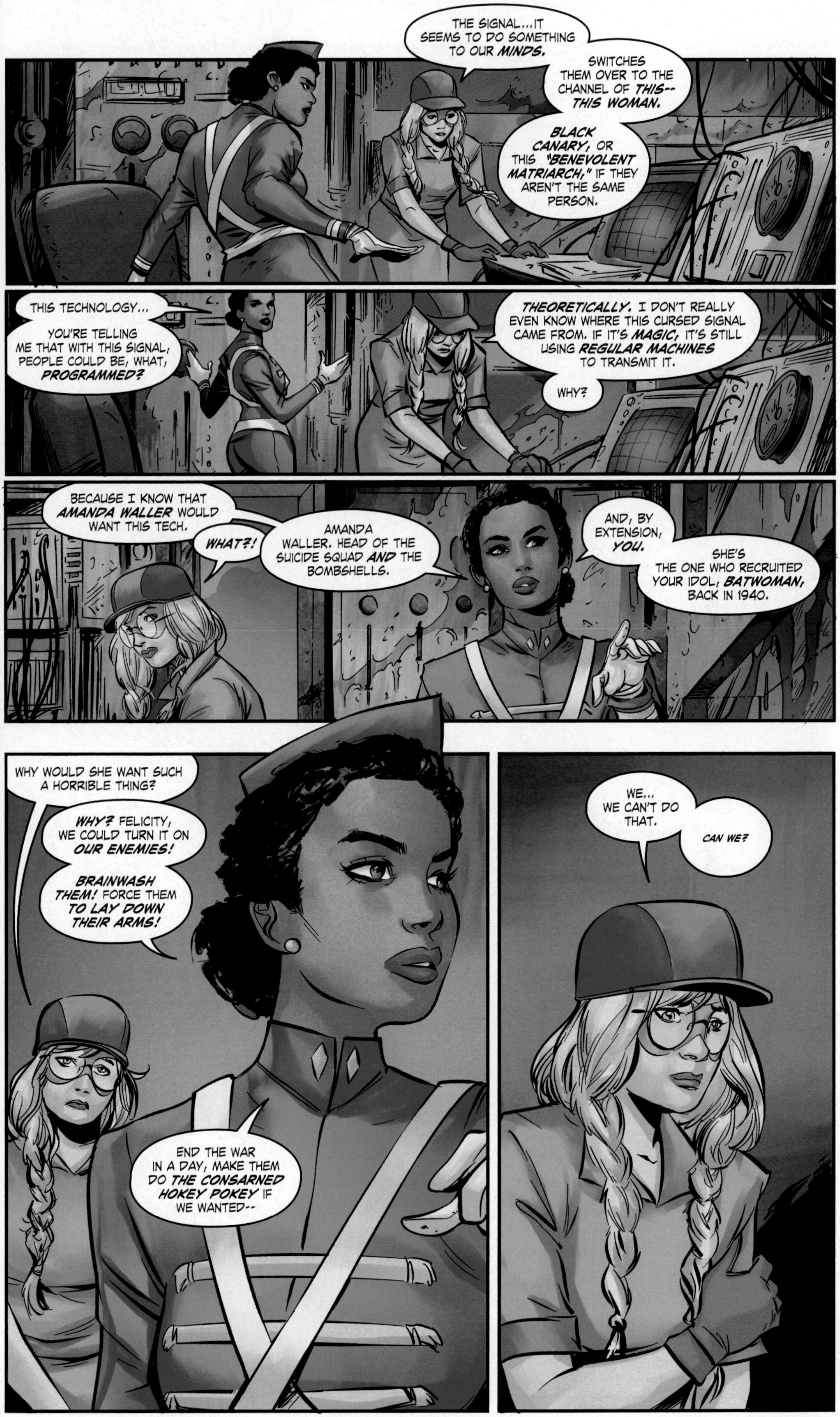
THE SIGNAL...IT SEEMS TO DO SOMETHING TO OUR MINDS.
SWITCHES THEM OVER TO THE CHANNEL OF THIS-- THIS WOMAN.
BLACK CANARY, OR THIS "BENEVOLENT MATRIARCH," IF THEY AREN'T THE SAME PERSON.
THIS TECHNOLOGY...
YOU'RE TELLING ME THAT WITH THIS SIGNAL, PEOPLE COULD BE, WHAT, PROGRAMMED?
THEORETICALLY. I DON'T REALLY EVEN KNOW WHERE THIS CURSED SIGNAL CAME FROM. IF IT'S MAGIC, IT'S STILL USING REGULAR MACHINES TO TRANSMIT IT.
WHY?
BECAUSE I KNOW THAT AMANDA WALLER WOULD WANT THIS TECH.
WHAT?!
AMANDA WALLER. HEAD OF THE SUICIDE SQUAD AND THE BOMBSHELLS.
AND, BY EXTENSION, YOU.
SHE'S THE ONE WHO RECRUITED YOUR IDOL, BATWOMAN, BACK IN 1940.
WHY WOULD SHE WANT SUCH A HORRIBLE THING?
WHY? FELICITY, WE COULD TURN IT ON OUR ENEMIES!
BRAINWASH THEM! FORCE THEM TO LAY DOWN THEIR ARMS!
END THE WAR IN A DAY, MAKE THEM DO THE CONSARNED HOKEY POKEY IF WE WANTED--
WE... WE CAN'T DO THAT.
CAN WE?

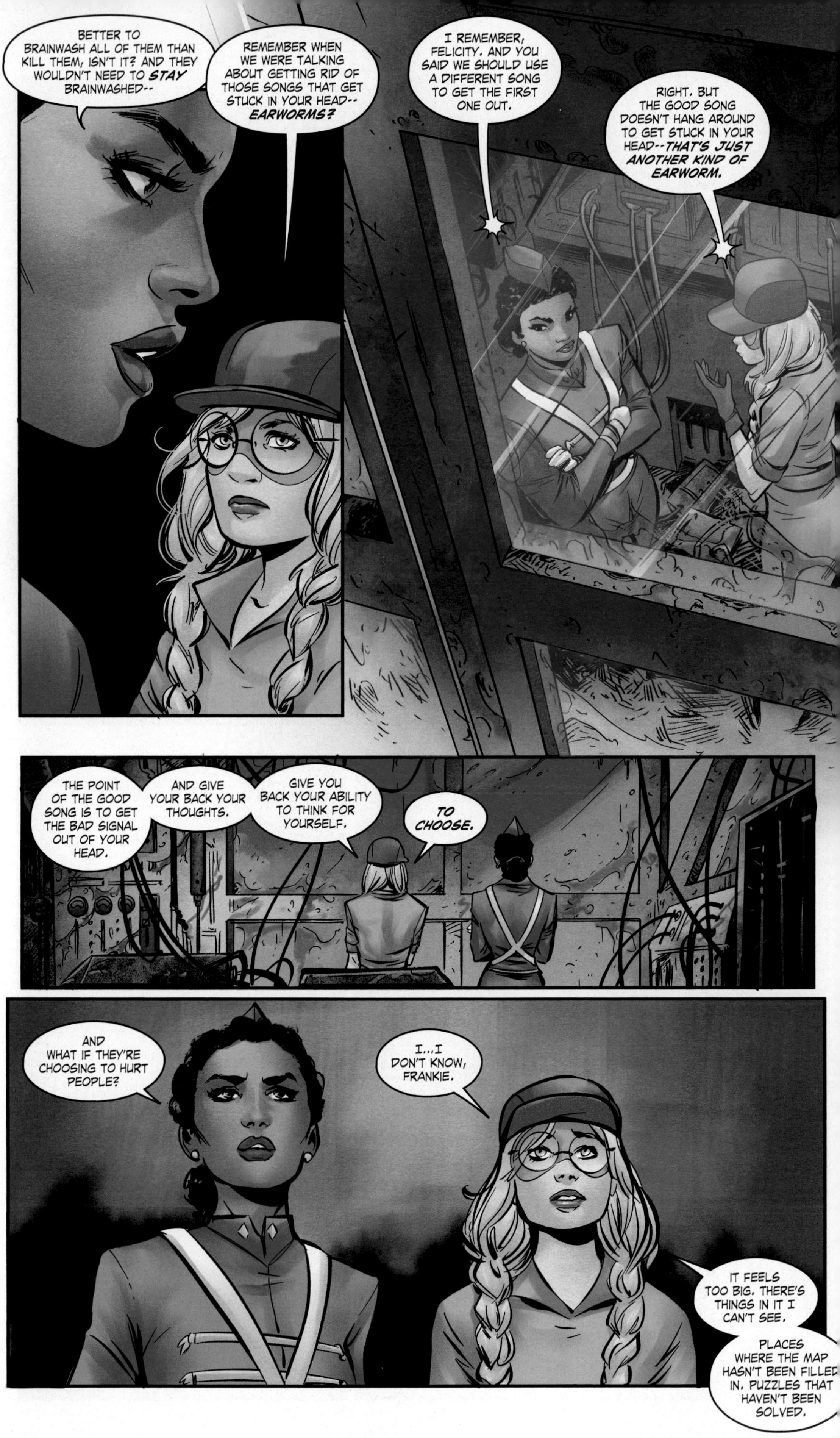
BETTER TO BRAINWASH ALL OF THEM THAN KILL THEM, ISN'T IT? AND THEY WOULDN'T NEED TO *STAY* BRAINWASHED--
REMEMBER WHEN WE WERE TALKING ABOUT GETTING RID OF THOSE SONGS THAT GET STUCK IN YOUR HEAD-- *EARWORMS?*
I REMEMBER, FELICITY. AND YOU SAID WE SHOULD USE A DIFFERENT SONG TO GET THE FIRST ONE OUT.
RIGHT. BUT THE GOOD SONG DOESN'T HANG AROUND TO GET STUCK IN YOUR HEAD--*THAT'S JUST ANOTHER KIND OF EARWORM.*
THE POINT OF THE GOOD SONG IS TO GET THE BAD SIGNAL OUT OF YOUR HEAD.
AND GIVE YOUR BACK YOUR THOUGHTS.
GIVE YOU BACK YOUR ABILITY TO THINK FOR YOURSELF.
TO CHOOSE.
AND WHAT IF THEY'RE CHOOSING TO HURT PEOPLE?
I...I DON'T KNOW, FRANKIE.
IT FEELS TOO BIG. THERE'S THINGS IN IT I CAN'T SEE.
PLACES WHERE THE MAP HASN'T BEEN FILLED IN. PUZZLES THAT HAVEN'T BEEN SOLVED.

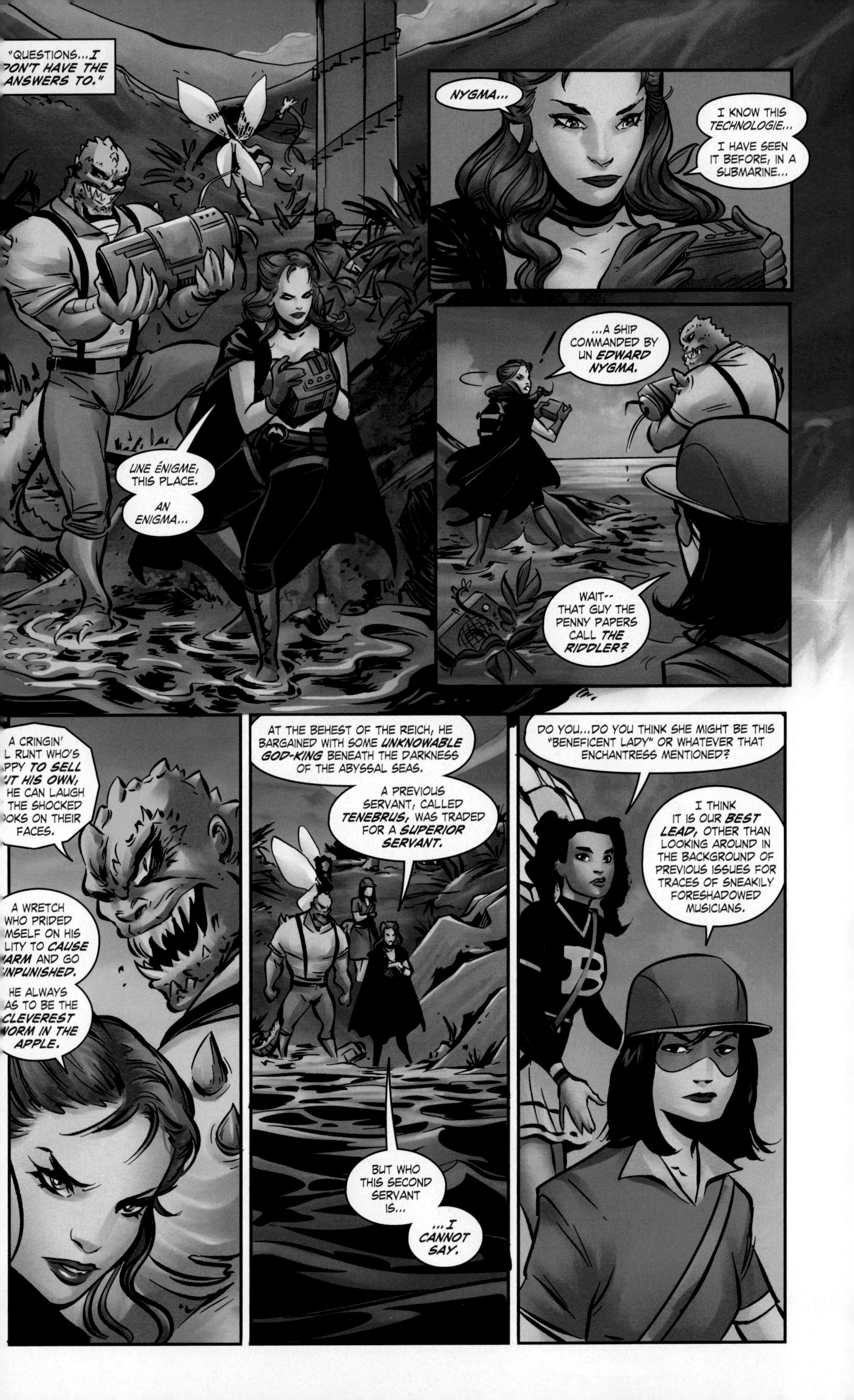
"QUESTIONS...I
DON'T HAVE THE
ANSWERS TO."
UNE ÉNIGME, THIS PLACE.
AN ENIGMA...
NYGMA...
I KNOW THIS TECHNOLOGIE...
I HAVE SEEN IT BEFORE, IN A SUBMARINE...
...A SHIP COMMANDED BY UN EDWARD NYGMA.
WAIT-- THAT GUY THE PENNY PAPERS CALL THE RIDDLER?
A CRINGIN' L RUNT WHO'S APPY TO SELL UT HIS OWN, HE CAN LAUGH THE SHOCKED OOKS ON THEIR FACES.
A WRETCH WHO PRIDED MSELF ON HIS LITY TO CAUSE ARM AND GO NPUNISHED.
HE ALWAYS AS TO BE THE CLEVEREST WORM IN THE APPLE.
AT THE BEHEST OF THE REICH, HE BARGAINED WITH SOME UNKNOWABLE GOD-KING BENEATH THE DARKNESS OF THE ABYSSAL SEAS.
A PREVIOUS SERVANT, CALLED TENEBRUS, WAS TRADED FOR A SUPERIOR SERVANT.
BUT WHO THIS SECOND SERVANT IS...
...I CANNOT SAY.
DO YOU...DO YOU THINK SHE MIGHT BE THIS "BENEFICENT LADY" OR WHATEVER THAT ENCHANTRESS MENTIONED?
I THINK IT IS OUR BEST LEAD, OTHER THAN LOOKING AROUND IN THE BACKGROUND OF PREVIOUS ISSUES FOR TRACES OF SNEAKILY FORESHADOWED MUSICIANS.

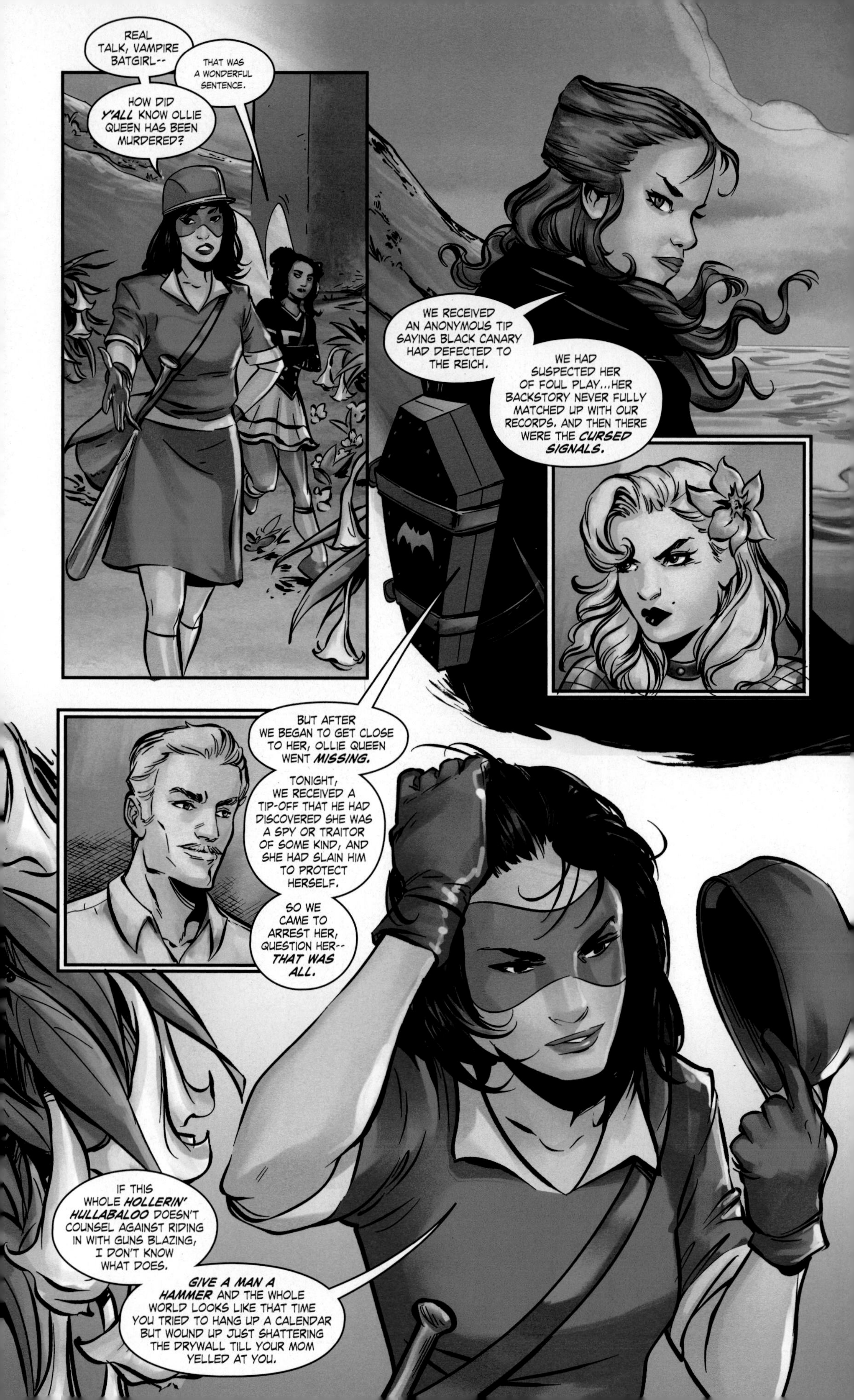
REAL TALK, VAMPIRE BATGIRL--
THAT WAS A WONDERFUL SENTENCE.
HOW DID Y'ALL KNOW OLLIE QUEEN HAS BEEN MURDERED?
WE RECEIVED AN ANONYMOUS TIP SAYING BLACK CANARY HAD DEFECTED TO THE REICH.
WE HAD SUSPECTED HER OF FOUL PLAY...HER BACKSTORY NEVER FULLY MATCHED UP WITH OUR RECORDS. AND THEN THERE WERE THE CURSED SIGNALS.
BUT AFTER WE BEGAN TO GET CLOSE TO HER, OLLIE QUEEN WENT MISSING.
TONIGHT, WE RECEIVED A TIP-OFF THAT HE HAD DISCOVERED SHE WAS A SPY OR TRAITOR OF SOME KIND, AND SHE HAD SLAIN HIM TO PROTECT HERSELF.
SO WE CAME TO ARREST HER, QUESTION HER-- THAT WAS ALL.
IF THIS WHOLE HOLLERIN' HULLABALOO DOESN'T COUNSEL AGAINST RIDING IN WITH GUNS BLAZING, I DON'T KNOW WHAT DOES.
GIVE A MAN A HAMMER AND THE WHOLE WORLD LOOKS LIKE THAT TIME YOU TRIED TO HANG UP A CALENDAR BUT WOUND UP JUST SHATTERING THE DRYWALL TILL YOUR MOM YELLED AT YOU.

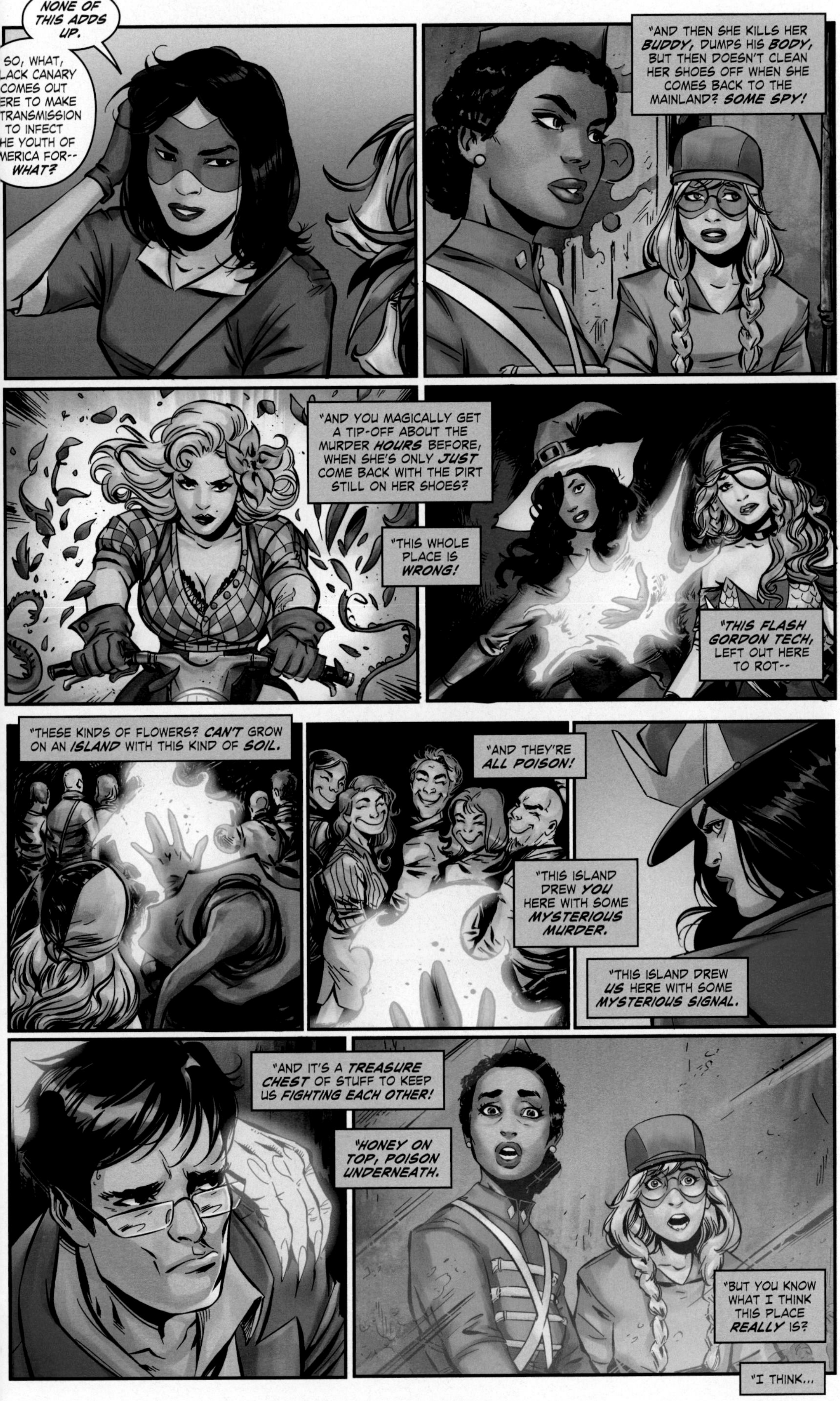
NONE OF THIS ADDS UP.
SO, WHAT, LACK CANARY COMES OUT ERE TO MAKE TRANSMISSION TO INFECT HE YOUTH OF MERICA FOR-- WHAT?
"AND THEN SHE KILLS HER BUDDY, DUMPS HIS BODY, BUT THEN DOESN'T CLEAN HER SHOES OFF WHEN SHE COMES BACK TO THE MAINLAND? SOME SPY!
"AND YOU MAGICALLY GET A TIP-OFF ABOUT THE MURDER HOURS BEFORE, WHEN SHE'S ONLY JUST COME BACK WITH THE DIRT STILL ON HER SHOES?
"THIS WHOLE PLACE IS WRONG!
"THIS FLASH GORDON TECH, LEFT OUT HERE TO ROT--
"THESE KINDS OF FLOWERS? CAN'T GROW ON AN ISLAND WITH THIS KIND OF SOIL.
"AND THEY'RE ALL POISON!
"THIS ISLAND DREW YOU HERE WITH SOME MYSTERIOUS MURDER.
"THIS ISLAND DREW US HERE WITH SOME MYSTERIOUS SIGNAL.
"AND IT'S A TREASURE CHEST OF STUFF TO KEEP US FIGHTING EACH OTHER!
"HONEY ON TOP, POISON UNDERNEATH.
"BUT YOU KNOW WHAT I THINK THIS PLACE REALLY IS?
"I THINK...

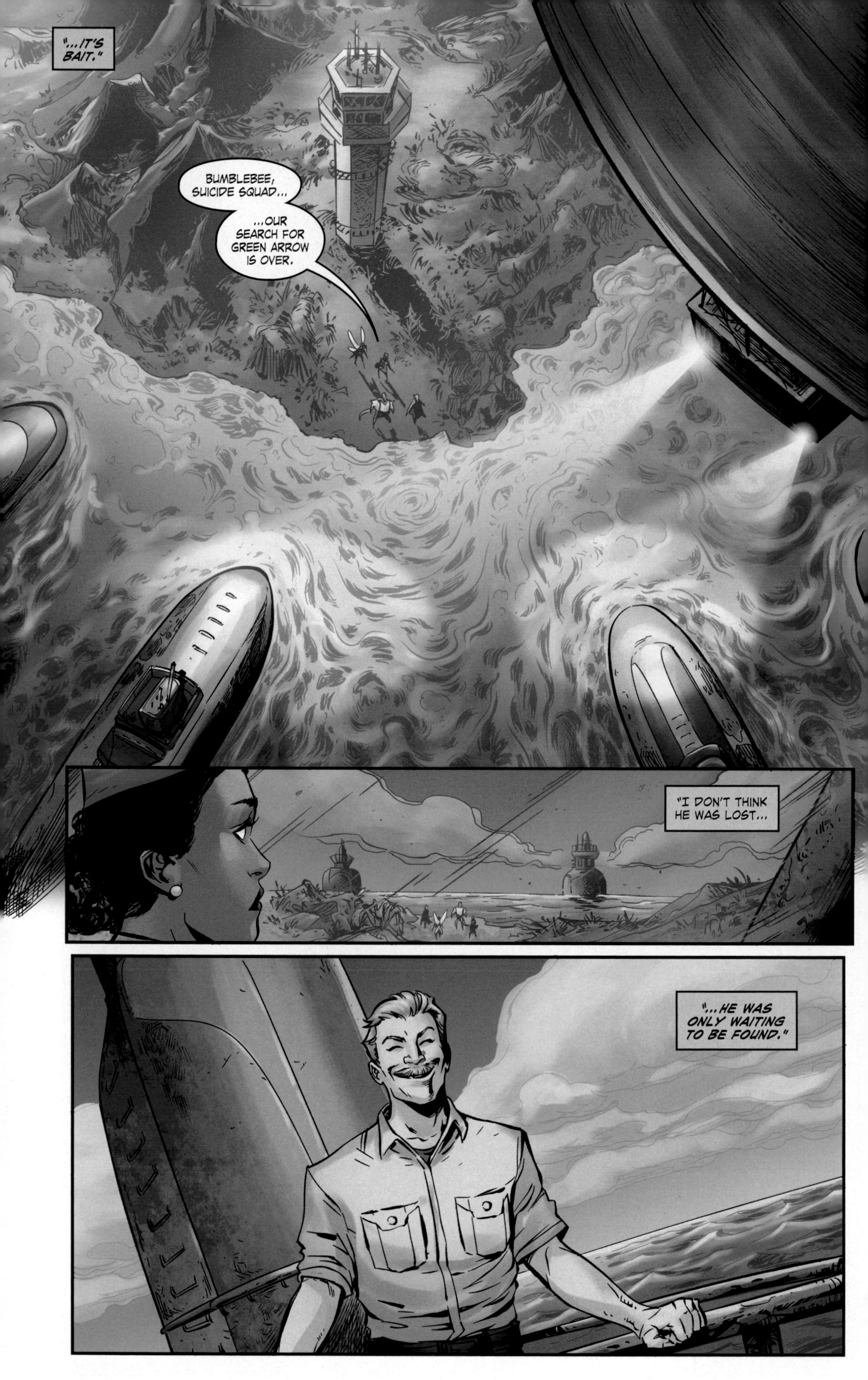
"...IT'S BAIT."
BUMBLEBEE, SUICIDE SQUAD...
...OUR SEARCH FOR GREEN ARROW IS OVER.
"I DON'T THINK HE WAS LOST...
"...HE WAS ONLY WAITING TO BE FOUND."

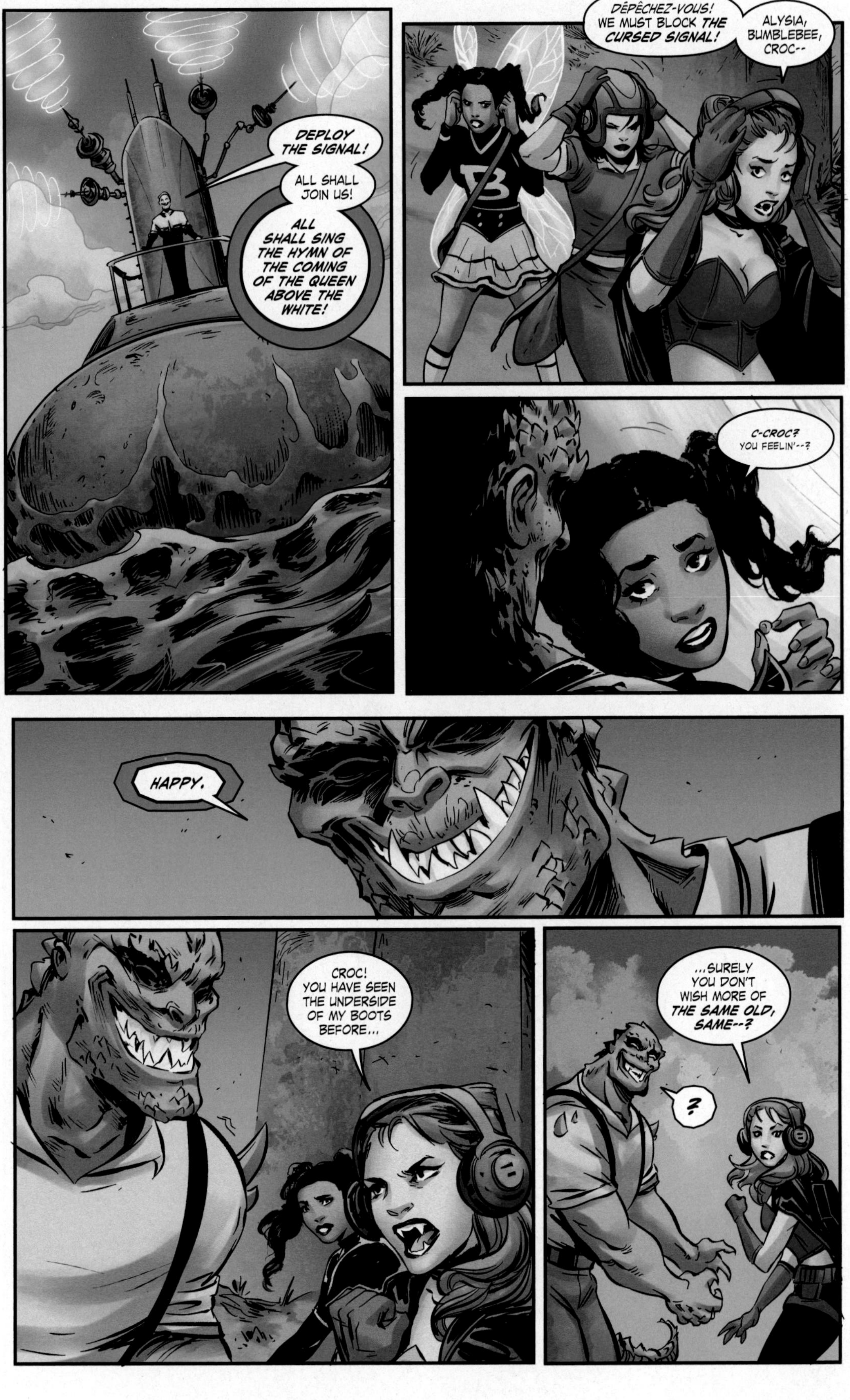
DEPLOY THE SIGNAL!
ALL SHALL JOIN US!
ALL SHALL SING THE HYMN OF THE COMING OF THE QUEEN ABOVE THE WHITE!
DÉPÊCHEZ-VOUS! WE MUST BLOCK THE CURSED SIGNAL!
ALYSIA, BUMBLEBEE, CROC--
C-CROC? YOU FEELIN'--?
HAPPY.
CROC! YOU HAVE SEEN THE UNDERSIDE OF MY BOOTS BEFORE...
...SURELY YOU DON'T WISH MORE OF THE SAME OLD, SAME--?
?

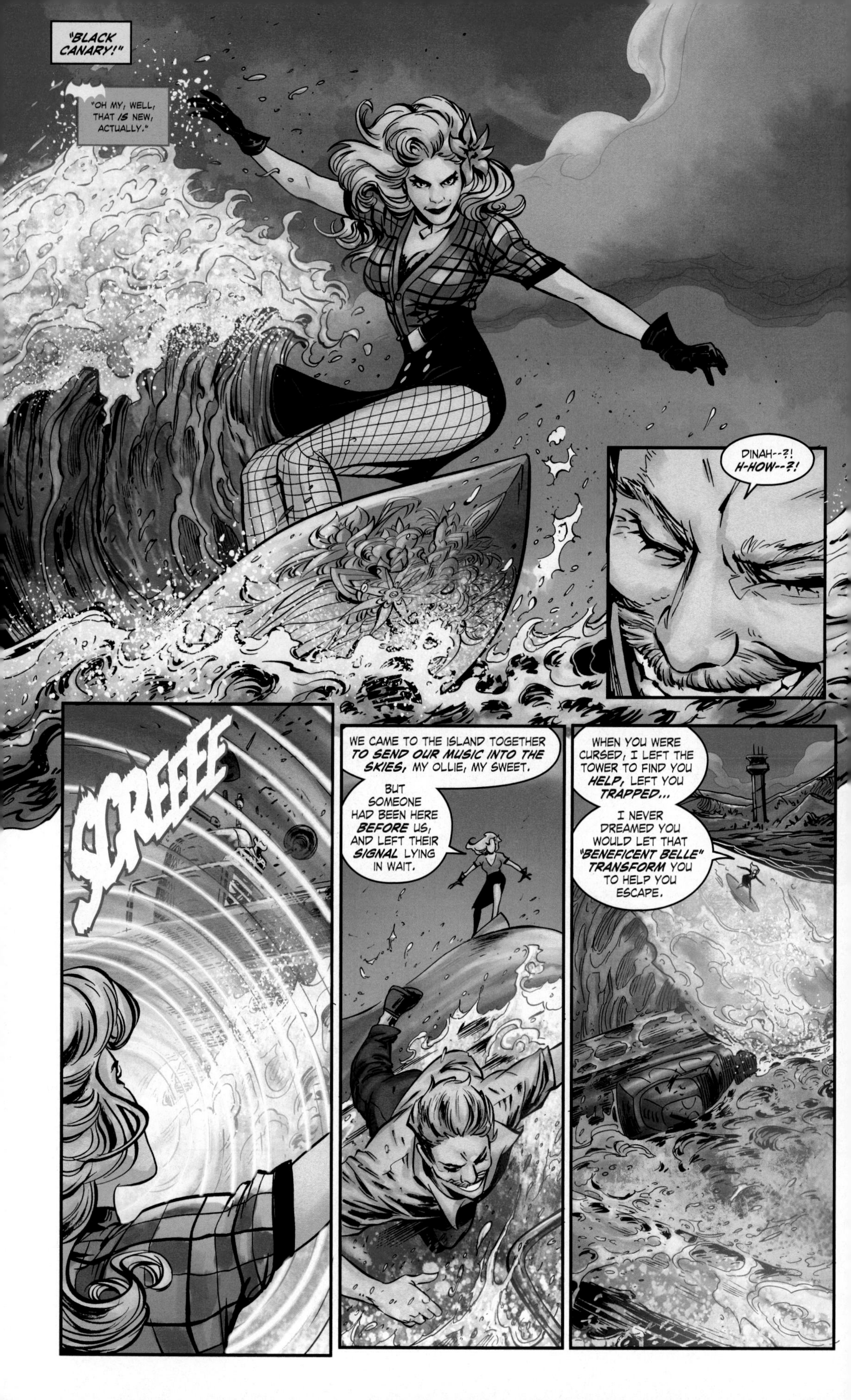
"BLACK CANARY!"
"OH MY, WELL, THAT IS NEW, ACTUALLY."
DINAH--?! H-HOW--?!
SCREEEE
WE CAME TO THE ISLAND TOGETHER TO SEND OUR MUSIC INTO THE SKIES, MY OLLIE, MY SWEET.
BUT SOMEONE HAD BEEN HERE BEFORE US, AND LEFT THEIR SIGNAL LYING IN WAIT.
WHEN YOU WERE CURSED, I LEFT THE TOWER TO FIND YOU HELP, LEFT YOU TRAPPED...
I NEVER DREAMED YOU WOULD LET THAT "BENEFICENT BELLE" TRANSFORM YOU TO HELP YOU ESCAPE.

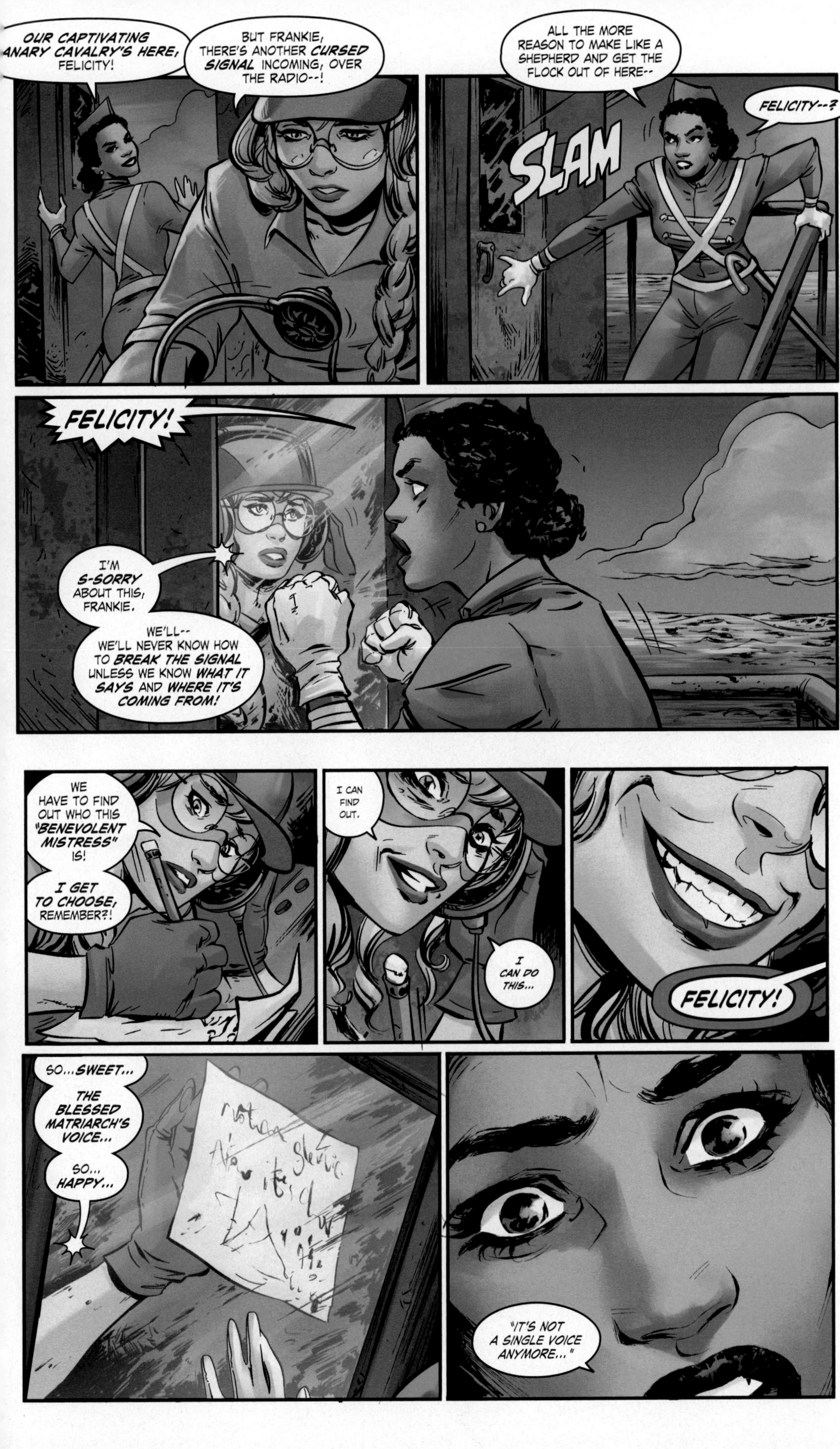
OUR CAPTIVATING ANARY CAVALRY'S HERE, FELICITY!
BUT FRANKIE, THERE'S ANOTHER CURSED SIGNAL INCOMING, OVER THE RADIO--!
ALL THE MORE REASON TO MAKE LIKE A SHEPHERD AND GET THE FLOCK OUT OF HERE--
SLAM
FELICITY--?
FELICITY!
I'M S-SORRY ABOUT THIS, FRANKIE.
WE'LL-- WE'LL NEVER KNOW HOW TO BREAK THE SIGNAL UNLESS WE KNOW WHAT IT SAYS AND WHERE IT'S COMING FROM!
WE HAVE TO FIND OUT WHO THIS "BENEVOLENT MISTRESS" IS!
I GET TO CHOOSE, REMEMBER?!
I CAN FIND OUT.
I CAN DO THIS...
FELICITY!
SO...SWEET...
THE BLESSED MATRIARCH'S VOICE...
SO... HAPPY...
"IT'S NOT A SINGLE VOICE ANYMORE..."

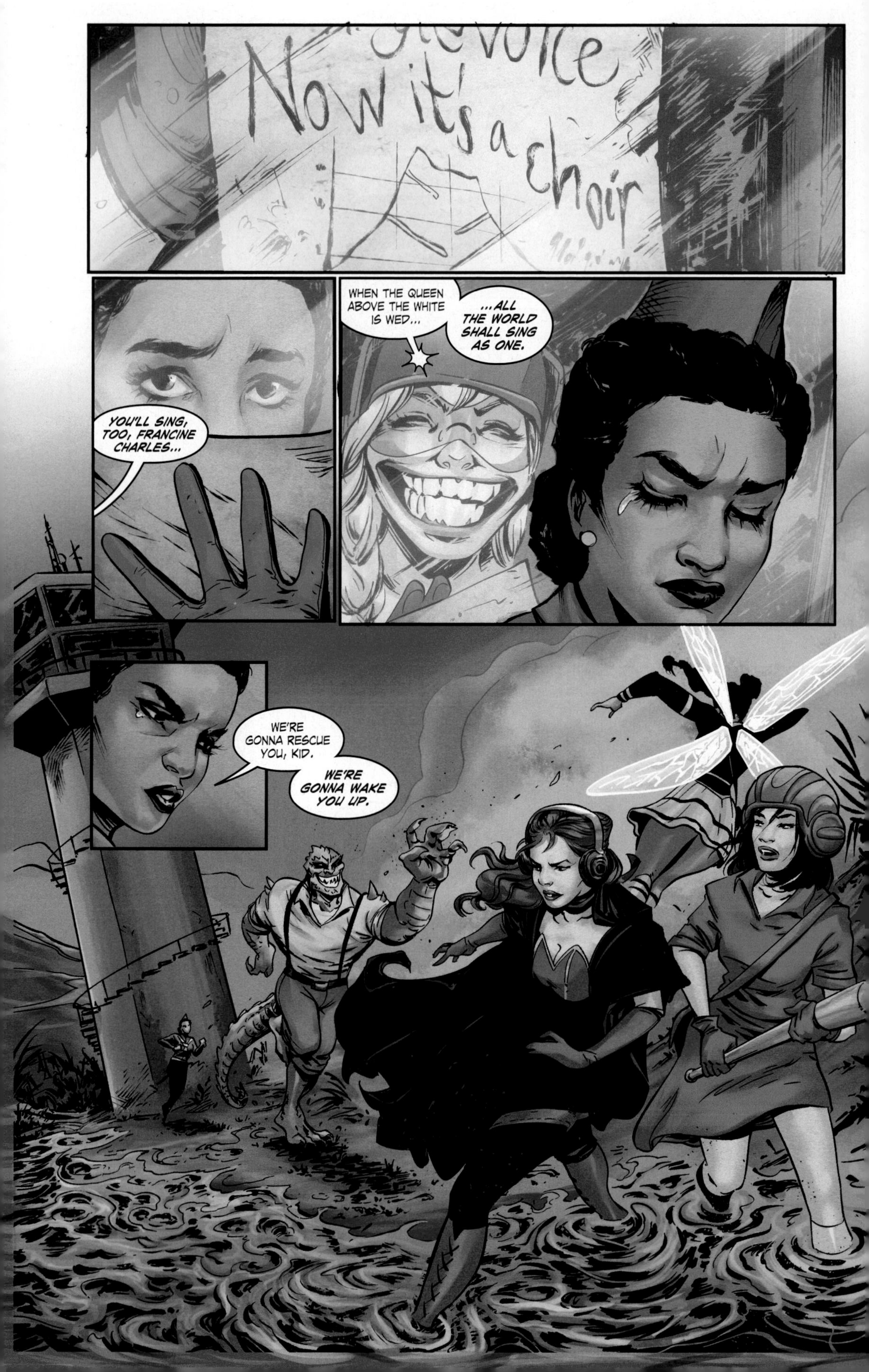
Now it's a choir
YOU'LL SING, TOO, FRANCINE CHARLES...
WHEN THE QUEEN ABOVE THE WHITE IS WED...
...ALL THE WORLD SHALL SING AS ONE.
WE'RE GONNA RESCUE YOU, KID.
WE'RE GONNA WAKE YOU UP.

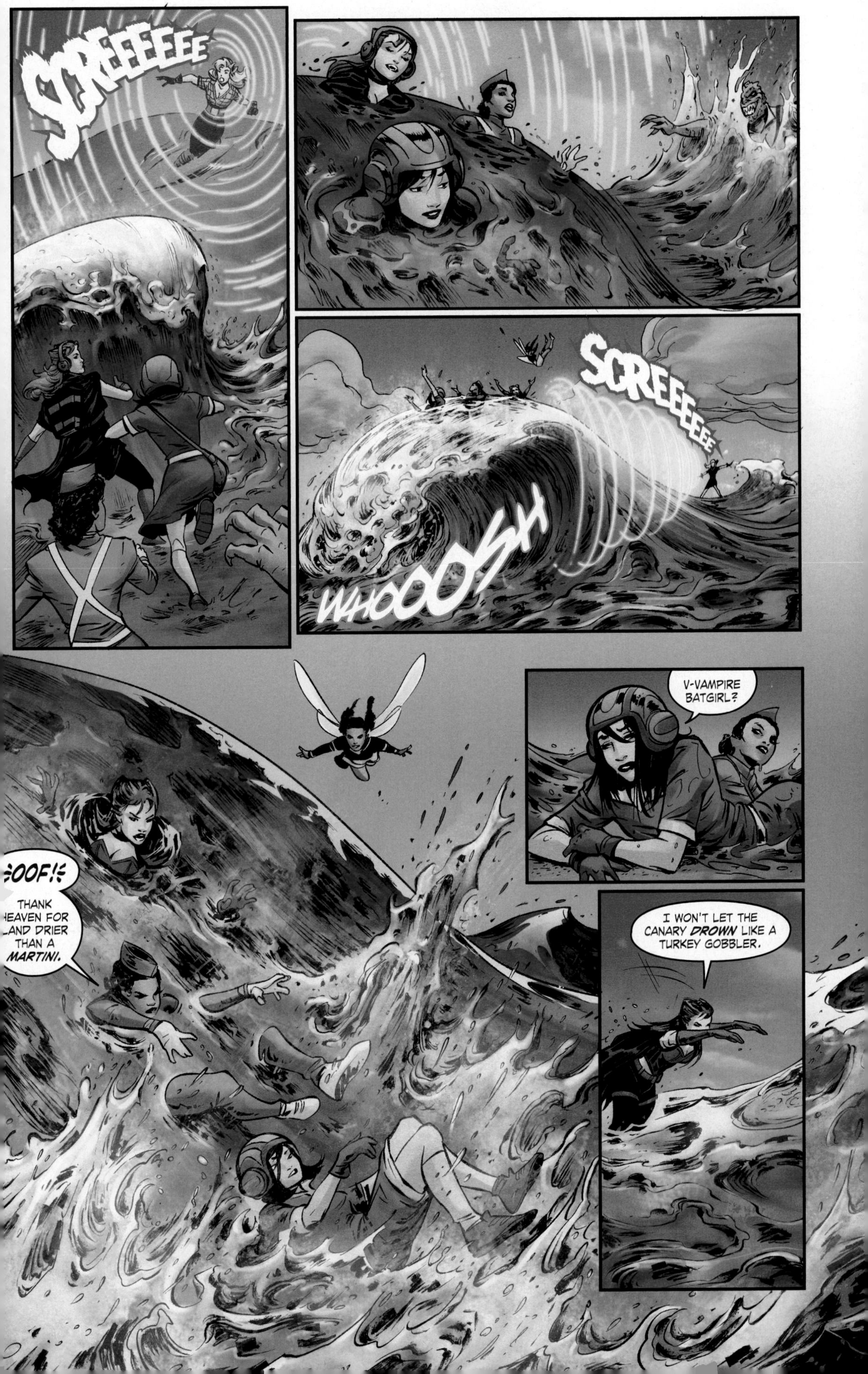
SCREEEEEEE
SCREEEEEEE
WHOOOOSH
V-VAMPIRE BATGIRL?
OOF!
THANK HEAVEN FOR LAND DRIER THAN A MARTINI.
I WON'T LET THE CANARY DROWN LIKE A TURKEY GOBBLER.

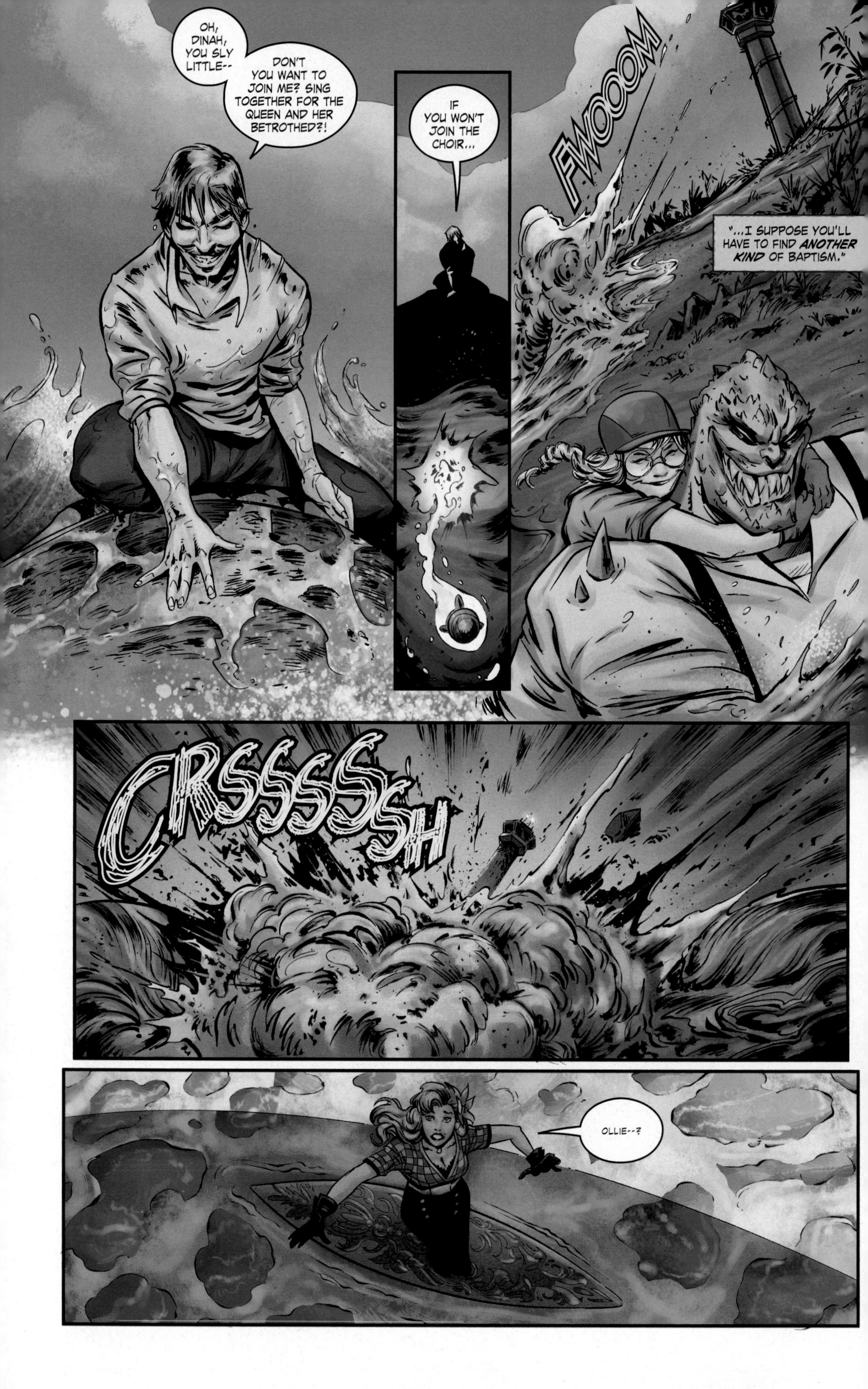
OH, DINAH, YOU SLY LITTLE--
DON'T YOU WANT TO JOIN ME? SING TOGETHER FOR THE QUEEN AND HER BETROTHED?!
IF YOU WON'T JOIN THE CHOIR...
FWOOOM
"...I SUPPOSE YOU'LL HAVE TO FIND ANOTHER KIND OF BAPTISM."
CRSSSSSSH
OLLIE--?

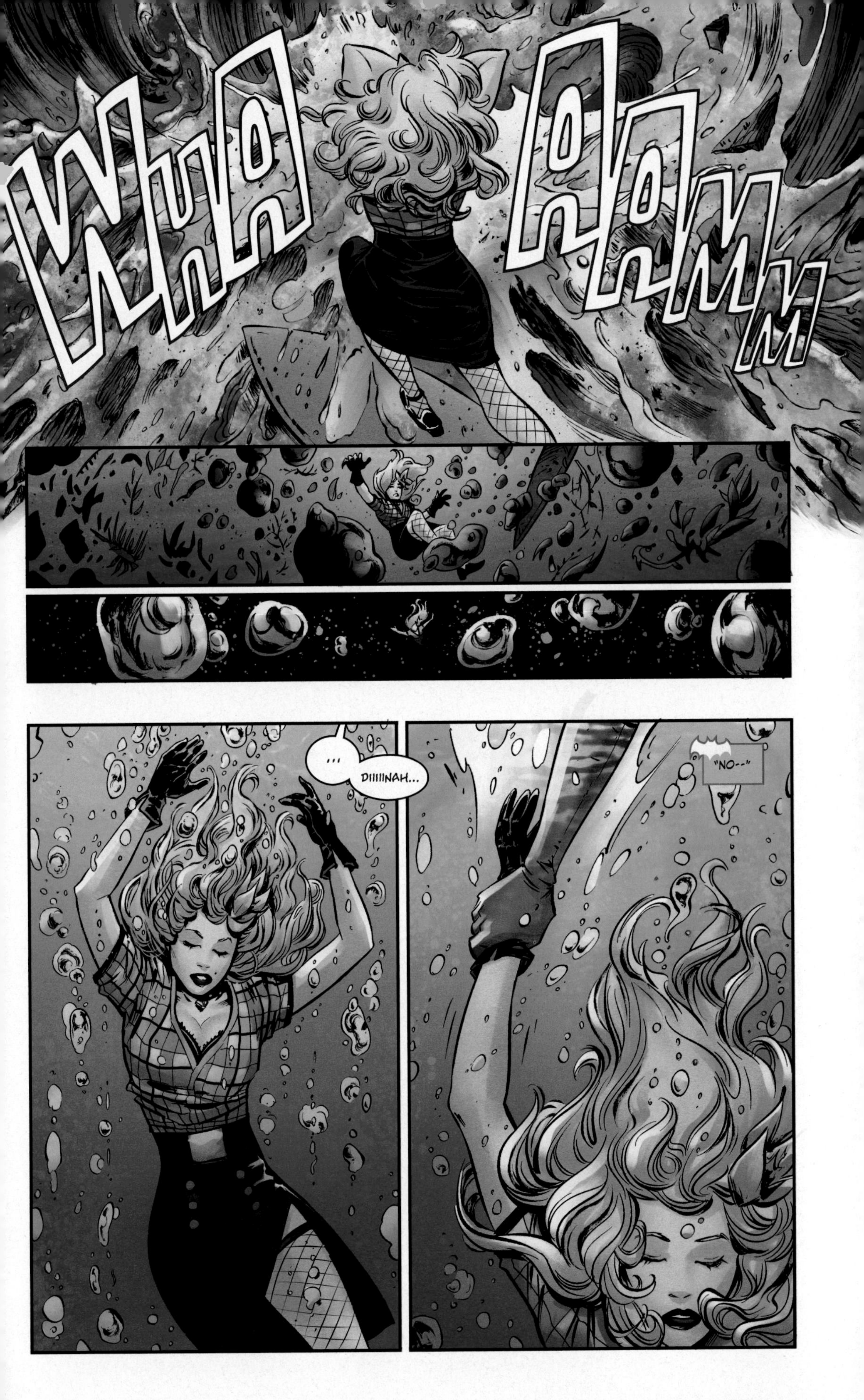
...
DIIIIINAH...
"NO--"

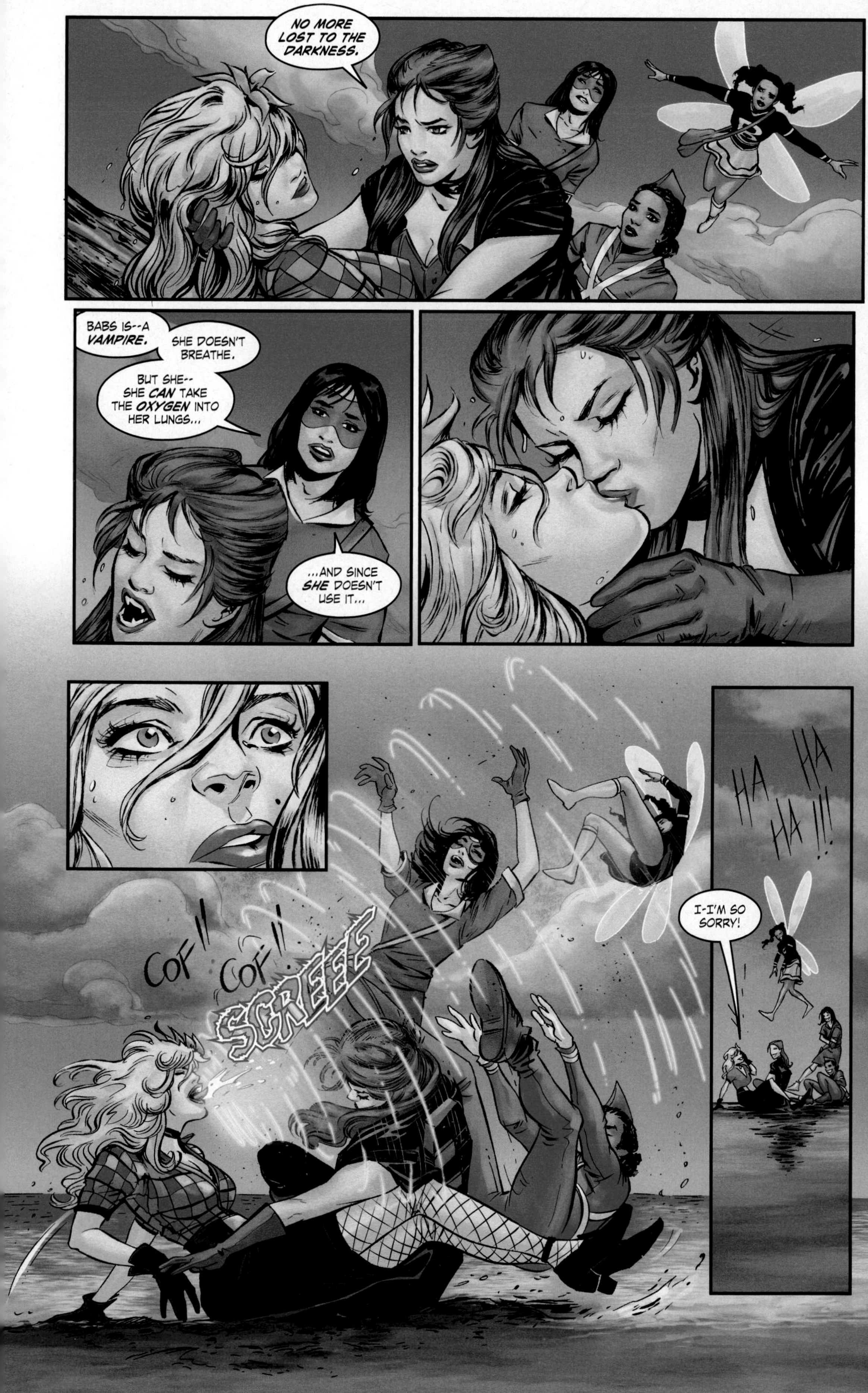
NO MORE LOST TO THE DARKNESS.
BABS IS--A VAMPIRE.
SHE DOESN'T BREATHE.
BUT SHE-- SHE CAN TAKE THE OXYGEN INTO HER LUNGS...
...AND SINCE SHE DOESN'T USE IT...
COF!! COF!!
SCREEE
HA HA HA!!!
I-I'M SO SORRY!

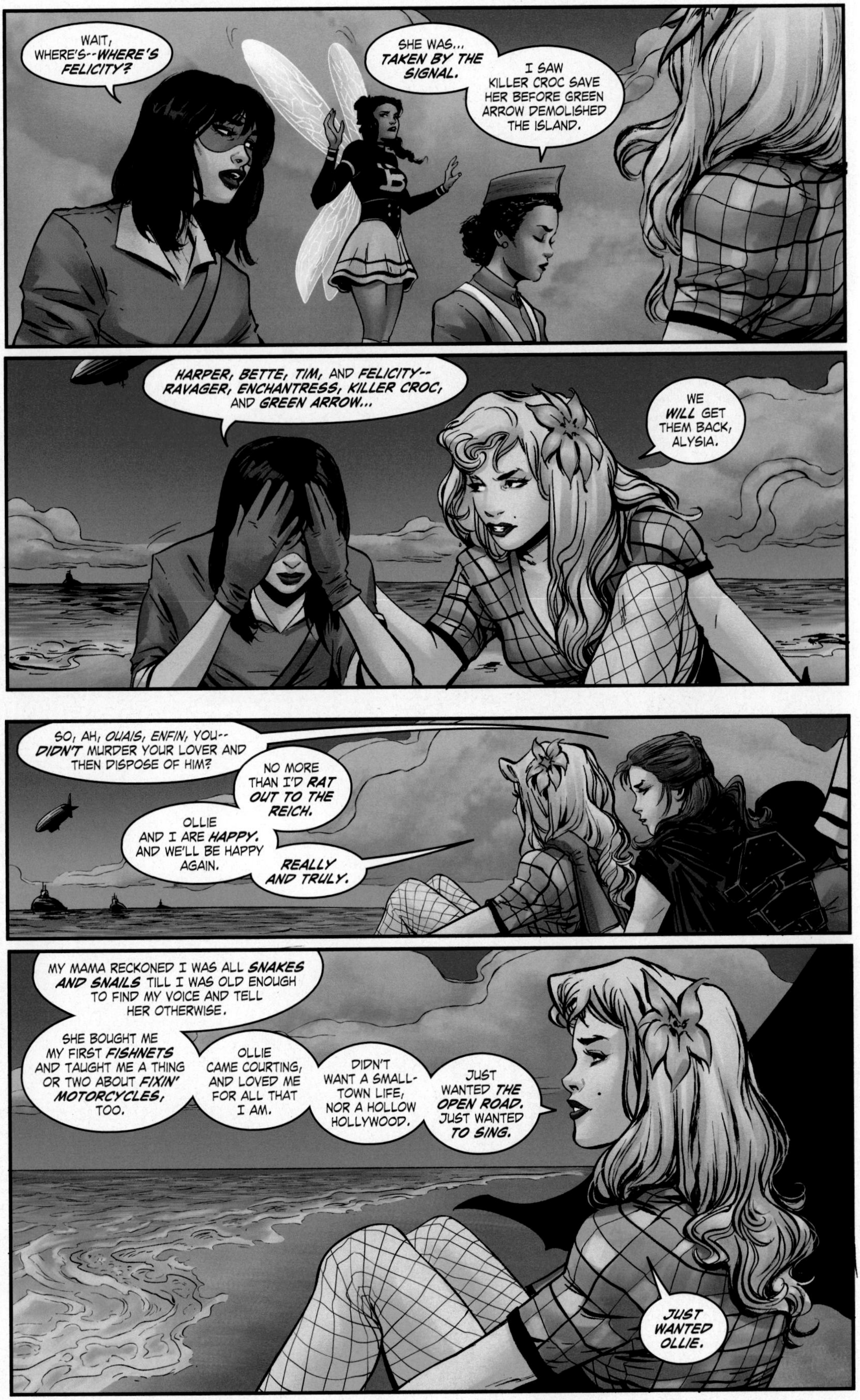
WAIT, WHERE'S--WHERE'S FELICITY?
SHE WAS... TAKEN BY THE SIGNAL.
I SAW KILLER CROC SAVE HER BEFORE GREEN ARROW DEMOLISHED THE ISLAND.
HARPER, BETTE, TIM, AND FELICITY-- RAVAGER, ENCHANTRESS, KILLER CROC, AND GREEN ARROW...
WE WILL GET THEM BACK, ALYSIA.
SO, AH, OUAIS, ENFIN, YOU-- DIDN'T MURDER YOUR LOVER AND THEN DISPOSE OF HIM?
NO MORE THAN I'D RAT OUT TO THE REICH.
OLLIE AND I ARE HAPPY. AND WE'LL BE HAPPY AGAIN.
REALLY AND TRULY.
MY MAMA RECKONED I WAS ALL SNAKES AND SNAILS TILL I WAS OLD ENOUGH TO FIND MY VOICE AND TELL HER OTHERWISE.
SHE BOUGHT ME MY FIRST FISHNETS AND TAUGHT ME A THING OR TWO ABOUT FIXIN' MOTORCYCLES, TOO.
OLLIE CAME COURTING, AND LOVED ME FOR ALL THAT I AM.
DIDN'T WANT A SMALL-TOWN LIFE, NOR A HOLLOW HOLLYWOOD.
JUST WANTED THE OPEN ROAD. JUST WANTED TO SING.
JUST WANTED OLLIE.

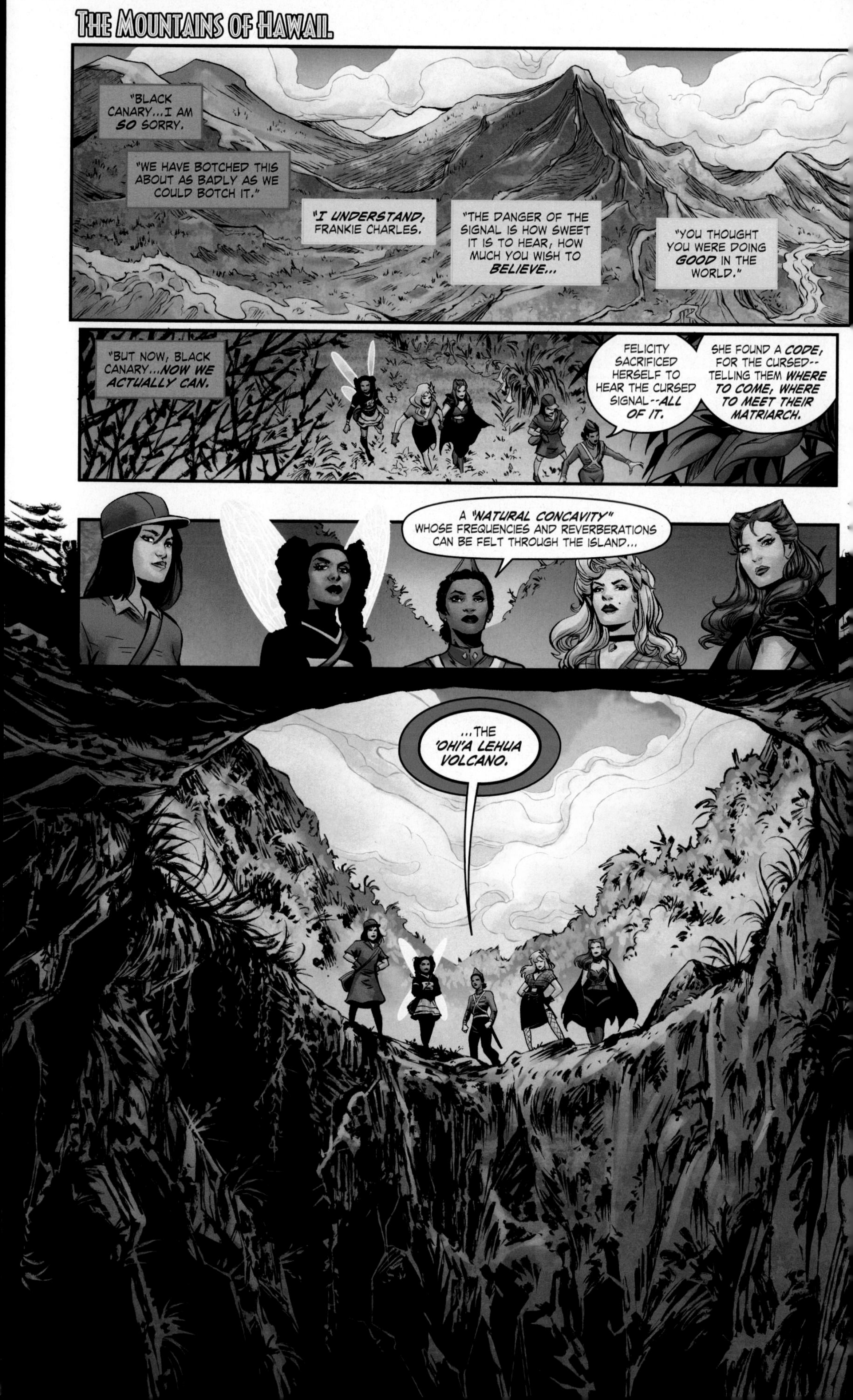
THE MOUNTAINS OF HAWAII.
"BLACK CANARY...I AM SO SORRY.
"WE HAVE BOTCHED THIS ABOUT AS BADLY AS WE COULD BOTCH IT."
"I UNDERSTAND, FRANKIE CHARLES.
"THE DANGER OF THE SIGNAL IS HOW SWEET IT IS TO HEAR, HOW MUCH YOU WISH TO BELIEVE...
"YOU THOUGHT YOU WERE DOING GOOD IN THE WORLD."
"BUT NOW, BLACK CANARY...NOW WE ACTUALLY CAN.
FELICITY SACRIFICED HERSELF TO HEAR THE CURSED SIGNAL--ALL OF IT.
SHE FOUND A CODE, FOR THE CURSED--TELLING THEM WHERE TO COME, WHERE TO MEET THEIR MATRIARCH.
A "NATURAL CONCAVITY" WHOSE FREQUENCIES AND REVERBERATIONS CAN BE FELT THROUGH THE ISLAND...
...THE 'OHI'A LEHUA VOLCANO.

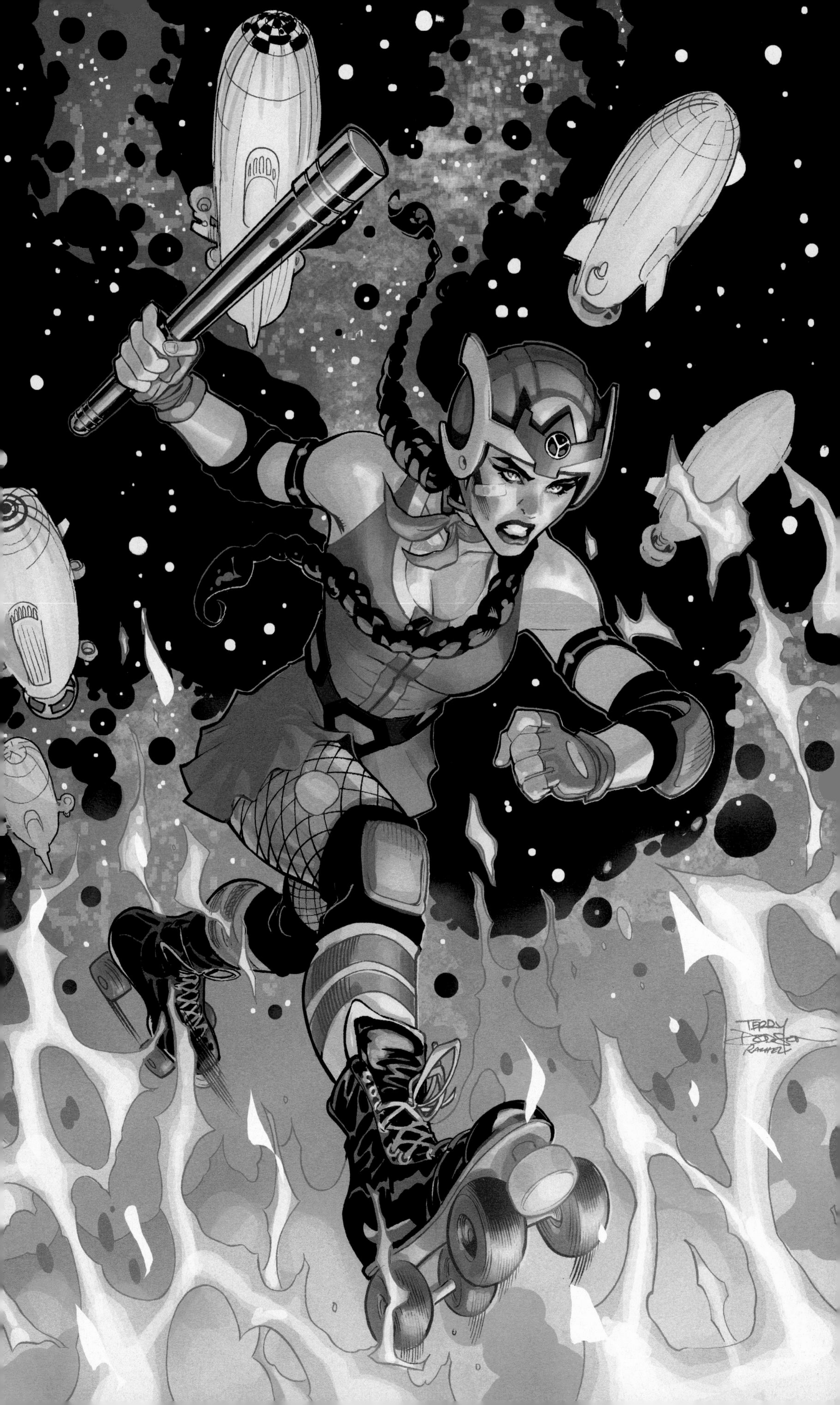
TERRY
DODSON
RACHEL

THE BLACK ISLAND

PARTS SEVEN and EIGHT

Written by
MARGUERITE BENNETT

Art by
SANDY JARRELL

Colors by
KELLY FITZPATRICK

Letters by
WES ABBOTT

Cover by
TERRY *and* **RACHEL DODSON**

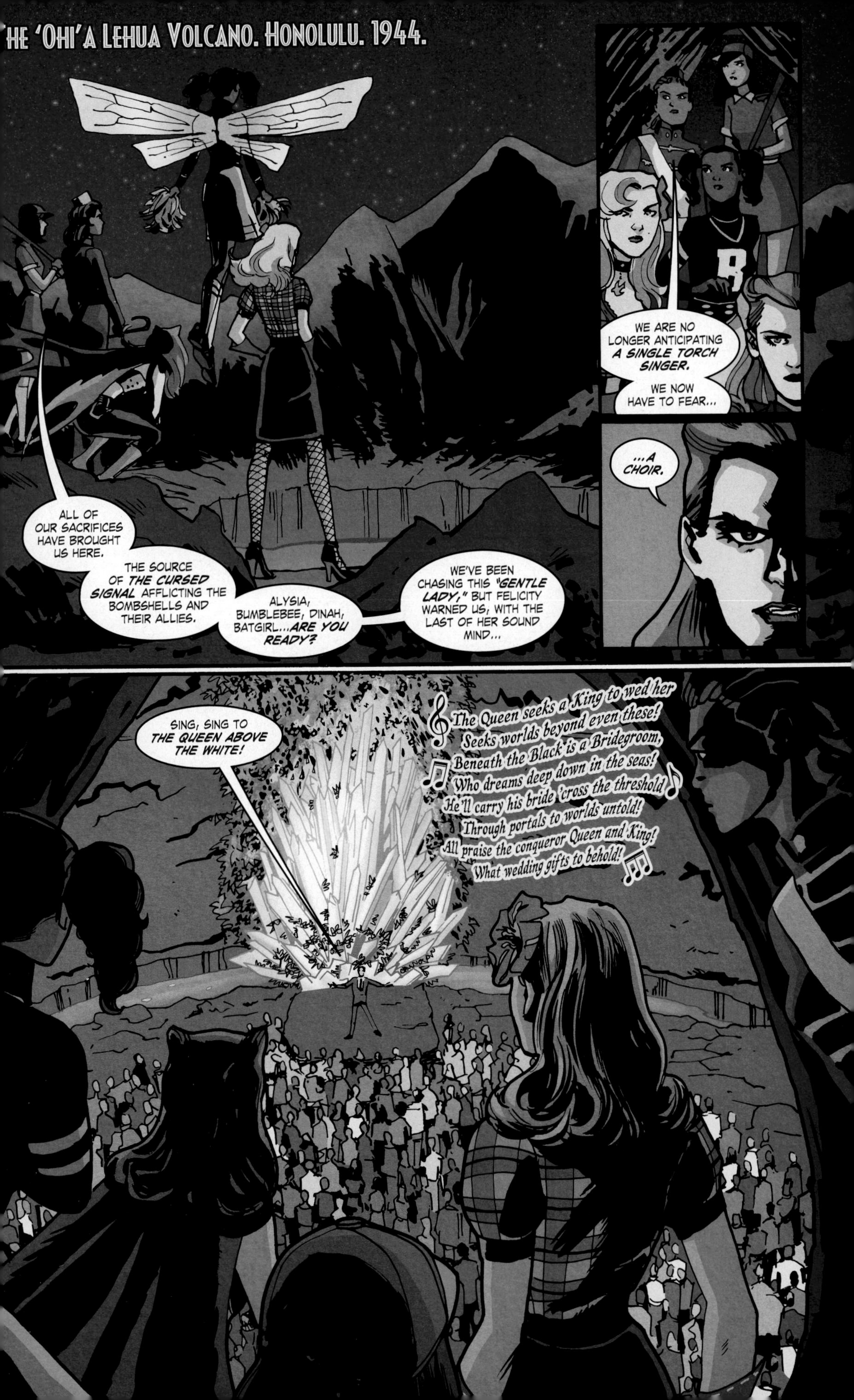

HE 'OHI'A LEHUA VOLCANO. HONOLULU. 1944.
ALL OF OUR SACRIFICES HAVE BROUGHT US HERE.
THE SOURCE OF THE CURSED SIGNAL AFFLICTING THE BOMBSHELLS AND THEIR ALLIES.
ALYSIA, BUMBLEBEE, DINAH, BATGIRL...ARE YOU READY?
WE'VE BEEN CHASING THIS "GENTLE LADY," BUT FELICITY WARNED US, WITH THE LAST OF HER SOUND MIND...
WE ARE NO LONGER ANTICIPATING A SINGLE TORCH SINGER.
WE NOW HAVE TO FEAR...
...A CHOIR.
SING, SING TO THE QUEEN ABOVE THE WHITE!
The Queen seeks a King to wed her
Seeks worlds beyond even these!
Seeks the Black is a Bridegroom,
Beneath the Black is a Bridegroom,
Who dreams deep down in the seas!
He'll carry his bride 'cross the threshold
Through portals to worlds untold!
All praise the conqueror Queen and King!
What wedding gifts to behold!

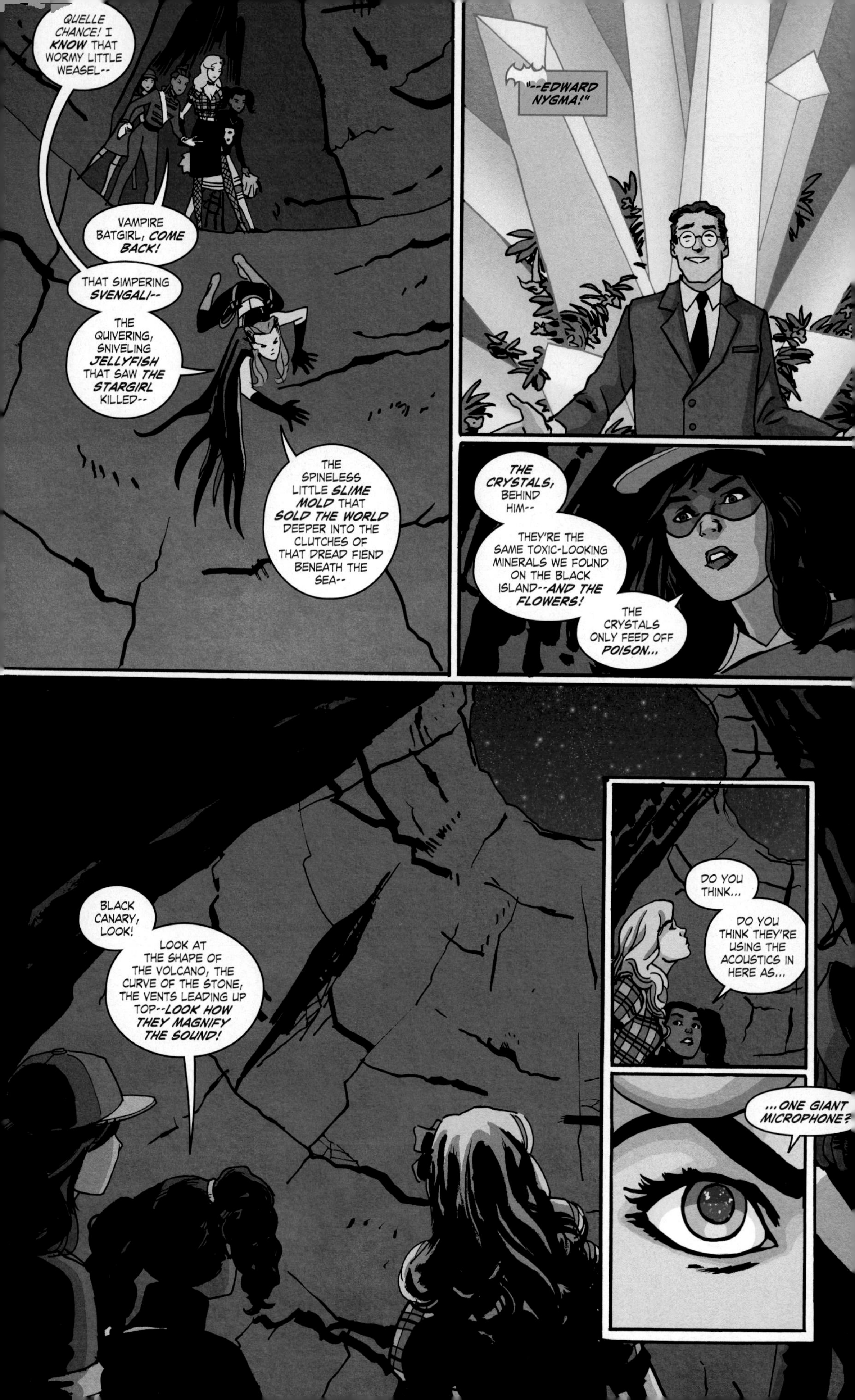

QUELLE CHANCE! I KNOW THAT WORMY LITTLE WEASEL--
VAMPIRE BATGIRL, COME BACK!
THAT SIMPERING SVENGALI--
THE QUIVERING, SNIVELING JELLYFISH THAT SAW THE STARGIRL KILLED--
THE SPINELESS LITTLE SLIME MOLD THAT SOLD THE WORLD DEEPER INTO THE CLUTCHES OF THAT DREAD FIEND BENEATH THE SEA--
"--EDWARD NYGMA!"
THE CRYSTALS, BEHIND HIM--
THEY'RE THE SAME TOXIC-LOOKING MINERALS WE FOUND ON THE BLACK ISLAND--AND THE FLOWERS!
THE CRYSTALS ONLY FEED OFF POISON...
BLACK CANARY, LOOK!
LOOK AT THE SHAPE OF THE VOLCANO, THE CURVE OF THE STONE, THE VENTS LEADING UP TOP--LOOK HOW THEY MAGNIFY THE SOUND!
DO YOU THINK...
DO YOU THINK THEY'RE USING THE ACOUSTICS IN HERE AS...
...ONE GIANT MICROPHONE?

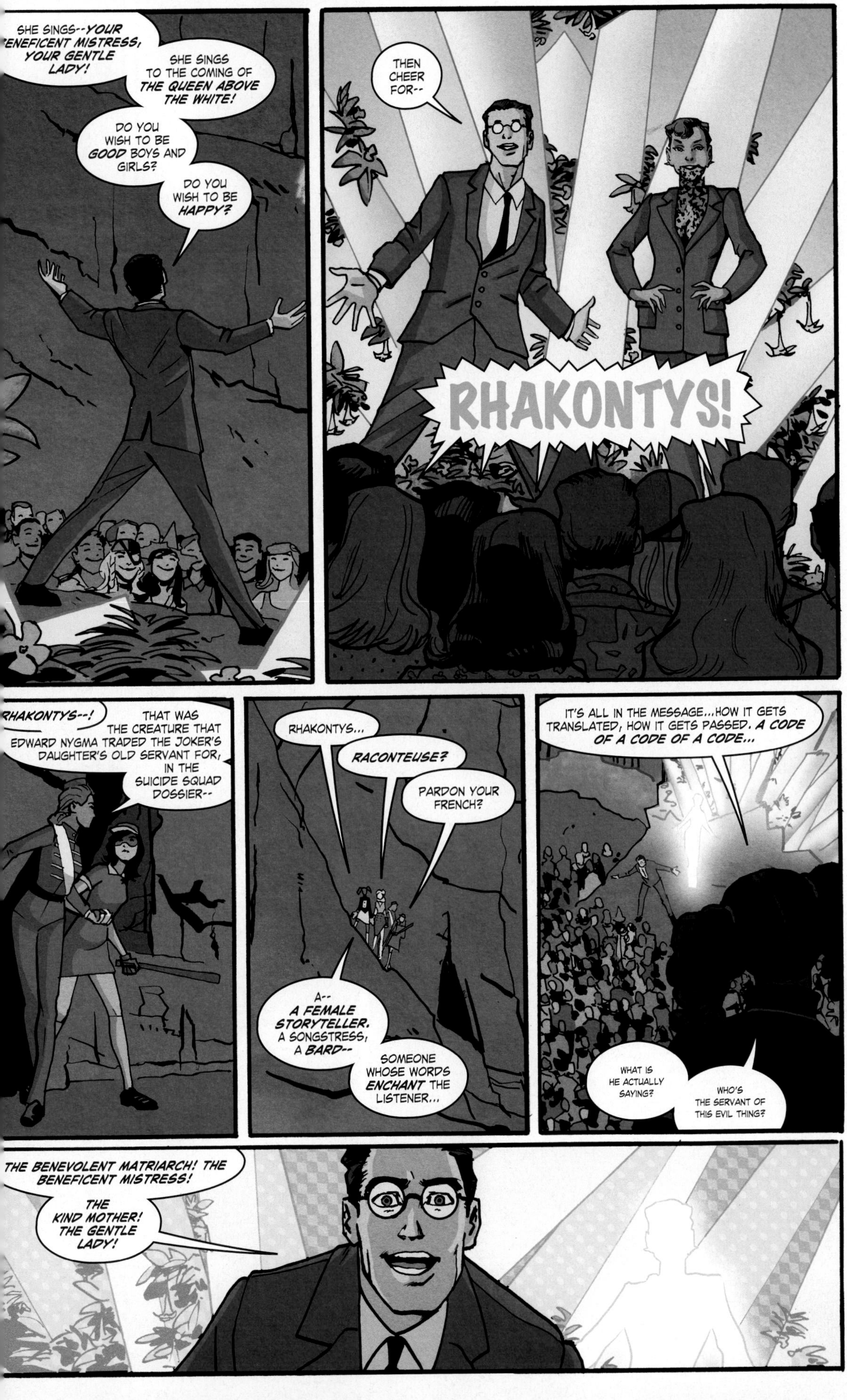

SHE SINGS--YOUR BENEFICENT MISTRESS, YOUR GENTLE LADY!
SHE SINGS TO THE COMING OF THE QUEEN ABOVE THE WHITE!
DO YOU WISH TO BE GOOD BOYS AND GIRLS?
DO YOU WISH TO BE HAPPY?
THEN CHEER FOR--
RHAKONTYS!
RHAKONTYS--!
THAT WAS THE CREATURE THAT EDWARD NYGMA TRADED THE JOKER'S DAUGHTER'S OLD SERVANT FOR, IN THE SUICIDE SQUAD DOSSIER--
RHAKONTYS...
RACONTEUSE?
PARDON YOUR FRENCH?
A-- A FEMALE STORYTELLER. A SONGSTRESS, A BARD--
SOMEONE WHOSE WORDS ENCHANT THE LISTENER...
IT'S ALL IN THE MESSAGE...HOW IT GETS TRANSLATED, HOW IT GETS PASSED. A CODE OF A CODE OF A CODE...
WHAT IS HE ACTUALLY SAYING?
WHO'S THE SERVANT OF THIS EVIL THING?
THE BENEVOLENT MATRIARCH! THE BENEFICENT MISTRESS!
THE KIND MOTHER! THE GENTLE LADY!

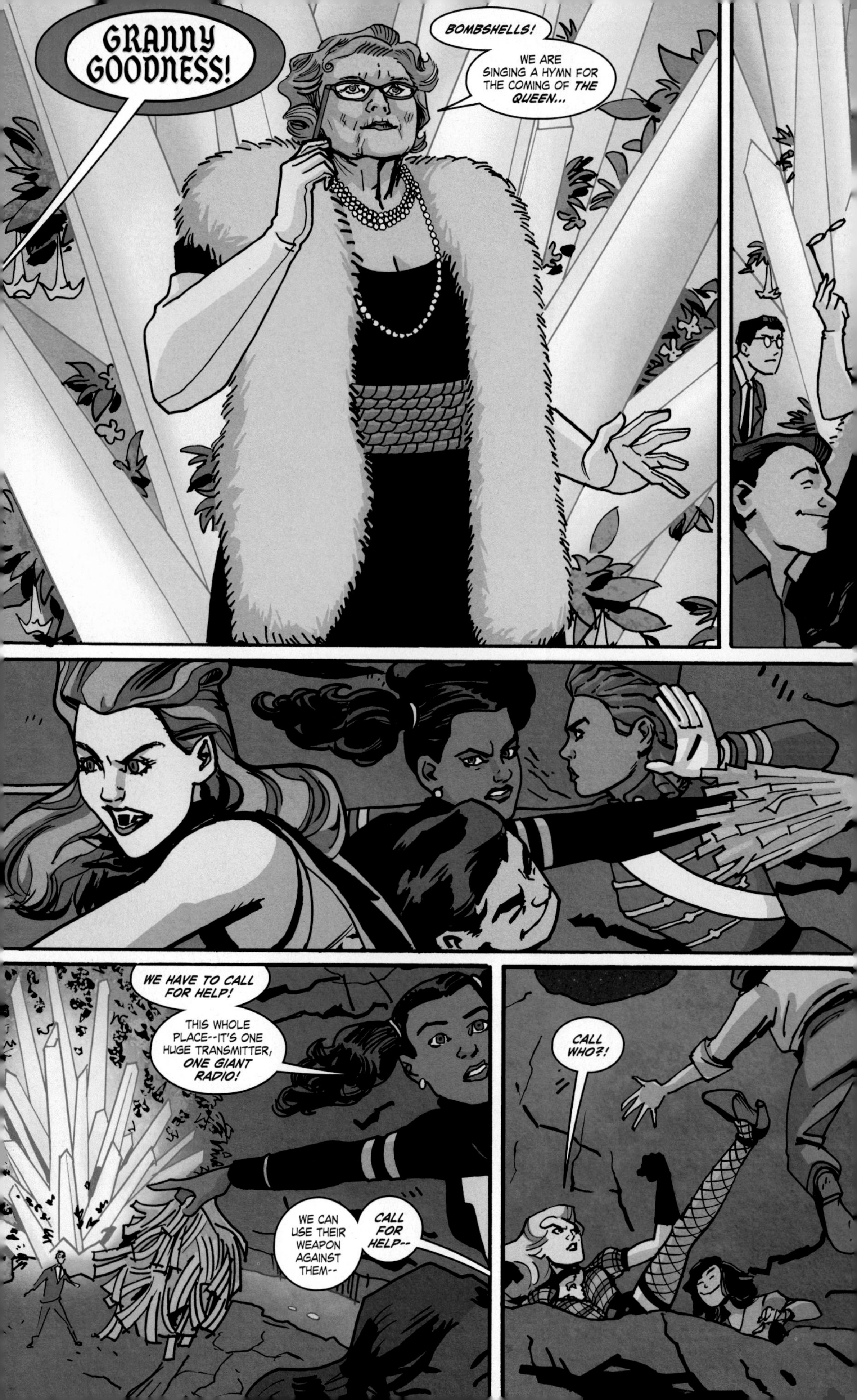
GRANNY GOODNESS!
BOMBSHELLS!
WE ARE SINGING A HYMN FOR THE COMING OF THE QUEEN...
WE HAVE TO CALL FOR HELP!
THIS WHOLE PLACE--IT'S ONE HUGE TRANSMITTER, ONE GIANT RADIO!
WE CAN USE THEIR WEAPON AGAINST THEM--
CALL FOR HELP--
CALL WHO?!

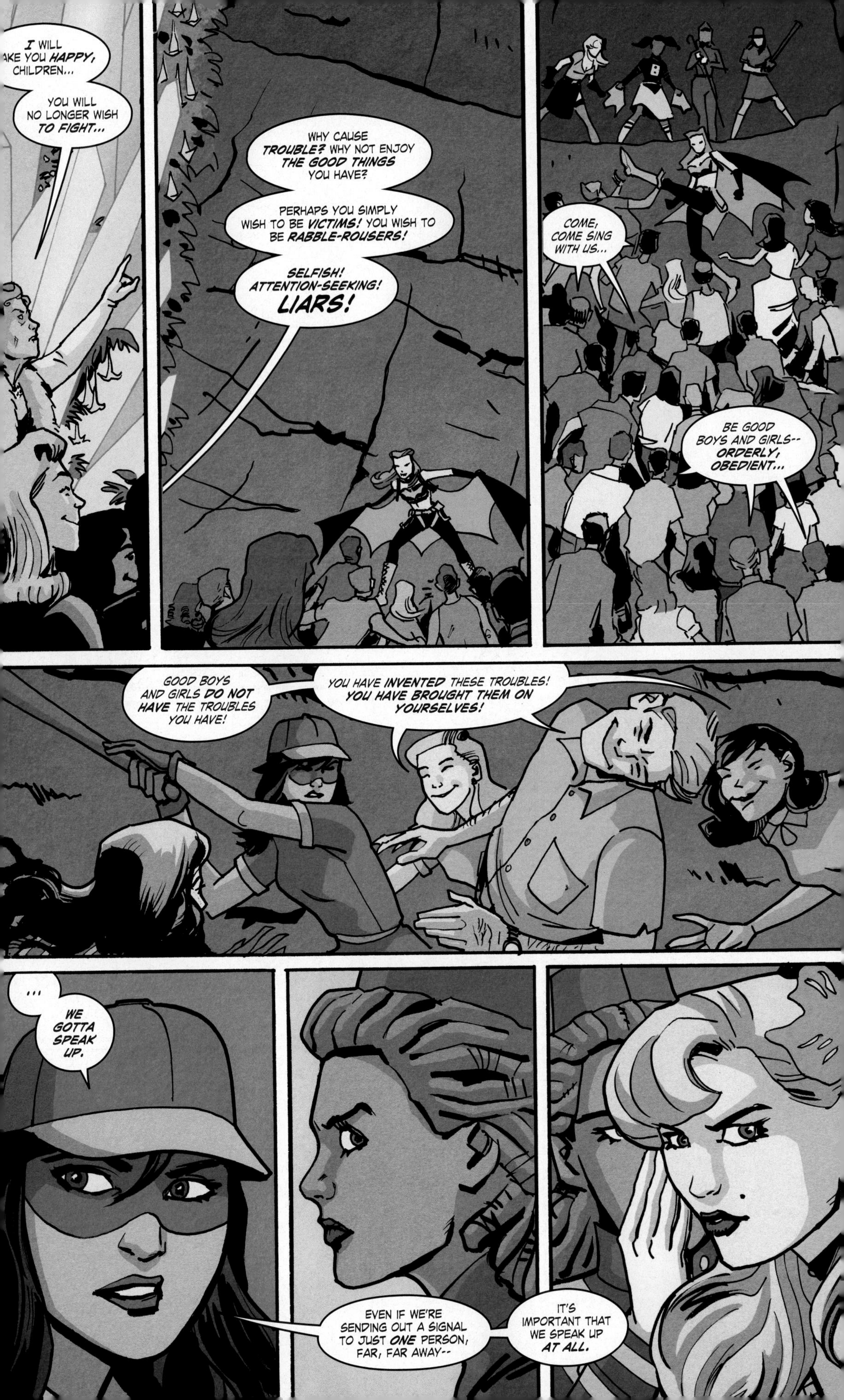
I WILL ...AKE YOU HAPPY, CHILDREN...
YOU WILL NO LONGER WISH TO FIGHT...
WHY CAUSE TROUBLE? WHY NOT ENJOY THE GOOD THINGS YOU HAVE?
PERHAPS YOU SIMPLY WISH TO BE VICTIMS! YOU WISH TO BE RABBLE-ROUSERS!
SELFISH! ATTENTION-SEEKING! LIARS!
COME, COME SING WITH US...
BE GOOD BOYS AND GIRLS-- ORDERLY, OBEDIENT...
GOOD BOYS AND GIRLS DO NOT HAVE THE TROUBLES YOU HAVE!
YOU HAVE INVENTED THESE TROUBLES! YOU HAVE BROUGHT THEM ON YOURSELVES!
...
WE GOTTA SPEAK UP.
EVEN IF WE'RE SENDING OUT A SIGNAL TO JUST ONE PERSON, FAR, FAR AWAY--
IT'S IMPORTANT THAT WE SPEAK UP AT ALL.

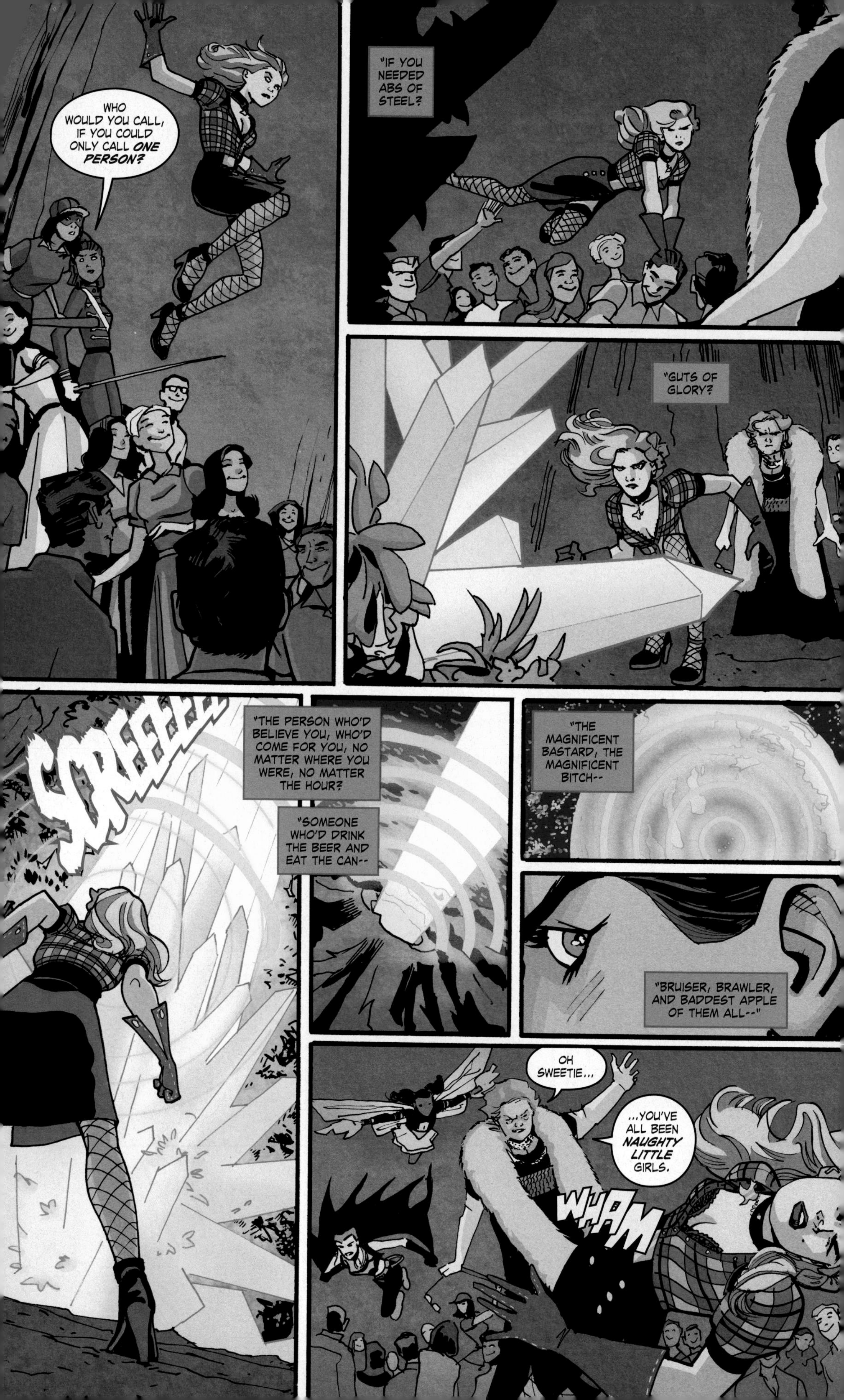
WHO WOULD YOU CALL, IF YOU COULD ONLY CALL *ONE PERSON?*
"IF YOU NEEDED ABS OF STEEL?
"GUTS OF GLORY?
SCREEEEE
"THE PERSON WHO'D BELIEVE YOU, WHO'D COME FOR YOU, NO MATTER WHERE YOU WERE, NO MATTER THE HOUR?
"SOMEONE WHO'D DRINK THE BEER AND EAT THE CAN--
"THE MAGNIFICENT BASTARD, THE MAGNIFICENT BITCH--
"BRUISER, BRAWLER, AND BADDEST APPLE OF THEM ALL--"
OH SWEETIE...
...YOU'VE ALL BEEN *NAUGHTY LITTLE* GIRLS.
WHAM

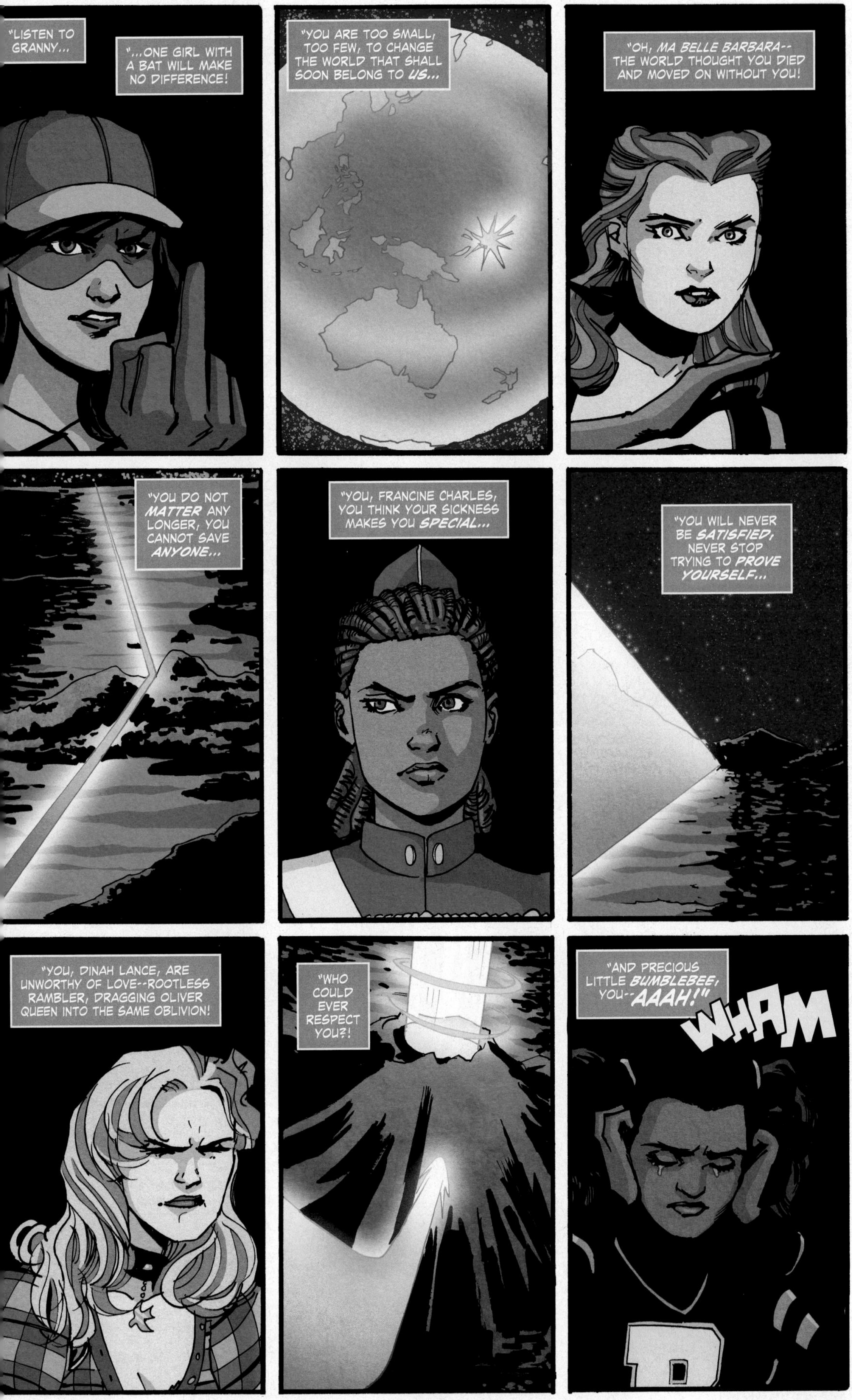
"LISTEN TO GRANNY...
"...ONE GIRL WITH A BAT WILL MAKE NO DIFFERENCE!
"YOU ARE TOO SMALL, TOO FEW, TO CHANGE THE WORLD THAT SHALL SOON BELONG TO US...
"OH, MA BELLE BARBARA-- THE WORLD THOUGHT YOU DIED AND MOVED ON WITHOUT YOU!
"YOU DO NOT MATTER ANY LONGER, YOU CANNOT SAVE ANYONE...
"YOU, FRANCINE CHARLES, YOU THINK YOUR SICKNESS MAKES YOU SPECIAL...
"YOU WILL NEVER BE SATISFIED, NEVER STOP TRYING TO PROVE YOURSELF...
"YOU, DINAH LANCE, ARE UNWORTHY OF LOVE--ROOTLESS RAMBLER, DRAGGING OLIVER QUEEN INTO THE SAME OBLIVION!
"WHO COULD EVER RESPECT YOU?!
"AND PRECIOUS LITTLE BUMBLEBEE, YOU--AAAH!"
WHAM

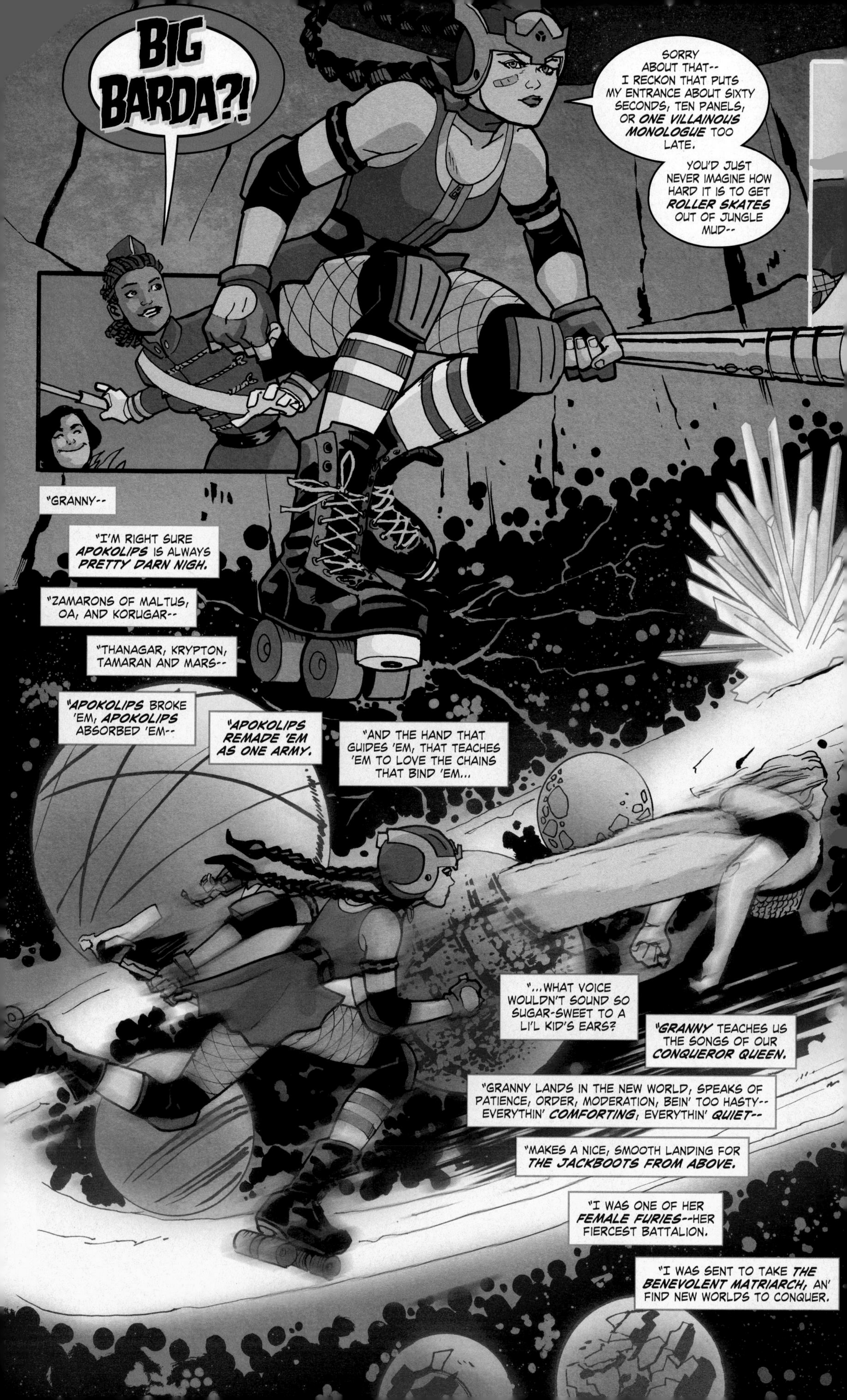
BIG BARDA?!
SORRY ABOUT THAT-- I RECKON THAT PUTS MY ENTRANCE ABOUT SIXTY SECONDS, TEN PANELS, OR ONE VILLAINOUS MONOLOGUE TOO LATE.
YOU'D JUST NEVER IMAGINE HOW HARD IT IS TO GET ROLLER SKATES OUT OF JUNGLE MUD--
"GRANNY--
"I'M RIGHT SURE APOKOLIPS IS ALWAYS PRETTY DARN NIGH.
"ZAMARONS OF MALTUS, OA, AND KORUGAR--
"THANAGAR, KRYPTON, TAMARAN AND MARS--
"APOKOLIPS BROKE 'EM, APOKOLIPS ABSORBED 'EM--
"APOKOLIPS REMADE 'EM AS ONE ARMY.
"AND THE HAND THAT GUIDES 'EM, THAT TEACHES 'EM TO LOVE THE CHAINS THAT BIND 'EM...
"...WHAT VOICE WOULDN'T SOUND SO SUGAR-SWEET TO A LI'L KID'S EARS?
"GRANNY TEACHES US THE SONGS OF OUR CONQUEROR QUEEN.
"GRANNY LANDS IN THE NEW WORLD, SPEAKS OF PATIENCE, ORDER, MODERATION, BEIN' TOO HASTY-- EVERYTHIN' COMFORTING, EVERYTHIN' QUIET--
"MAKES A NICE, SMOOTH LANDING FOR THE JACKBOOTS FROM ABOVE.
"I WAS ONE OF HER FEMALE FURIES--HER FIERCEST BATTALION.
"I WAS SENT TO TAKE THE BENEVOLENT MATRIARCH, AN' FIND NEW WORLDS TO CONQUER.

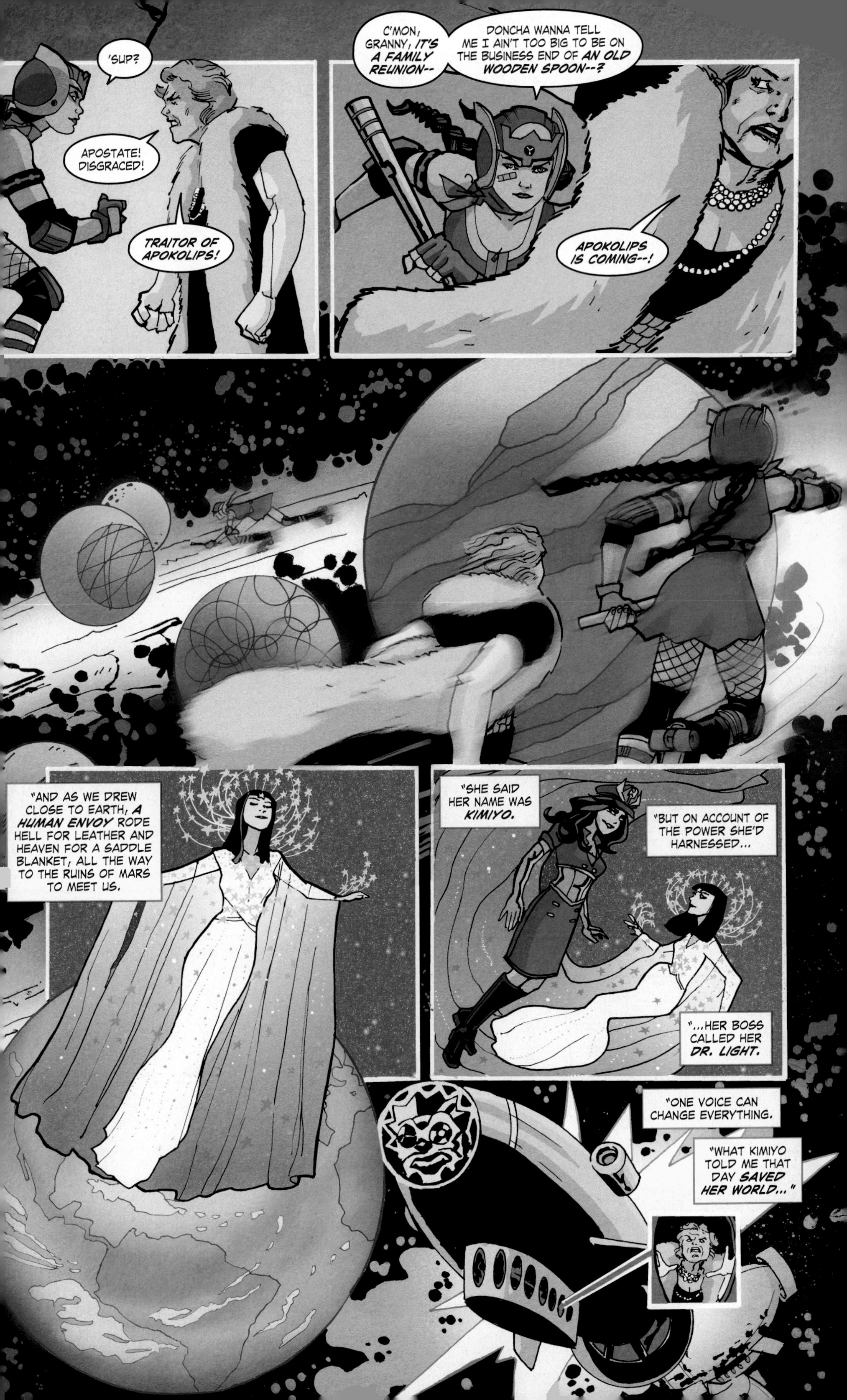
'SUP?
APOSTATE! DISGRACED!
TRAITOR OF APOKOLIPS!
C'MON, GRANNY, IT'S A FAMILY REUNION--
DONCHA WANNA TELL ME I AIN'T TOO BIG TO BE ON THE BUSINESS END OF AN OLD WOODEN SPOON--?
APOKOLIPS IS COMING--!
"AND AS WE DREW CLOSE TO EARTH, A HUMAN ENVOY RODE HELL FOR LEATHER AND HEAVEN FOR A SADDLE BLANKET, ALL THE WAY TO THE RUINS OF MARS TO MEET US.
"SHE SAID HER NAME WAS KIMIYO.
"BUT ON ACCOUNT OF THE POWER SHE'D HARNESSED...
"...HER BOSS CALLED HER DR. LIGHT.
"ONE VOICE CAN CHANGE EVERYTHING.
"WHAT KIMIYO TOLD ME THAT DAY SAVED HER WORLD..."

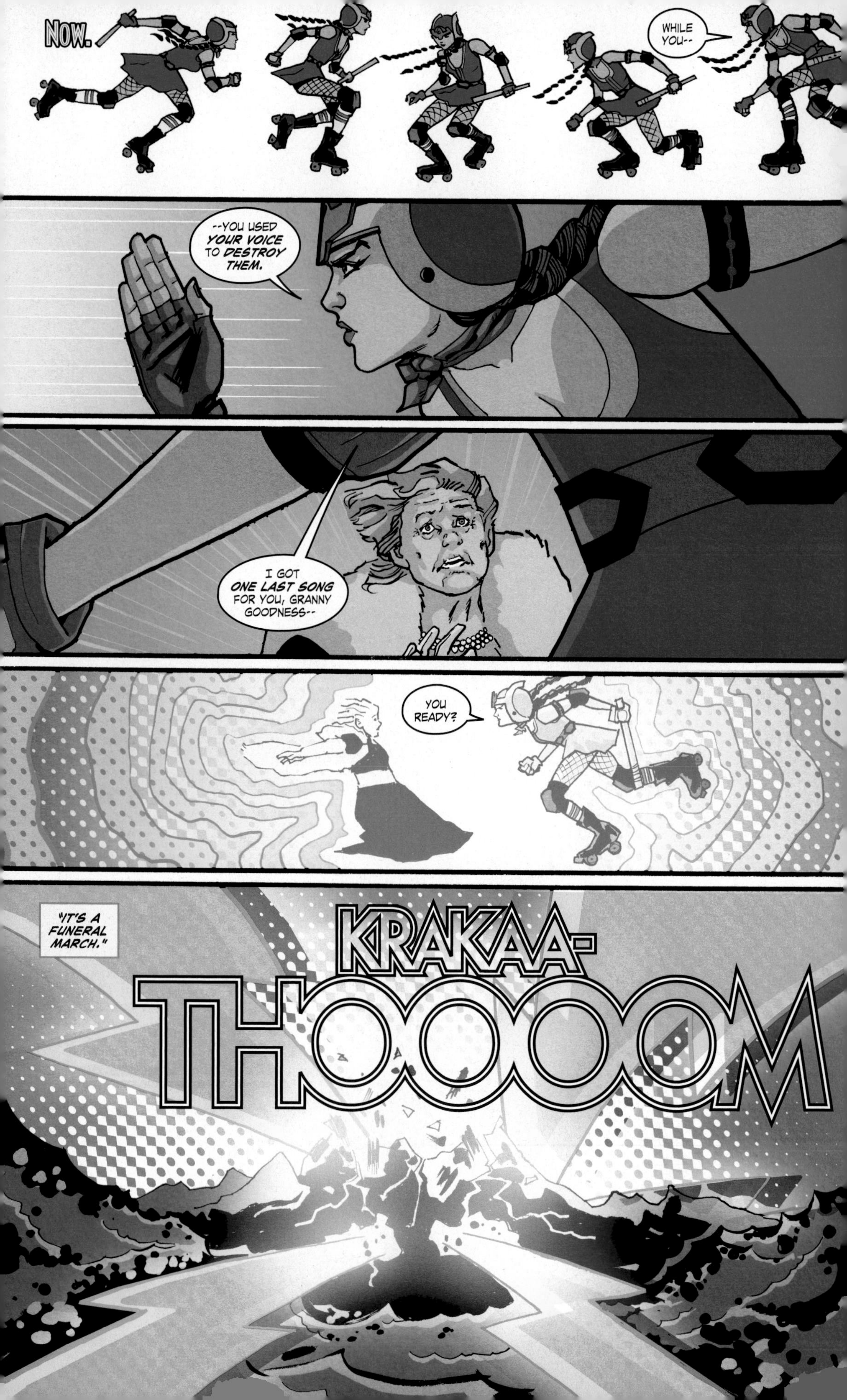
NOW.
WHILE YOU--
--YOU USED YOUR VOICE TO DESTROY THEM.
I GOT ONE LAST SONG FOR YOU, GRANNY GOODNESS--
YOU READY?
"IT'S A FUNERAL MARCH."
KRAKAA-THOOOOM

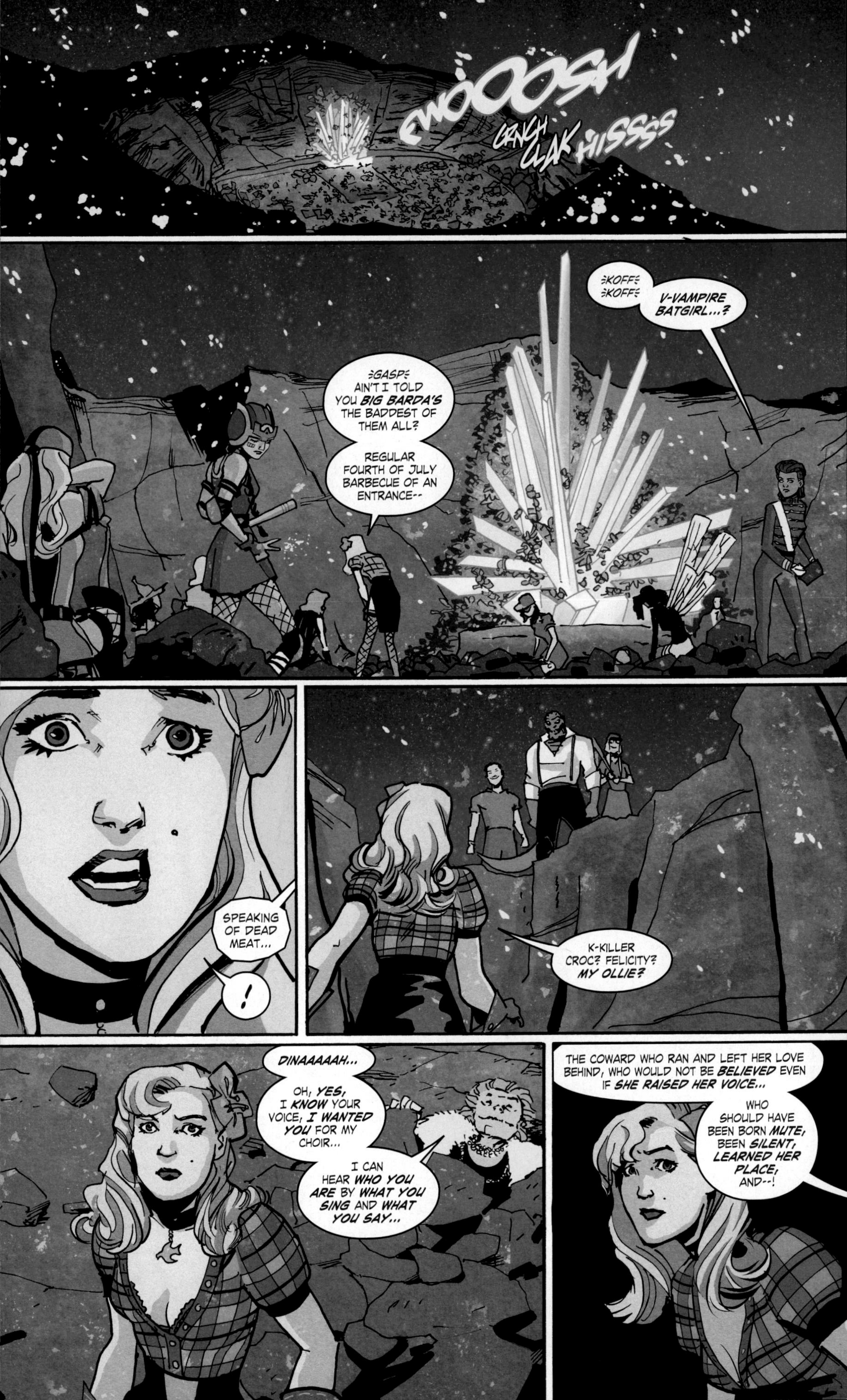
FWOOOSH
CRNCH CLAK HIISSSS
GASP
AIN'T I TOLD YOU BIG BARDA'S THE BADDEST OF THEM ALL?
REGULAR FOURTH OF JULY BARBECUE OF AN ENTRANCE--
KOFF KOFF
V-VAMPIRE BATGIRL...?
SPEAKING OF DEAD MEAT...
!
K-KILLER CROC? FELICITY? MY OLLIE?
DINAAAAAH...
OH, YES, I KNOW YOUR VOICE; I WANTED YOU FOR MY CHOIR...
I CAN HEAR WHO YOU ARE BY WHAT YOU SING AND WHAT YOU SAY...
THE COWARD WHO RAN AND LEFT HER LOVE BEHIND, WHO WOULD NOT BE BELIEVED EVEN IF SHE RAISED HER VOICE...
WHO SHOULD HAVE BEEN BORN MUTE, BEEN SILENT, LEARNED HER PLACE, AND--!

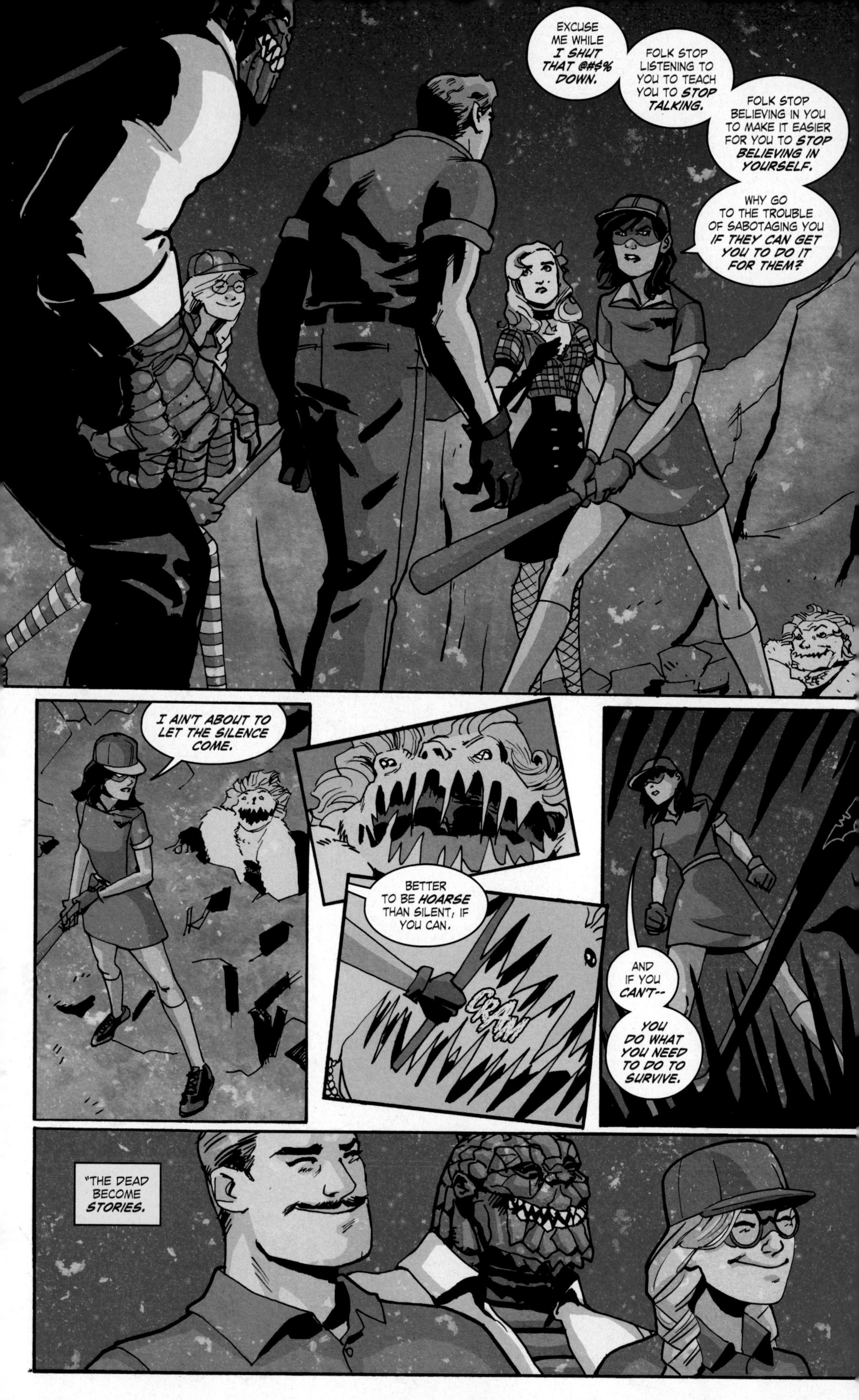
EXCUSE ME WHILE I SHUT THAT @#$% DOWN.
FOLK STOP LISTENING TO YOU TO TEACH YOU TO STOP TALKING.
FOLK STOP BELIEVING IN YOU TO MAKE IT EASIER FOR YOU TO STOP BELIEVING IN YOURSELF.
WHY GO TO THE TROUBLE OF SABOTAGING YOU IF THEY CAN GET YOU TO DO IT FOR THEM?
I AIN'T ABOUT TO LET THE SILENCE COME.
BETTER TO BE HOARSE THAN SILENT, IF YOU CAN.
CRAM
AND IF YOU CAN'T--
YOU DO WHAT YOU NEED TO DO TO SURVIVE.
"THE DEAD BECOME STORIES.

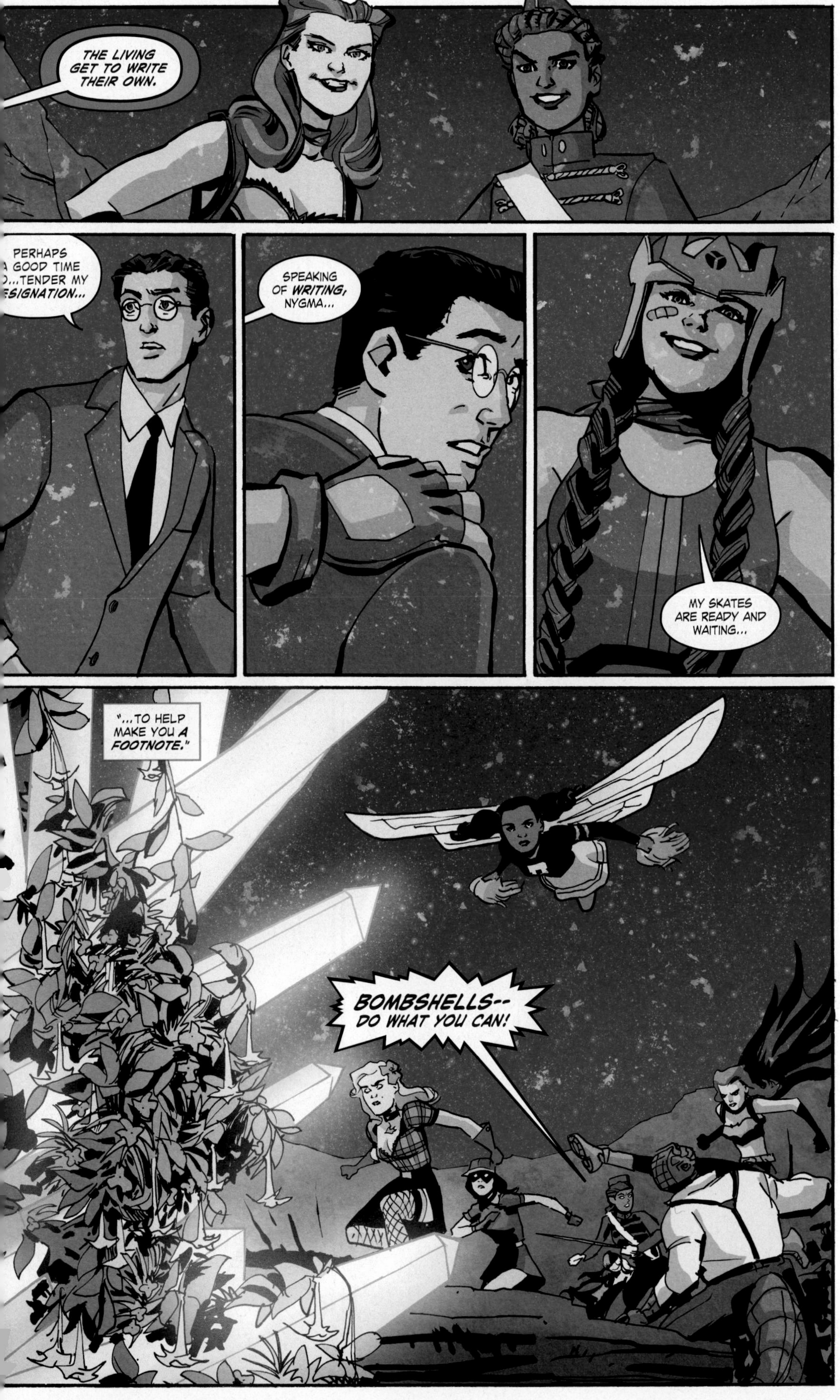
THE LIVING GET TO WRITE THEIR OWN.
PERHAPS A GOOD TIME TO...TENDER MY RESIGNATION...
SPEAKING OF WRITING, NYGMA...
MY SKATES ARE READY AND WAITING...
"...TO HELP MAKE YOU A FOOTNOTE."
BOMBSHELLS-- DO WHAT YOU CAN!

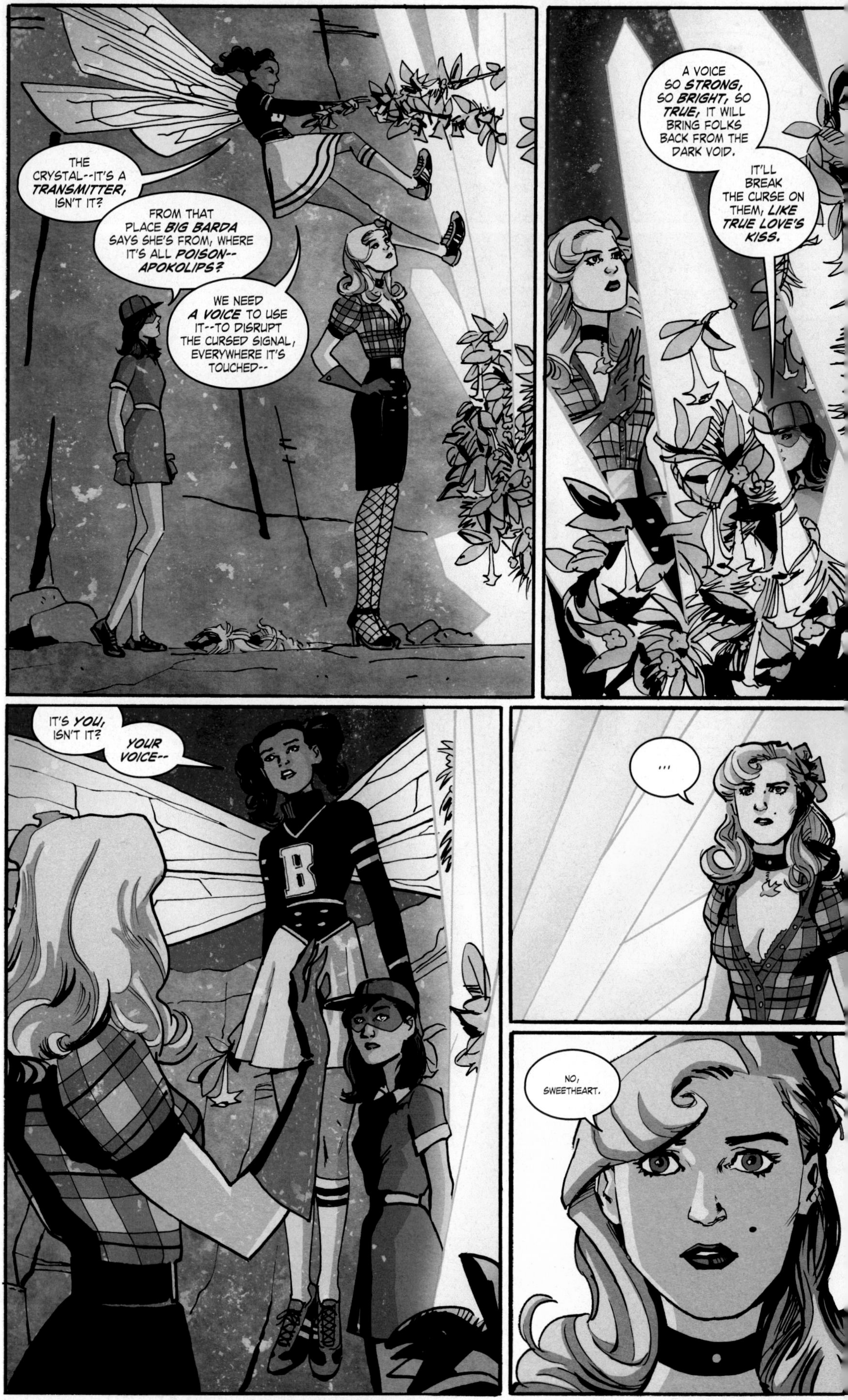
THE CRYSTAL--IT'S A TRANSMITTER, ISN'T IT?
FROM THAT PLACE BIG BARDA SAYS SHE'S FROM, WHERE IT'S ALL POISON-- APOKOLIPS?
WE NEED A VOICE TO USE IT--TO DISRUPT THE CURSED SIGNAL, EVERYWHERE IT'S TOUCHED--
A VOICE SO STRONG, SO BRIGHT, SO TRUE, IT WILL BRING FOLKS BACK FROM THE DARK VOID.
IT'LL BREAK THE CURSE ON THEM, LIKE TRUE LOVE'S KISS.
IT'S YOU, ISN'T IT?
YOUR VOICE--
...
NO, SWEETHEART.

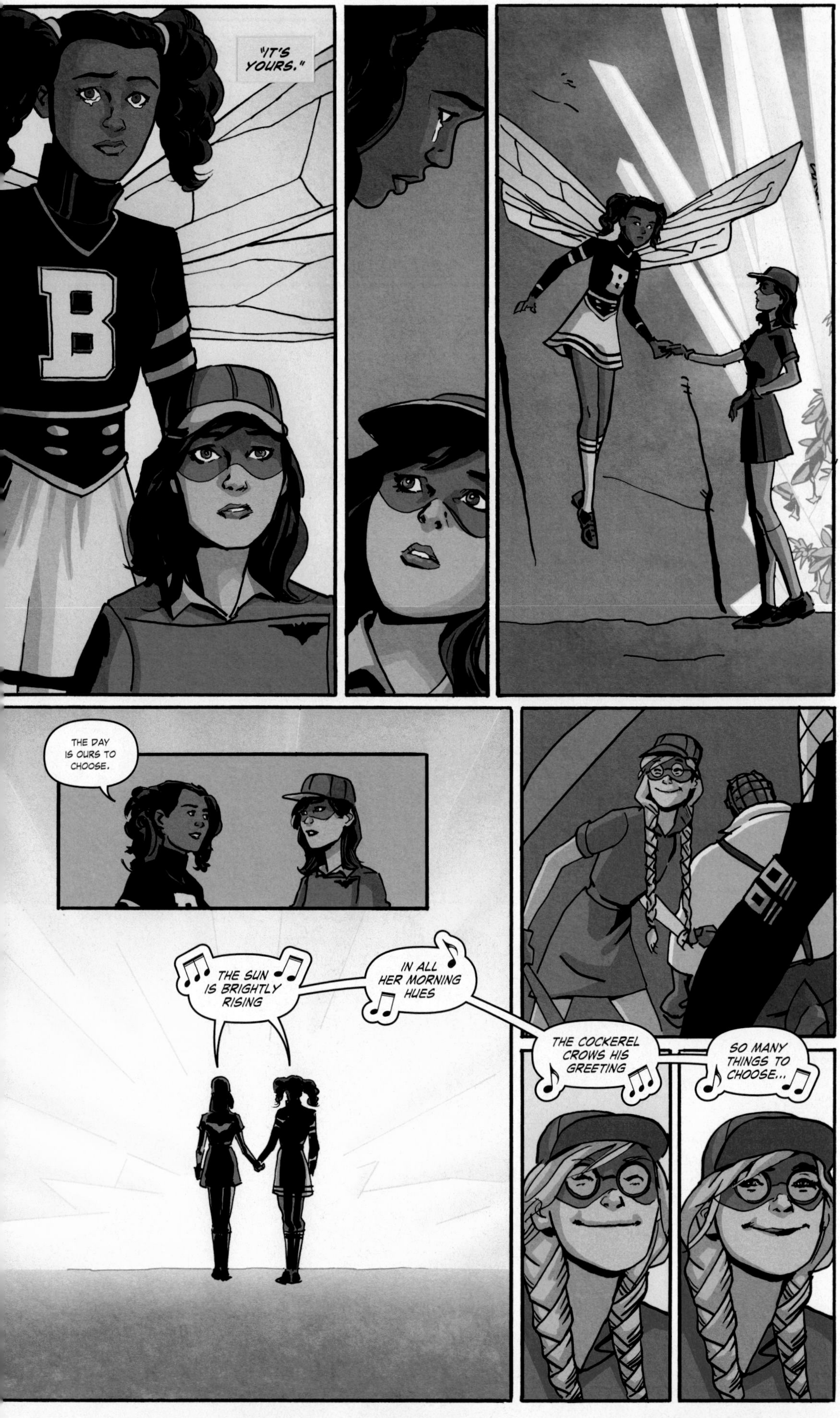
"IT'S YOURS."
THE DAY IS OURS TO CHOOSE.
THE SUN IS BRIGHTLY RISING
IN ALL HER MORNING HUES
THE COCKEREL CROWS HIS GREETING
SO MANY THINGS TO CHOOSE...

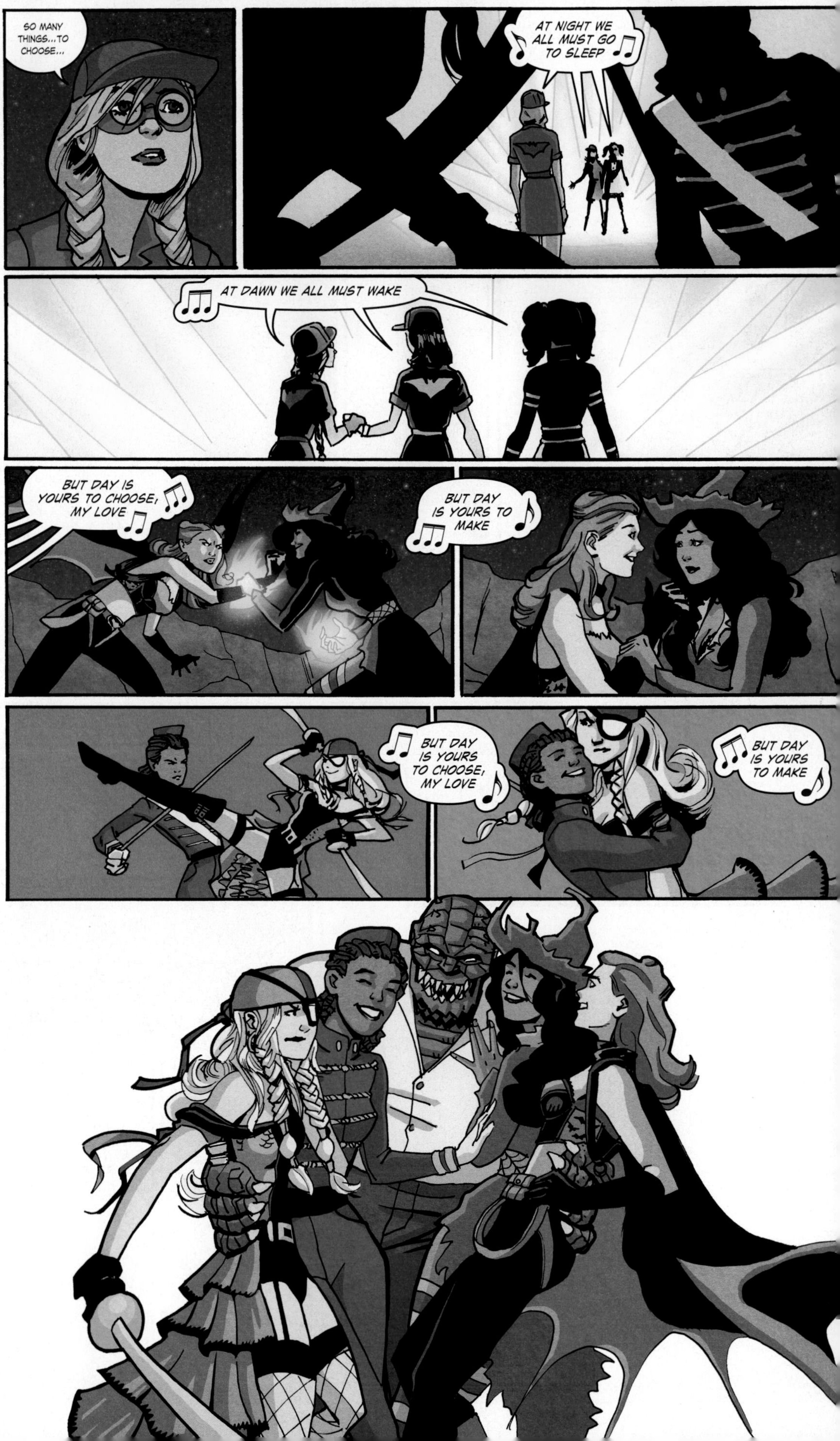
SO MANY THINGS...TO CHOOSE...
AT NIGHT WE ALL MUST GO TO SLEEP
AT DAWN WE ALL MUST WAKE
BUT DAY IS YOURS TO CHOOSE, MY LOVE
BUT DAY IS YOURS TO MAKE
BUT DAY IS YOURS TO CHOOSE, MY LOVE
BUT DAY IS YOURS TO MAKE

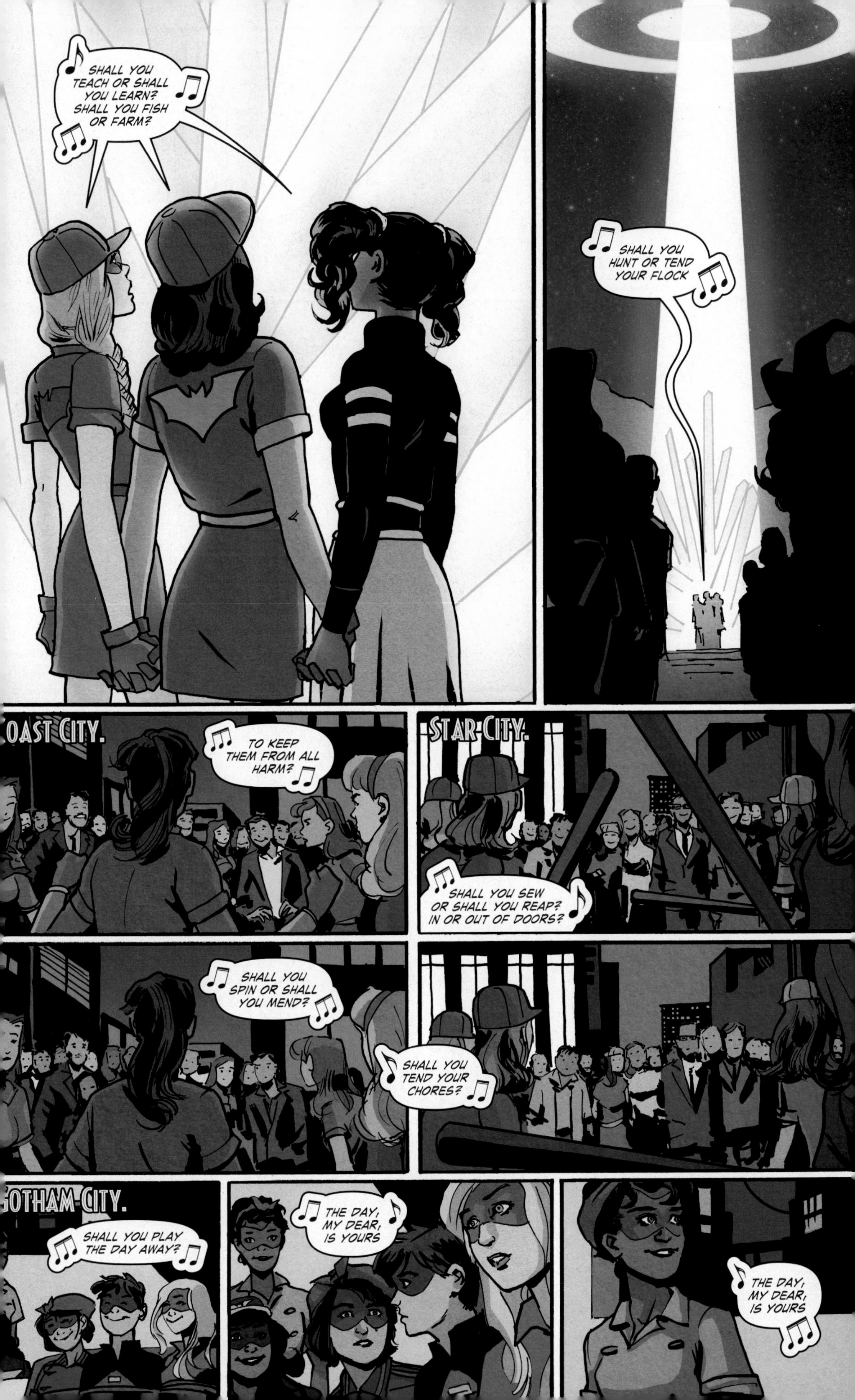
SHALL YOU TEACH OR SHALL YOU LEARN? SHALL YOU FISH OR FARM?
SHALL YOU HUNT OR TEND YOUR FLOCK
OAST CITY.
TO KEEP THEM FROM ALL HARM?
STAR CITY.
SHALL YOU SEW OR SHALL YOU REAP? IN OR OUT OF DOORS?
SHALL YOU SPIN OR SHALL YOU MEND?
SHALL YOU TEND YOUR CHORES?
GOTHAM CITY.
SHALL YOU PLAY THE DAY AWAY?
THE DAY, MY DEAR, IS YOURS
THE DAY, MY DEAR, IS YOURS

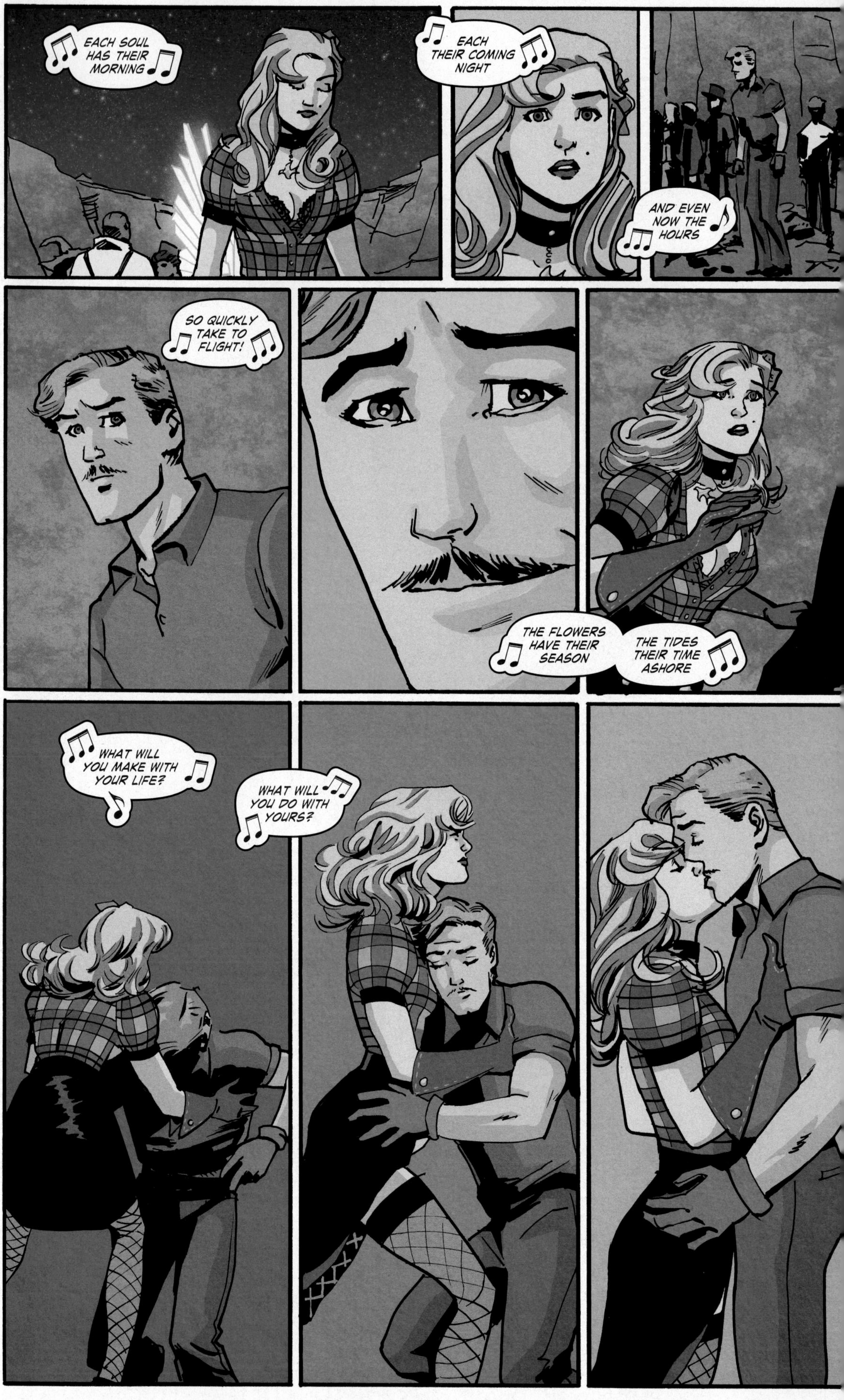
EACH SOUL HAS THEIR MORNING
EACH THEIR COMING NIGHT
AND EVEN NOW THE HOURS
SO QUICKLY TAKE TO FLIGHT!
THE FLOWERS HAVE THEIR SEASON
THE TIDES THEIR TIME ASHORE
WHAT WILL YOU MAKE WITH YOUR LIFE?
WHAT WILL YOU DO WITH YOURS?

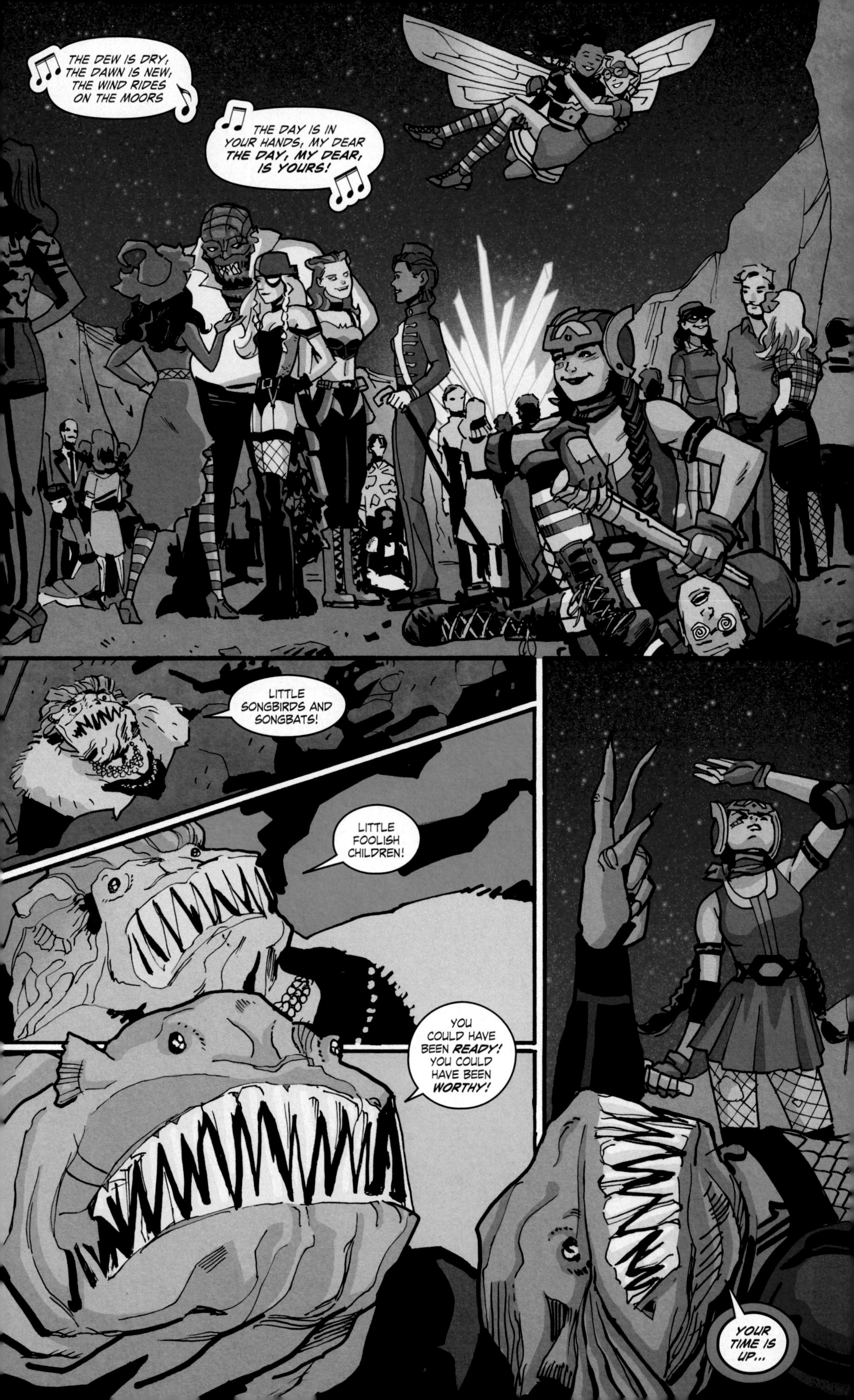
THE DEW IS DRY, THE DAWN IS NEW, THE WIND RIDES ON THE MOORS
THE DAY IS IN YOUR HANDS, MY DEAR THE DAY, MY DEAR, IS YOURS!
LITTLE SONGBIRDS AND SONGBATS!
LITTLE FOOLISH CHILDREN!
YOU COULD HAVE BEEN READY! YOU COULD HAVE BEEN WORTHY!
YOUR TIME IS UP...

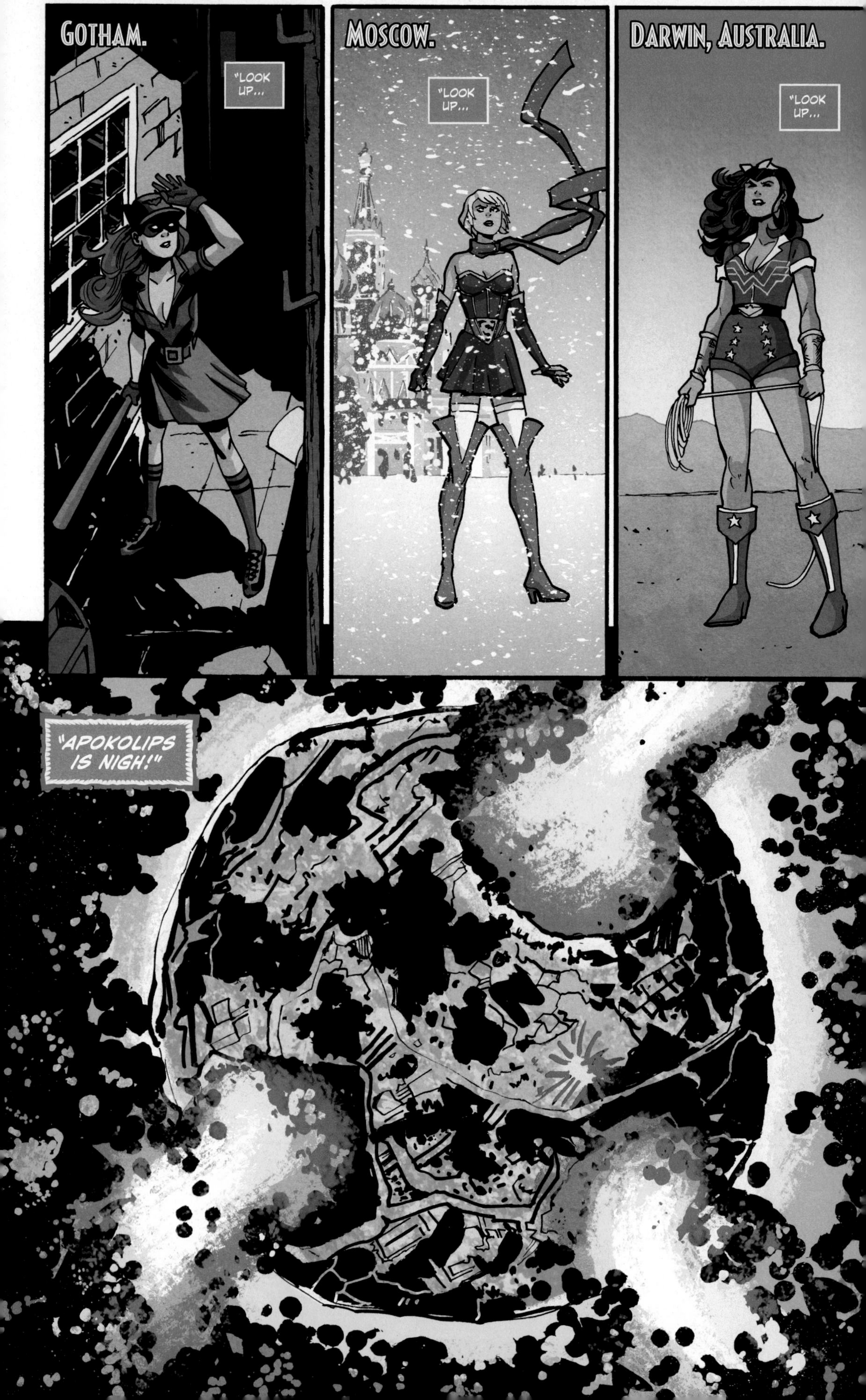
GOTHAM.
"LOOK UP...
MOSCOW.
"LOOK UP...
DARWIN, AUSTRALIA.
"LOOK UP...
"APOKOLIPS IS NIGH!"

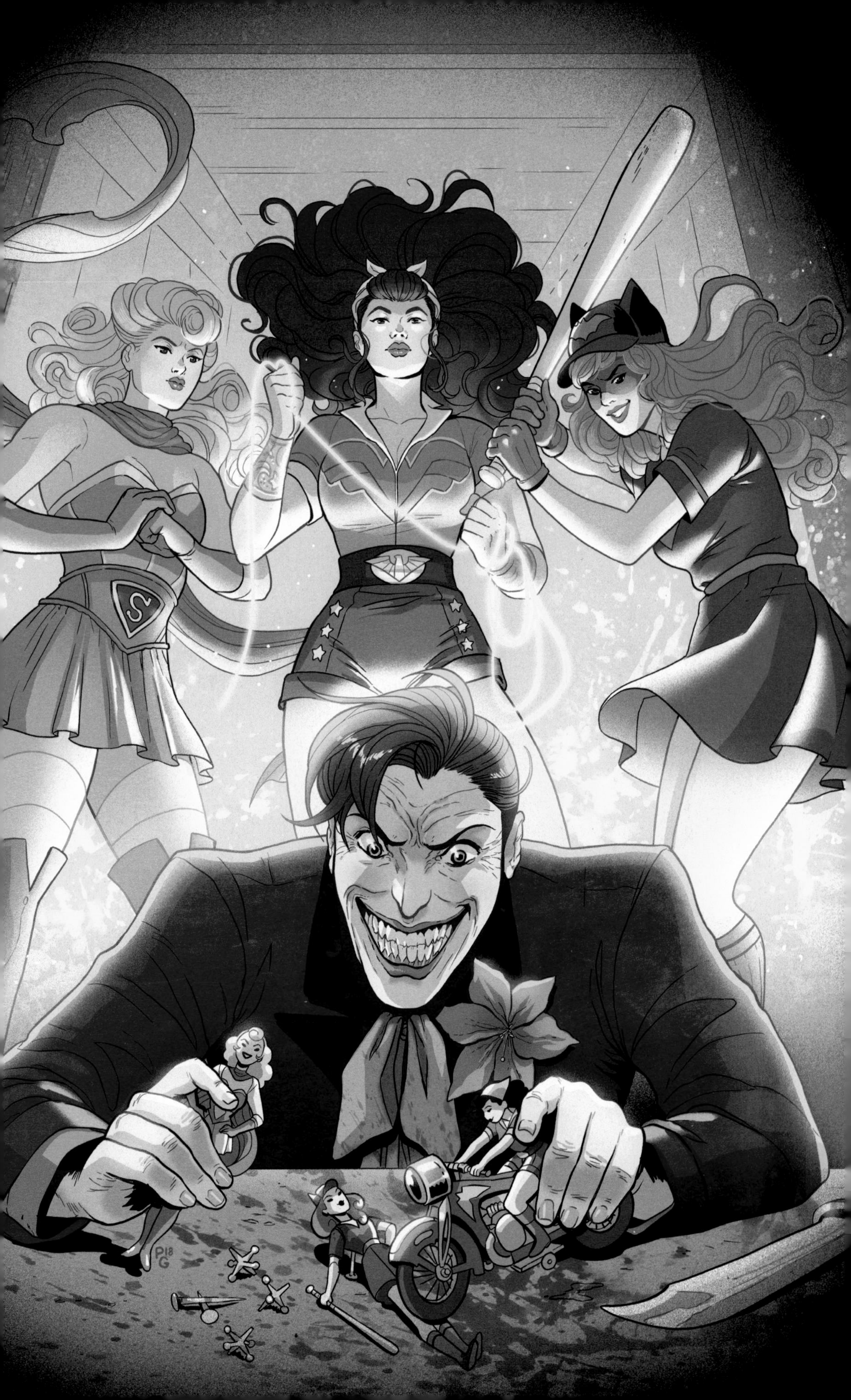

TAPS
PARTS ONE and TWO

Written by
MARGUERITE BENNETT

Art by
SIYA OUM

Colors by
J. NANJAN

Letters by
WES ABBOTT

Cover by
PAULINA GANUCHEAU

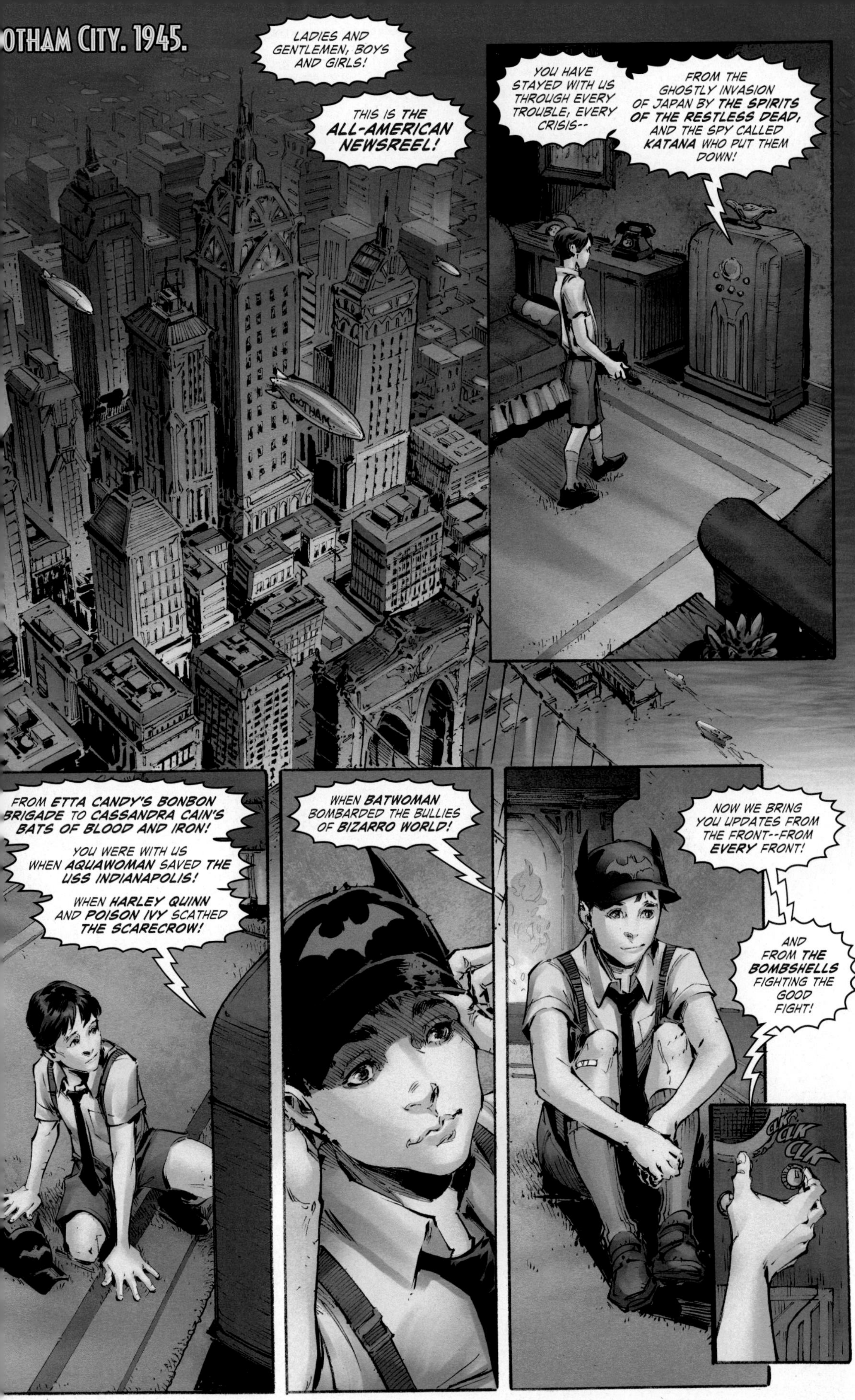
OTHAM CITY. 1945.
LADIES AND GENTLEMEN, BOYS AND GIRLS!
THIS IS THE ALL-AMERICAN NEWSREEL!
YOU HAVE STAYED WITH US THROUGH EVERY TROUBLE, EVERY CRISIS--
FROM THE GHOSTLY INVASION OF JAPAN BY THE SPIRITS OF THE RESTLESS DEAD, AND THE SPY CALLED KATANA WHO PUT THEM DOWN!
FROM ETTA CANDY'S BONBON BRIGADE TO CASSANDRA CAIN'S BATS OF BLOOD AND IRON!
YOU WERE WITH US WHEN AQUAWOMAN SAVED THE USS INDIANAPOLIS!
WHEN HARLEY QUINN AND POISON IVY SCATHED THE SCARECROW!
WHEN BATWOMAN BOMBARDED THE BULLIES OF BIZARRO WORLD!
NOW WE BRING YOU UPDATES FROM THE FRONT--FROM EVERY FRONT!
AND FROM THE BOMBSHELLS FIGHTING THE GOOD FIGHT!

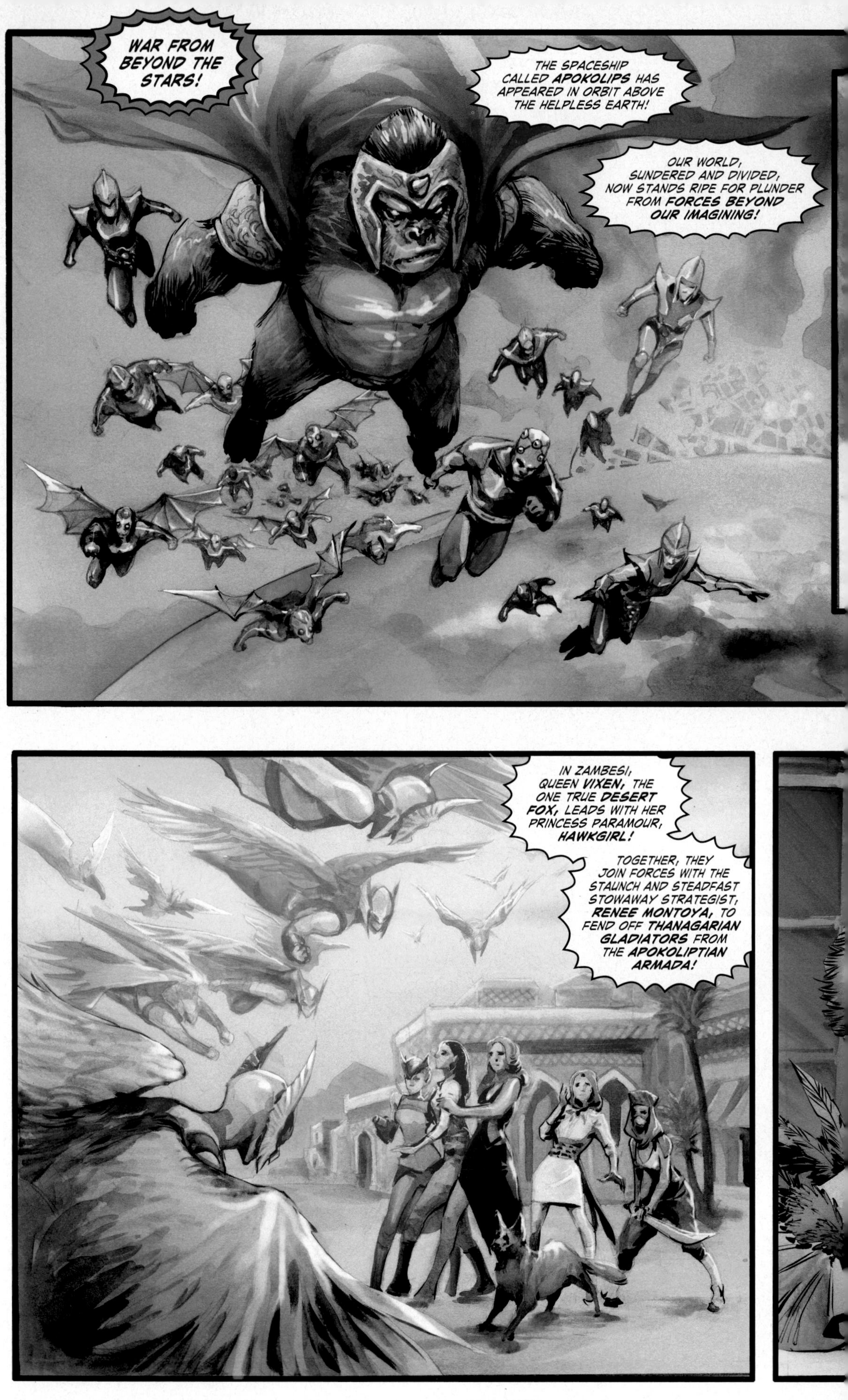

WAR FROM BEYOND THE STARS!
THE SPACESHIP CALLED **APOKOLIPS** HAS APPEARED IN ORBIT ABOVE THE HELPLESS EARTH!
OUR WORLD, SUNDERED AND DIVIDED, NOW STANDS RIPE FOR PLUNDER FROM **FORCES BEYOND OUR IMAGINING!**
IN ZAMBESI, QUEEN **VIXEN,** THE ONE TRUE **DESERT FOX,** LEADS WITH HER PRINCESS PARAMOUR, **HAWKGIRL!**
TOGETHER, THEY JOIN FORCES WITH THE STAUNCH AND STEADFAST STOWAWAY STRATEGIST, **RENEE MONTOYA,** TO FEND OFF **THANAGARIAN GLADIATORS** FROM THE **APOKOLIPTIAN ARMADA!**

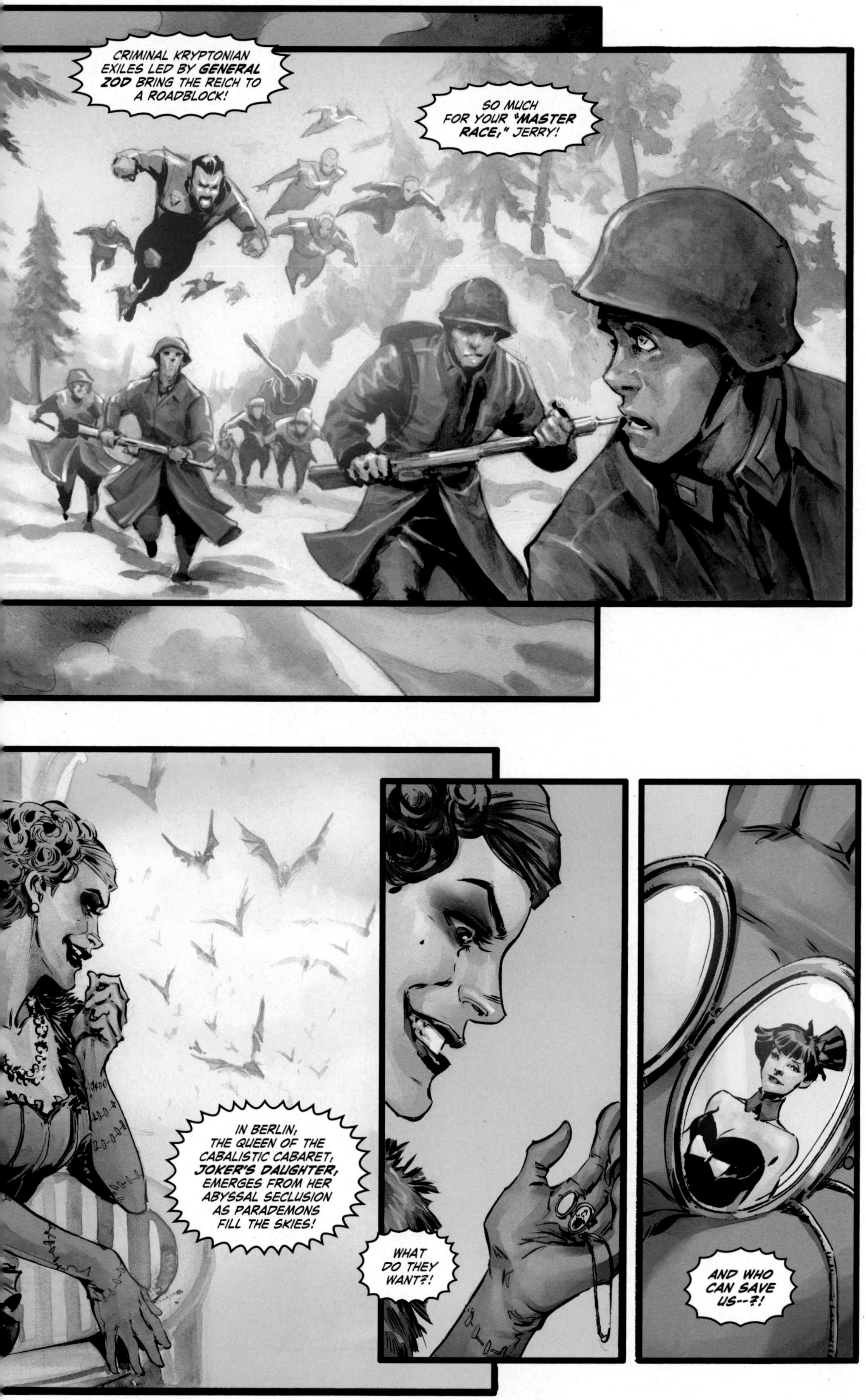
CRIMINAL KRYPTONIAN EXILES LED BY GENERAL ZOD BRING THE REICH TO A ROADBLOCK!
SO MUCH FOR YOUR "MASTER RACE," JERRY!
IN BERLIN, THE QUEEN OF THE CABALISTIC CABARET, JOKER'S DAUGHTER, EMERGES FROM HER ABYSSAL SECLUSION AS PARADEMONS FILL THE SKIES!
WHAT DO THEY WANT?!
AND WHO CAN SAVE US--?!

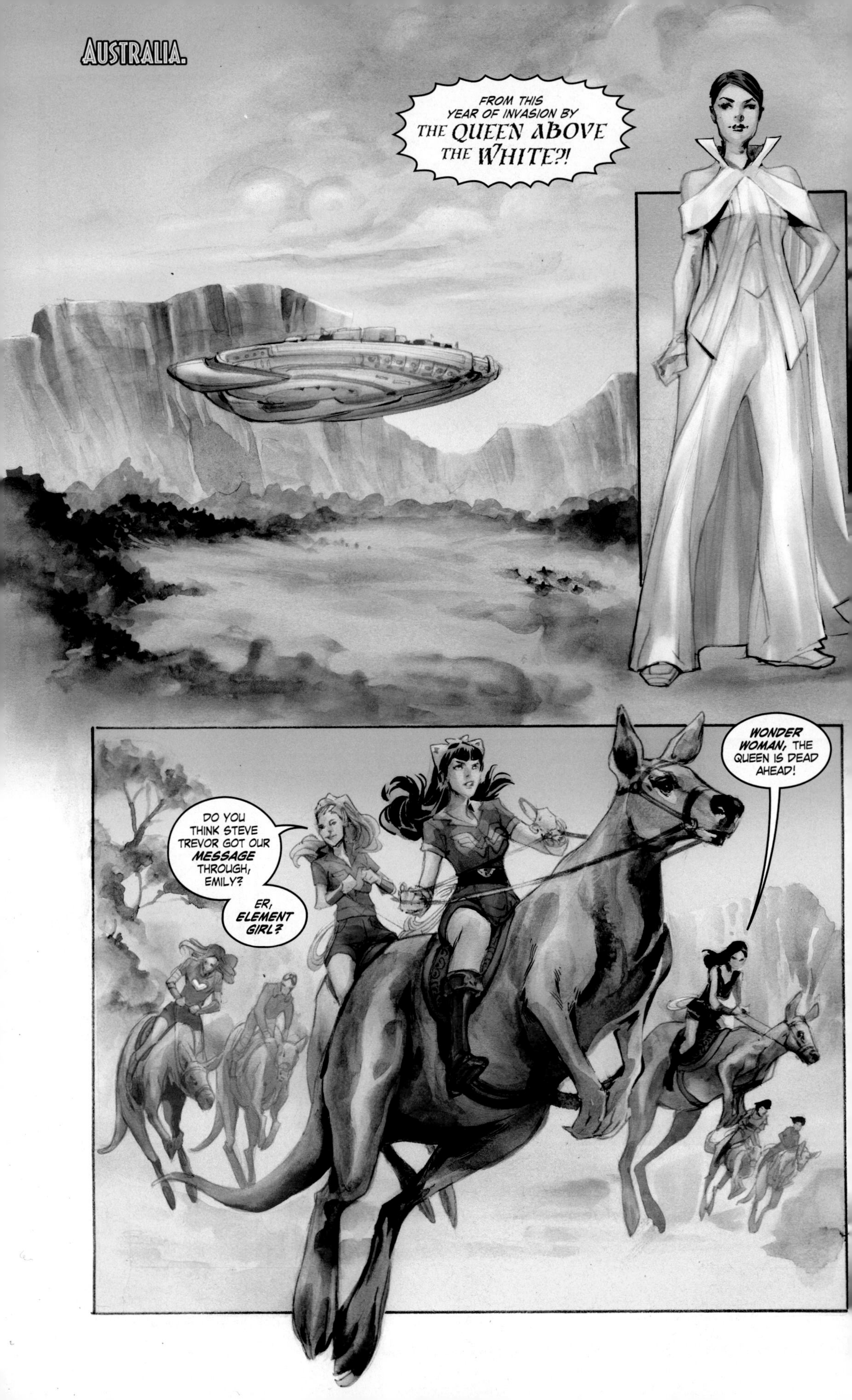
AUSTRALIA.
FROM THIS YEAR OF INVASION BY THE QUEEN ABOVE THE WHITE?!
DO YOU THINK STEVE TREVOR GOT OUR MESSAGE THROUGH, EMILY?
ER, ELEMENT GIRL?
WONDER WOMAN, THE QUEEN IS DEAD AHEAD!

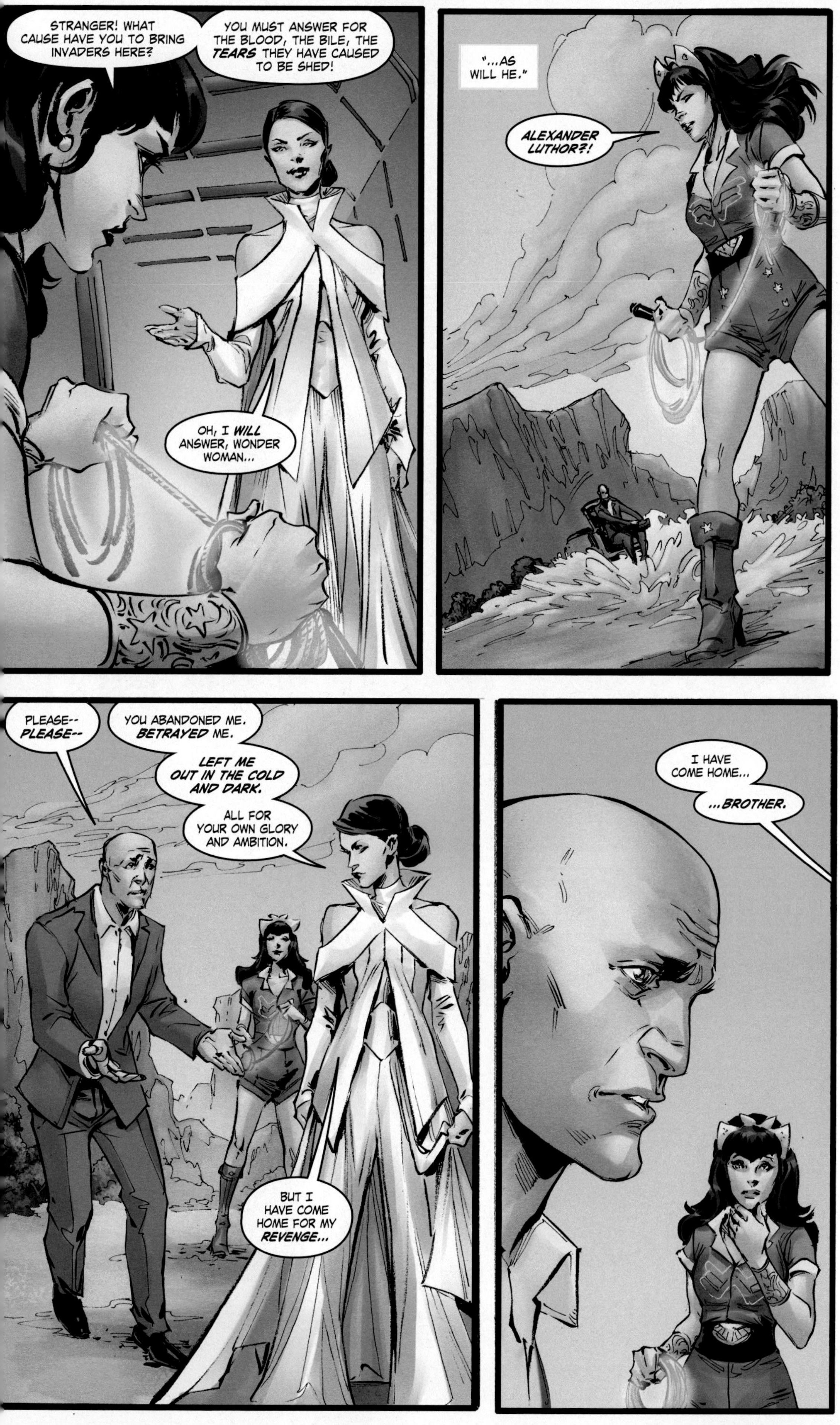
STRANGER! WHAT CAUSE HAVE YOU TO BRING INVADERS HERE?
YOU MUST ANSWER FOR THE BLOOD, THE BILE, THE *TEARS* THEY HAVE CAUSED TO BE SHED!
OH, I *WILL* ANSWER, WONDER WOMAN...
"...AS WILL HE."
ALEXANDER LUTHOR?!
PLEASE-- *PLEASE--*
YOU ABANDONED ME. *BETRAYED* ME.
LEFT ME OUT IN THE COLD AND DARK.
ALL FOR YOUR OWN GLORY AND AMBITION.
BUT I HAVE COME HOME FOR MY *REVENGE...*
I HAVE COME HOME...
...BROTHER.

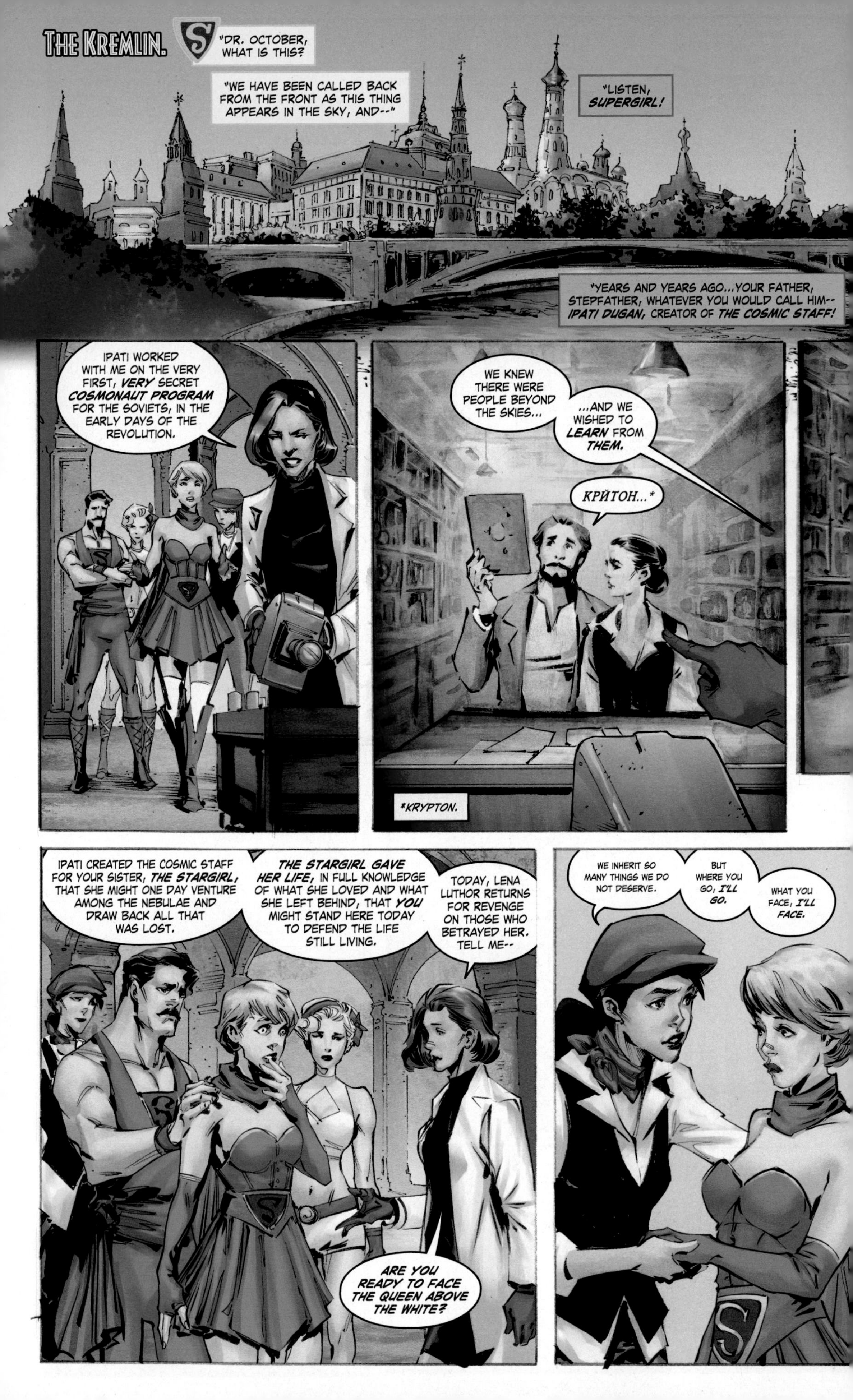
THE KREMLIN.
"DR. OCTOBER, WHAT IS THIS?
"WE HAVE BEEN CALLED BACK FROM THE FRONT AS THIS THING APPEARS IN THE SKY, AND--"
"LISTEN, SUPERGIRL!
"YEARS AND YEARS AGO...YOUR FATHER, STEPFATHER, WHATEVER YOU WOULD CALL HIM-- IPATI DUGAN, CREATOR OF THE COSMIC STAFF!
IPATI WORKED WITH ME ON THE VERY FIRST, VERY SECRET COSMONAUT PROGRAM FOR THE SOVIETS, IN THE EARLY DAYS OF THE REVOLUTION.
WE KNEW THERE WERE PEOPLE BEYOND THE SKIES...
...AND WE WISHED TO LEARN FROM THEM.
КРИТОН...*
*KRYPTON.
IPATI CREATED THE COSMIC STAFF FOR YOUR SISTER, THE STARGIRL, THAT SHE MIGHT ONE DAY VENTURE AMONG THE NEBULAE AND DRAW BACK ALL THAT WAS LOST.
THE STARGIRL GAVE HER LIFE, IN FULL KNOWLEDGE OF WHAT SHE LOVED AND WHAT SHE LEFT BEHIND, THAT YOU MIGHT STAND HERE TODAY TO DEFEND THE LIFE STILL LIVING.
TODAY, LENA LUTHOR RETURNS FOR REVENGE ON THOSE WHO BETRAYED HER. TELL ME--
ARE YOU READY TO FACE THE QUEEN ABOVE THE WHITE?
WE INHERIT SO MANY THINGS WE DO NOT DESERVE.
BUT WHERE YOU GO, I'LL GO.
WHAT YOU FACE, I'LL FACE.

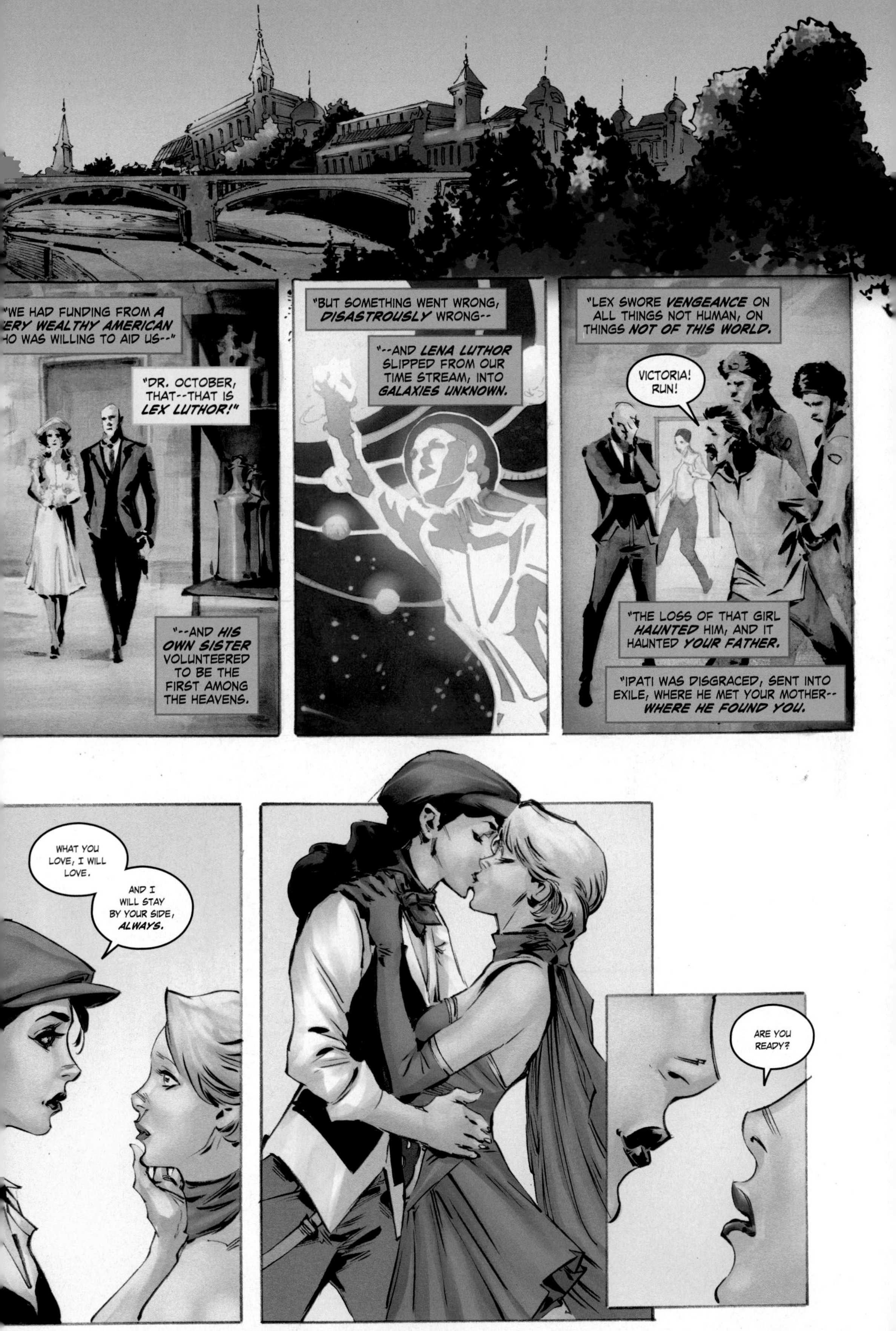
"WE HAD FUNDING FROM A ...ERY WEALTHY AMERICAN ...HO WAS WILLING TO AID US--"
"DR. OCTOBER, THAT--THAT IS LEX LUTHOR!"
"--AND HIS OWN SISTER VOLUNTEERED TO BE THE FIRST AMONG THE HEAVENS.
"BUT SOMETHING WENT WRONG, DISASTROUSLY WRONG--
"--AND LENA LUTHOR SLIPPED FROM OUR TIME STREAM, INTO GALAXIES UNKNOWN.
"LEX SWORE VENGEANCE ON ALL THINGS NOT HUMAN, ON THINGS NOT OF THIS WORLD.
VICTORIA! RUN!
"THE LOSS OF THAT GIRL HAUNTED HIM, AND IT HAUNTED YOUR FATHER.
"IPATI WAS DISGRACED, SENT INTO EXILE, WHERE HE MET YOUR MOTHER-- WHERE HE FOUND YOU.
WHAT YOU LOVE, I WILL LOVE.
AND I WILL STAY BY YOUR SIDE, ALWAYS.
ARE YOU READY?

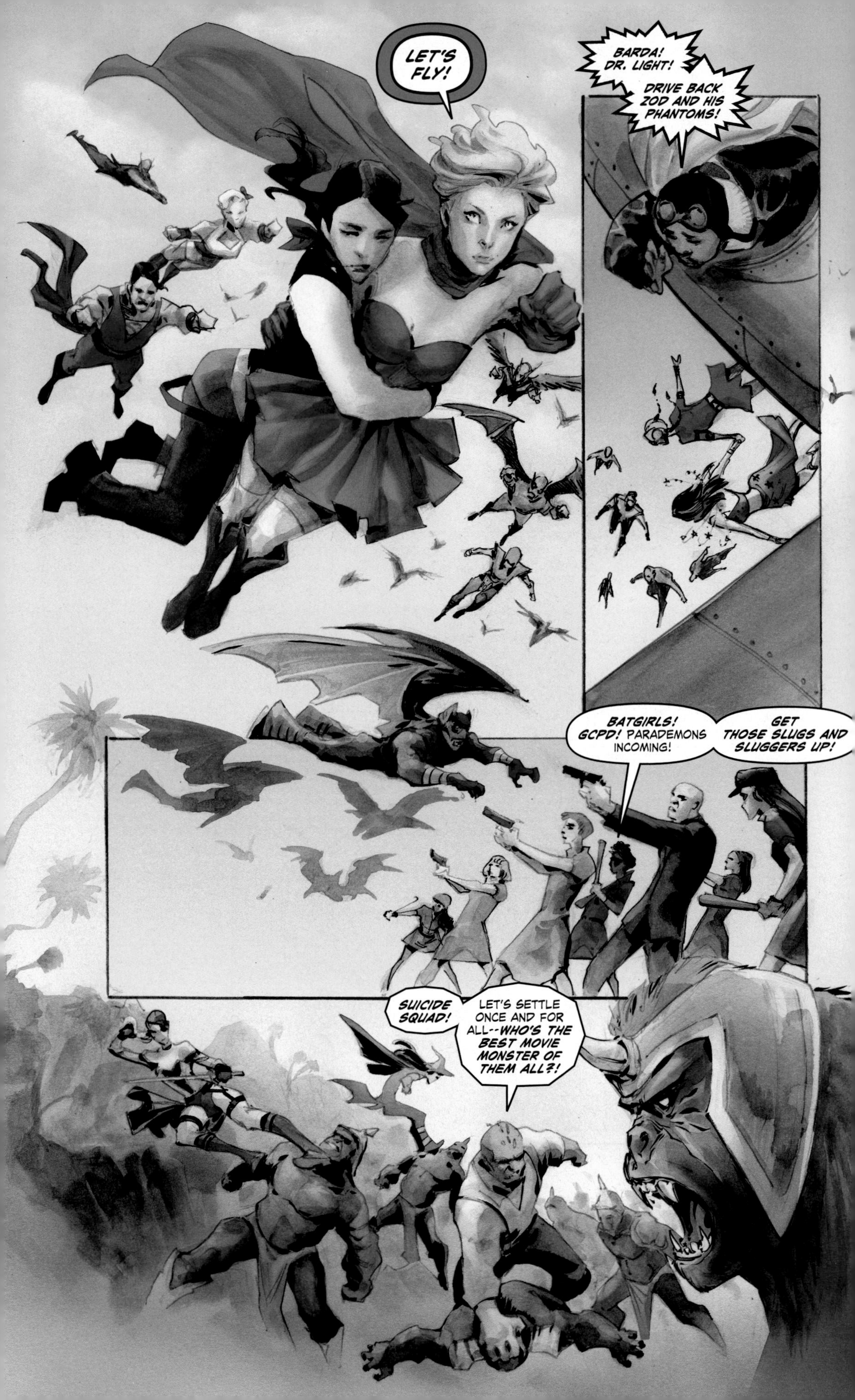
LET'S FLY!
BARDA! DR. LIGHT!
DRIVE BACK ZOD AND HIS PHANTOMS!
BATGIRLS! GCPD! PARADEMONS INCOMING!
GET THOSE SLUGS AND SLUGGERS UP!
SUICIDE SQUAD!
LET'S SETTLE ONCE AND FOR ALL--WHO'S THE BEST MOVIE MONSTER OF THEM ALL?!

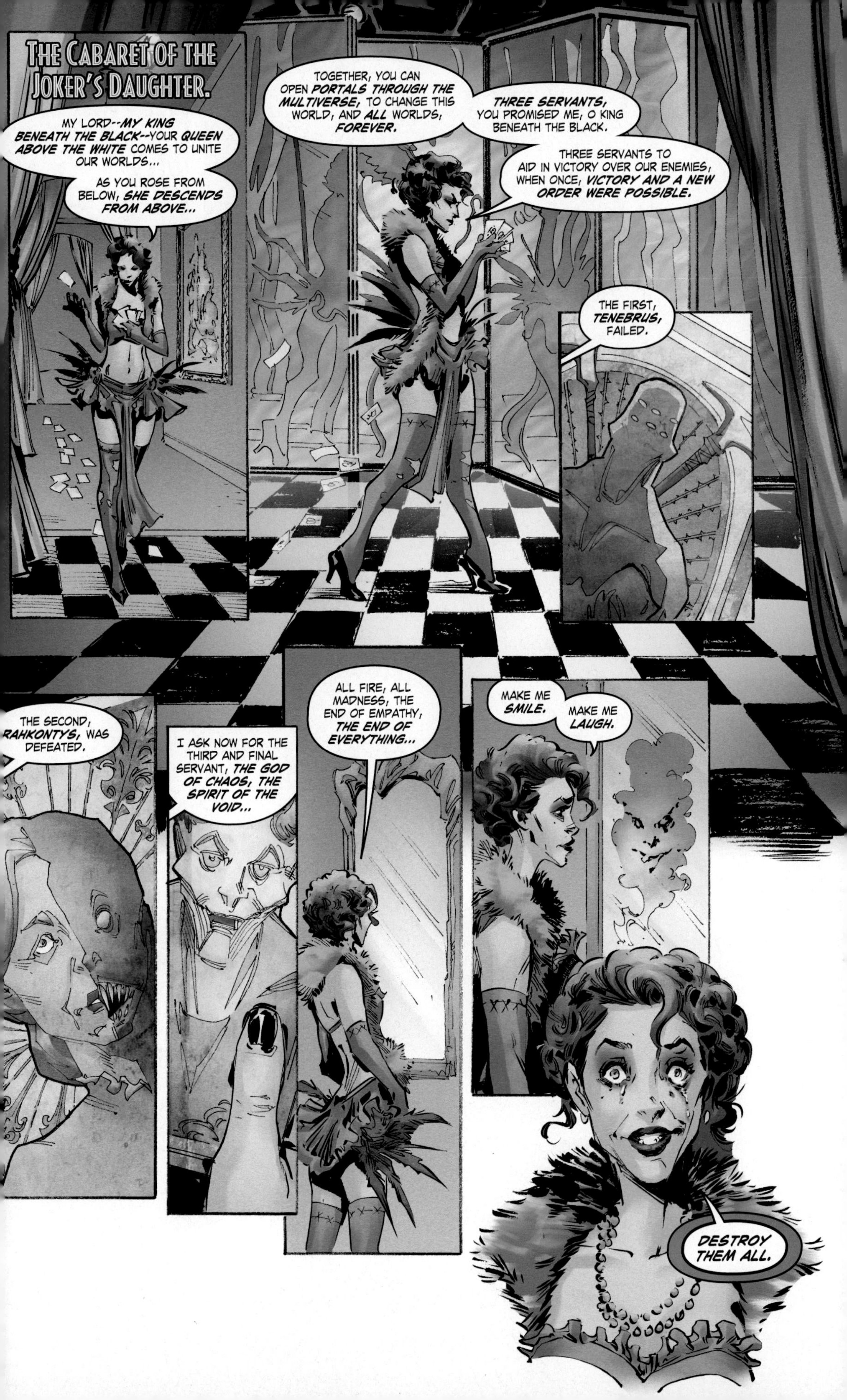
THE CABARET OF THE JOKER'S DAUGHTER.
MY LORD--MY KING BENEATH THE BLACK--YOUR QUEEN ABOVE THE WHITE COMES TO UNITE OUR WORLDS...
AS YOU ROSE FROM BELOW, SHE DESCENDS FROM ABOVE...
TOGETHER, YOU CAN OPEN PORTALS THROUGH THE MULTIVERSE, TO CHANGE THIS WORLD, AND ALL WORLDS, FOREVER.
THREE SERVANTS, YOU PROMISED ME, O KING BENEATH THE BLACK.
THREE SERVANTS TO AID IN VICTORY OVER OUR ENEMIES, WHEN ONCE, VICTORY AND A NEW ORDER WERE POSSIBLE.
THE FIRST, TENEBRUS, FAILED.
THE SECOND, RAHKONTYS, WAS DEFEATED.
I ASK NOW FOR THE THIRD AND FINAL SERVANT, THE GOD OF CHAOS, THE SPIRIT OF THE VOID...
ALL FIRE, ALL MADNESS, THE END OF EMPATHY, THE END OF EVERYTHING...
MAKE ME SMILE.
MAKE ME LAUGH.
DESTROY THEM ALL.

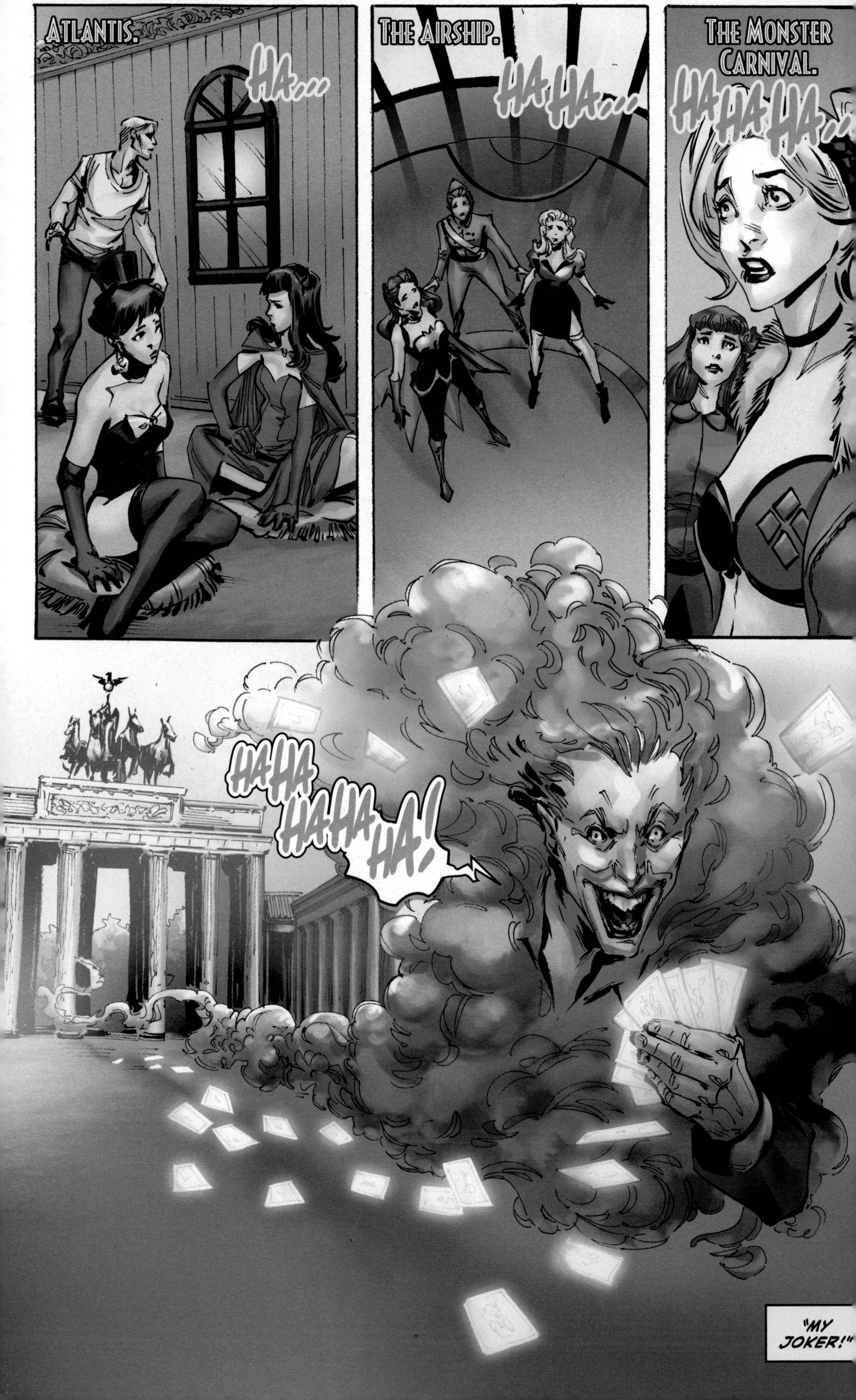
Atlantis.
HA...
The airship.
HA HA...
The Monster Carnival.
HA HA HA...
HA HA HA HA HA!
"MY JOKER!"

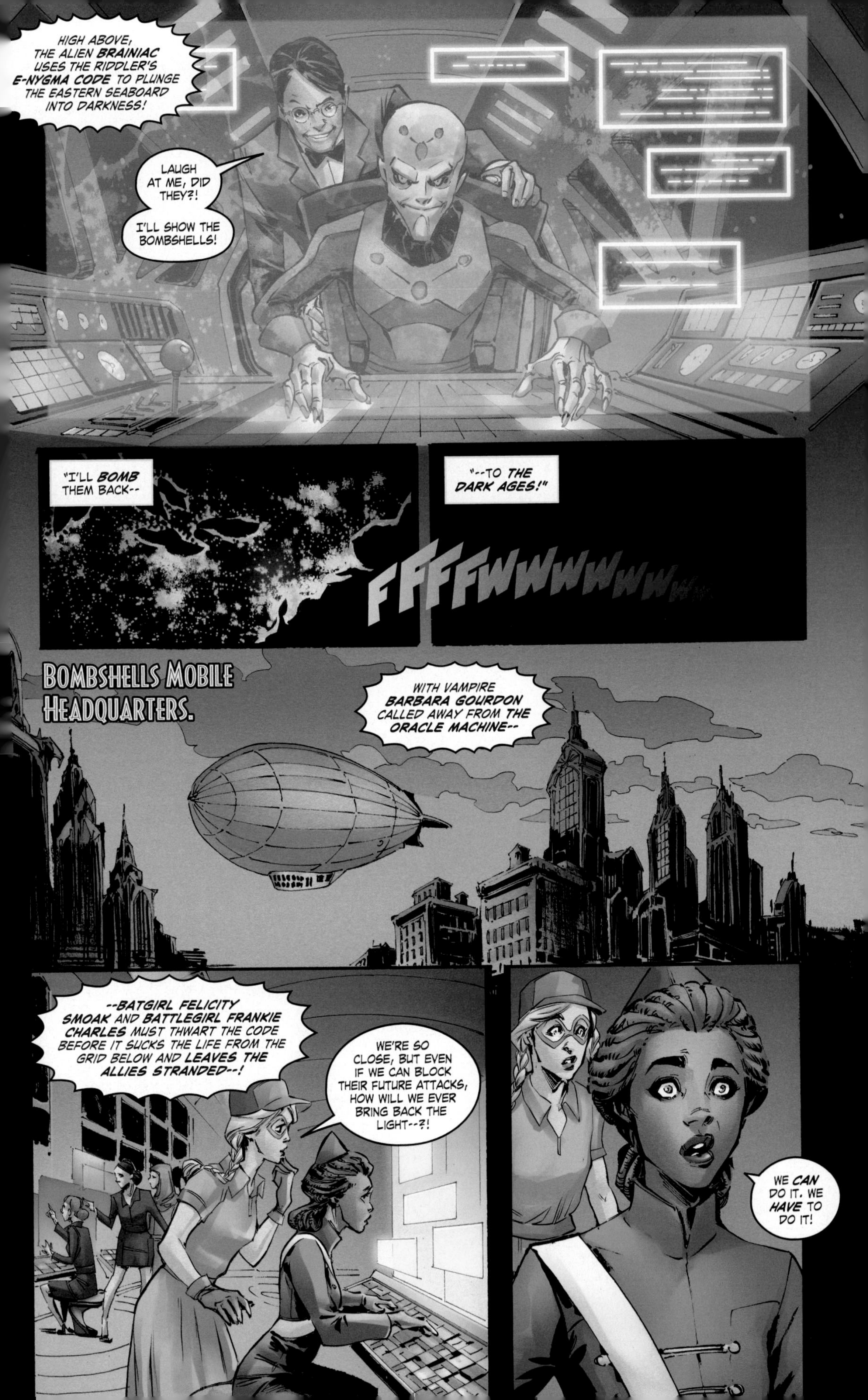

HIGH ABOVE, THE ALIEN BRAINIAC USES THE RIDDLER'S E-NYGMA CODE TO PLUNGE THE EASTERN SEABOARD INTO DARKNESS!
LAUGH AT ME, DID THEY?!
I'LL SHOW THE BOMBSHELLS!
"I'LL BOMB THEM BACK--
"--TO THE DARK AGES!"
FFFFWWWWWWWW
BOMBSHELLS MOBILE HEADQUARTERS.
WITH VAMPIRE BARBARA GOURDON CALLED AWAY FROM THE ORACLE MACHINE--
--BATGIRL FELICITY SMOAK AND BATTLEGIRL FRANKIE CHARLES MUST THWART THE CODE BEFORE IT SUCKS THE LIFE FROM THE GRID BELOW AND LEAVES THE ALLIES STRANDED--!
WE'RE SO CLOSE, BUT EVEN IF WE CAN BLOCK THEIR FUTURE ATTACKS, HOW WILL WE EVER BRING BACK THE LIGHT--?!
WE CAN DO IT. WE HAVE TO DO IT!

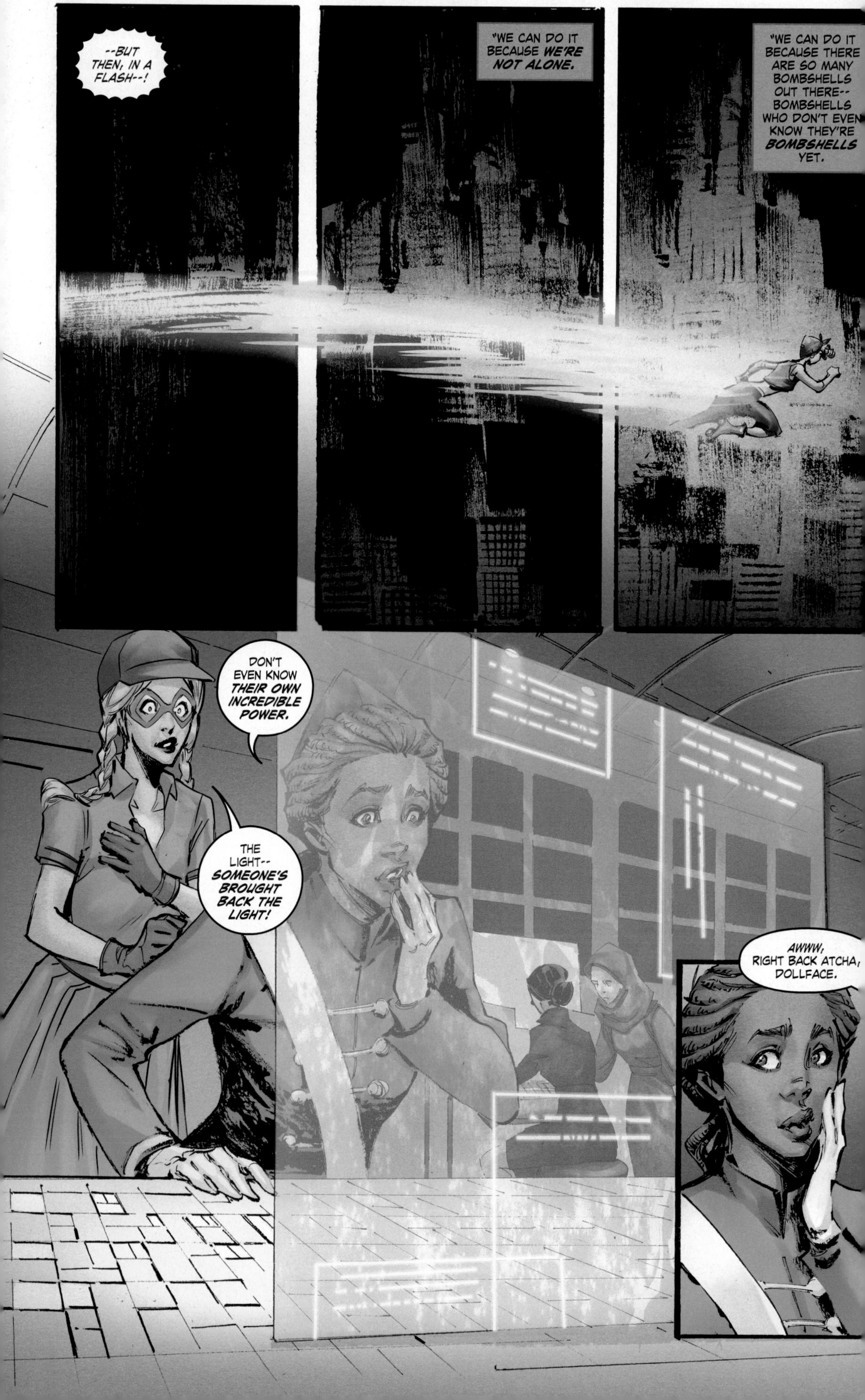
--BUT THEN, IN A FLASH--!
"WE CAN DO IT BECAUSE WE'RE NOT ALONE.
"WE CAN DO IT BECAUSE THERE ARE SO MANY BOMBSHELLS OUT THERE--BOMBSHELLS WHO DON'T EVEN KNOW THEY'RE BOMBSHELLS YET.
DON'T EVEN KNOW THEIR OWN INCREDIBLE POWER.
THE LIGHT--SOMEONE'S BROUGHT BACK THE LIGHT!
AWWW, RIGHT BACK ATCHA, DOLLFACE.

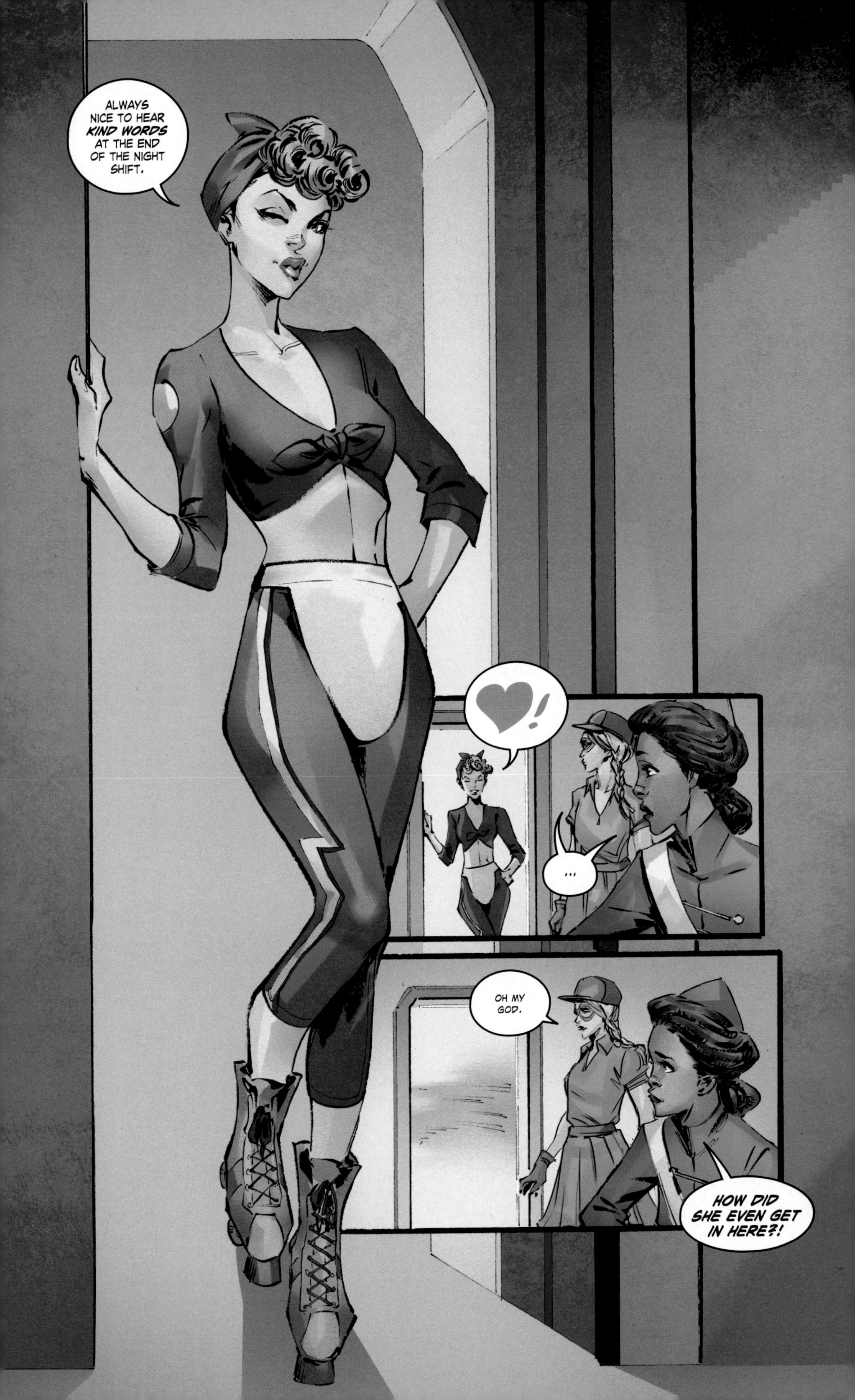
ALWAYS NICE TO HEAR KIND WORDS AT THE END OF THE NIGHT SHIFT.
!
...
OH MY GOD.
HOW DID SHE EVEN GET IN HERE?!

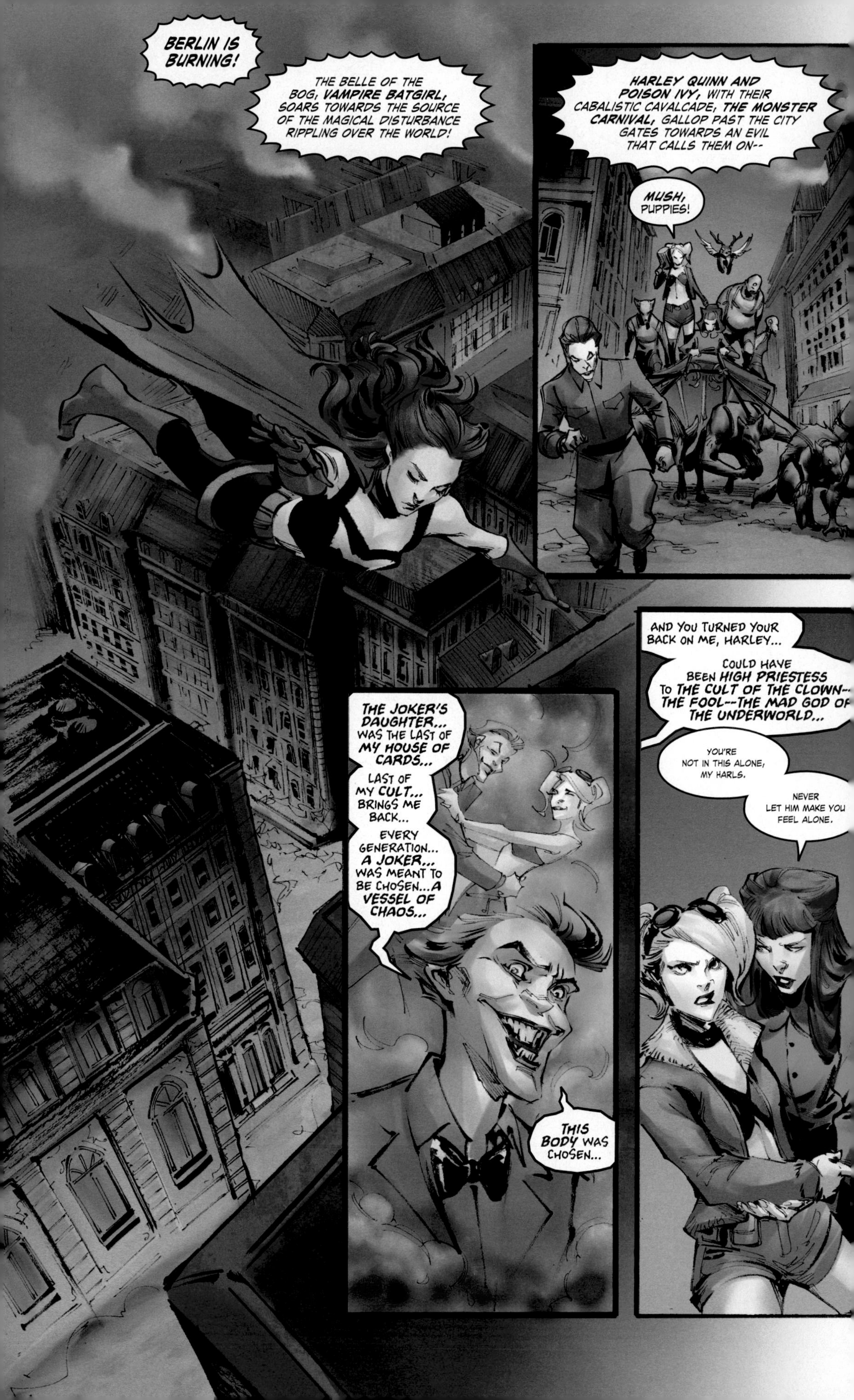
BERLIN IS BURNING!
THE BELLE OF THE BOG, VAMPIRE BATGIRL, SOARS TOWARDS THE SOURCE OF THE MAGICAL DISTURBANCE RIPPLING OVER THE WORLD!
HARLEY QUINN AND POISON IVY, WITH THEIR CABALISTIC CAVALCADE, THE MONSTER CARNIVAL, GALLOP PAST THE CITY GATES TOWARDS AN EVIL THAT CALLS THEM ON--
MUSH, PUPPIES!
THE JOKER'S DAUGHTER... WAS THE LAST OF MY HOUSE OF CARDS...
LAST OF MY CULT... BRINGS ME BACK...
EVERY GENERATION... A JOKER... WAS MEANT TO BE CHOSEN...A VESSEL OF CHAOS...
THIS BODY WAS CHOSEN...
AND YOU TURNED YOUR BACK ON ME, HARLEY...
COULD HAVE BEEN HIGH PRIESTESS TO THE CULT OF THE CLOWN-- THE FOOL--THE MAD GOD OF THE UNDERWORLD...
YOU'RE NOT IN THIS ALONE, MY HARLS.
NEVER LET HIM MAKE YOU FEEL ALONE.

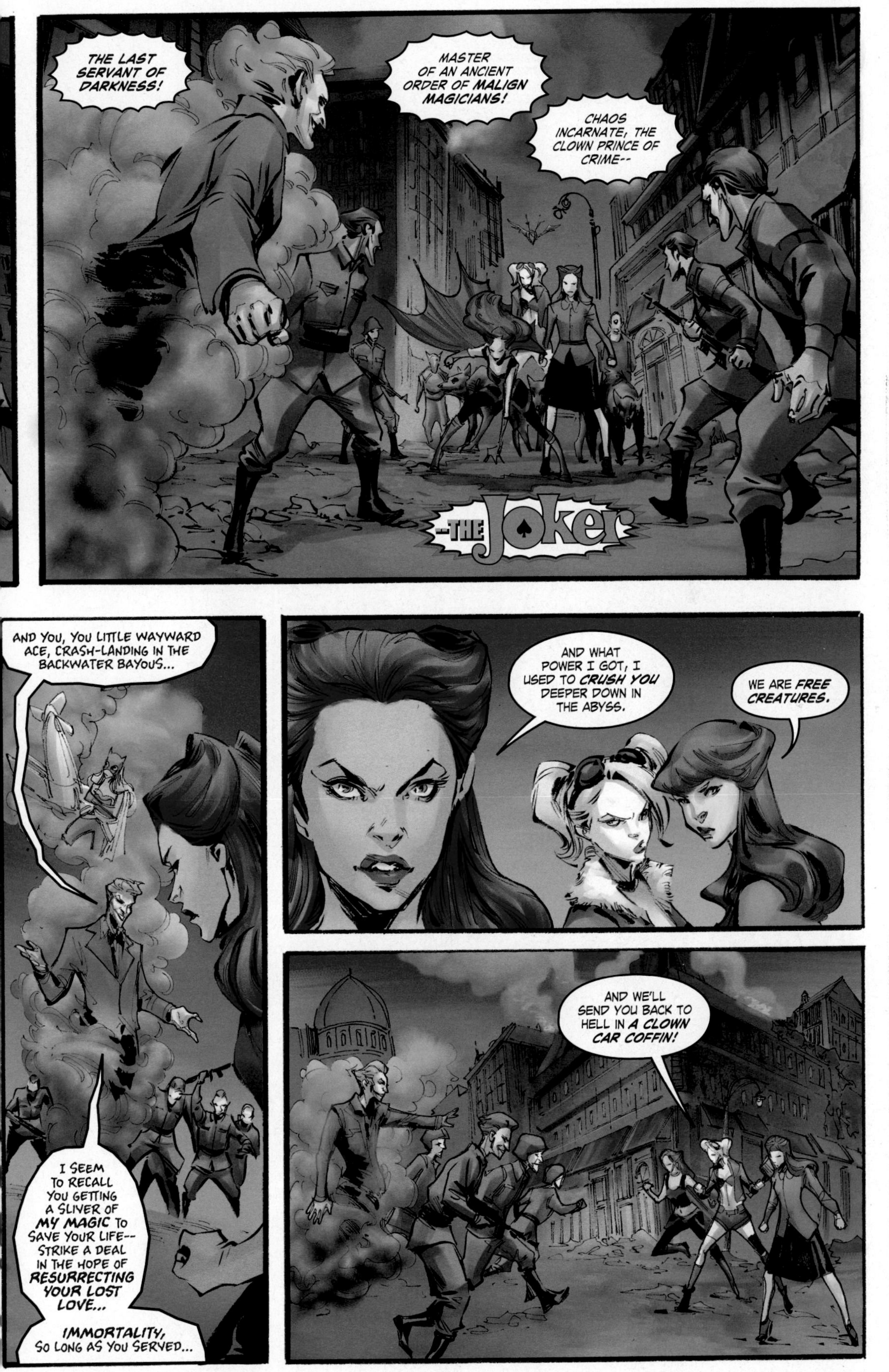
THE LAST SERVANT OF DARKNESS!
MASTER OF AN ANCIENT ORDER OF MALIGN MAGICIANS!
CHAOS INCARNATE, THE CLOWN PRINCE OF CRIME--
--THE Joker
AND YOU, YOU LITTLE WAYWARD ACE, CRASH-LANDING IN THE BACKWATER BAYOUS...
I SEEM TO RECALL YOU GETTING A SLIVER OF MY MAGIC TO SAVE YOUR LIFE-- STRIKE A DEAL IN THE HOPE OF RESURRECTING YOUR LOST LOVE...
IMMORTALITY, SO LONG AS YOU SERVED...
AND WHAT POWER I GOT, I USED TO CRUSH YOU DEEPER DOWN IN THE ABYSS.
WE ARE FREE CREATURES.
AND WE'LL SEND YOU BACK TO HELL IN A CLOWN CAR COFFIN!

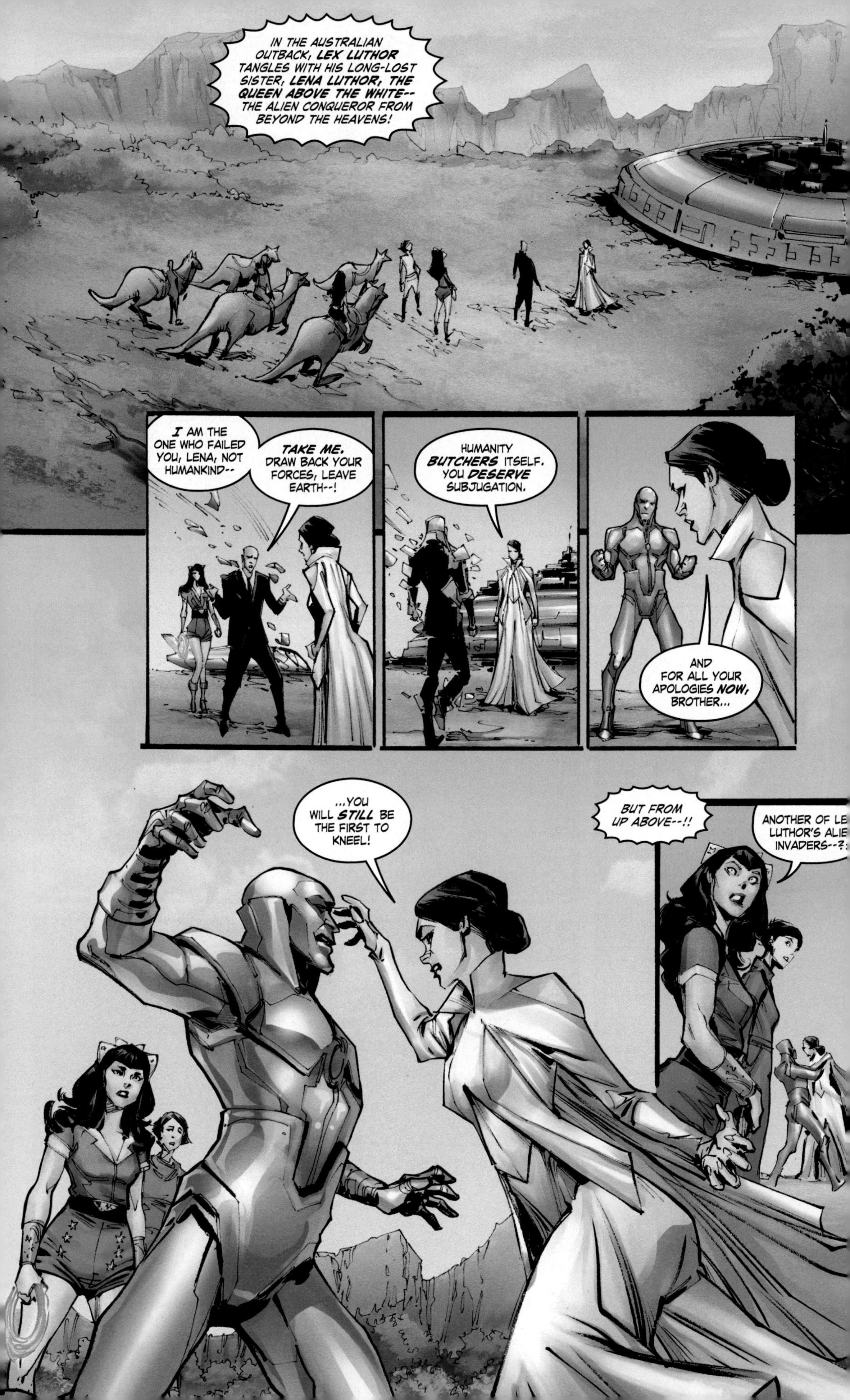
IN THE AUSTRALIAN OUTBACK, LEX LUTHOR TANGLES WITH HIS LONG-LOST SISTER, LENA LUTHOR, THE QUEEN ABOVE THE WHITE-- THE ALIEN CONQUEROR FROM BEYOND THE HEAVENS!
I AM THE ONE WHO FAILED YOU, LENA, NOT HUMANKIND--
TAKE ME. DRAW BACK YOUR FORCES, LEAVE EARTH--!
HUMANITY BUTCHERS ITSELF. YOU DESERVE SUBJUGATION.
AND FOR ALL YOUR APOLOGIES NOW, BROTHER...
...YOU WILL STILL BE THE FIRST TO KNEEL!
BUT FROM UP ABOVE--!!

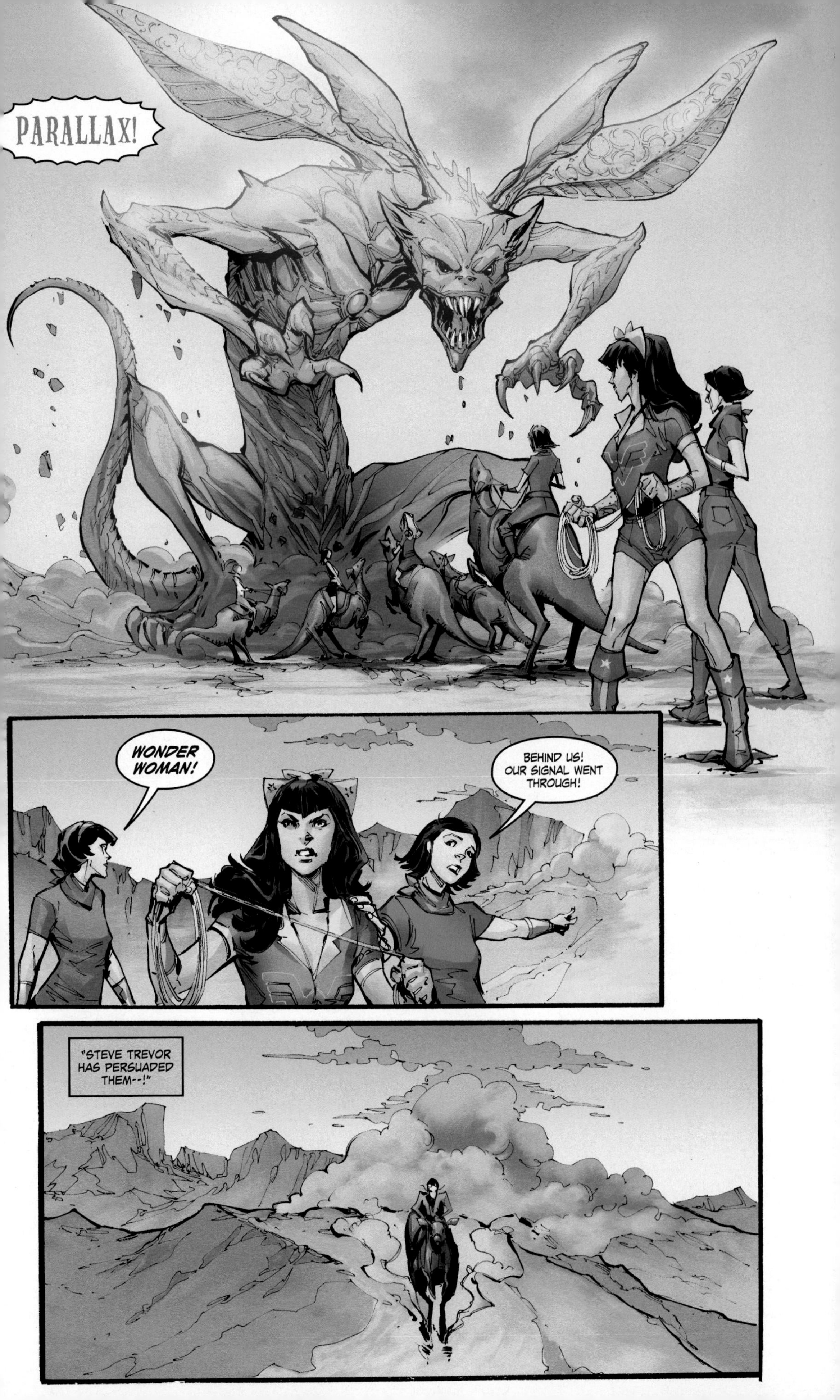
PARALLAX!
WONDER WOMAN!
BEHIND US! OUR SIGNAL WENT THROUGH!
"STEVE TREVOR HAS PERSUADED THEM--!"

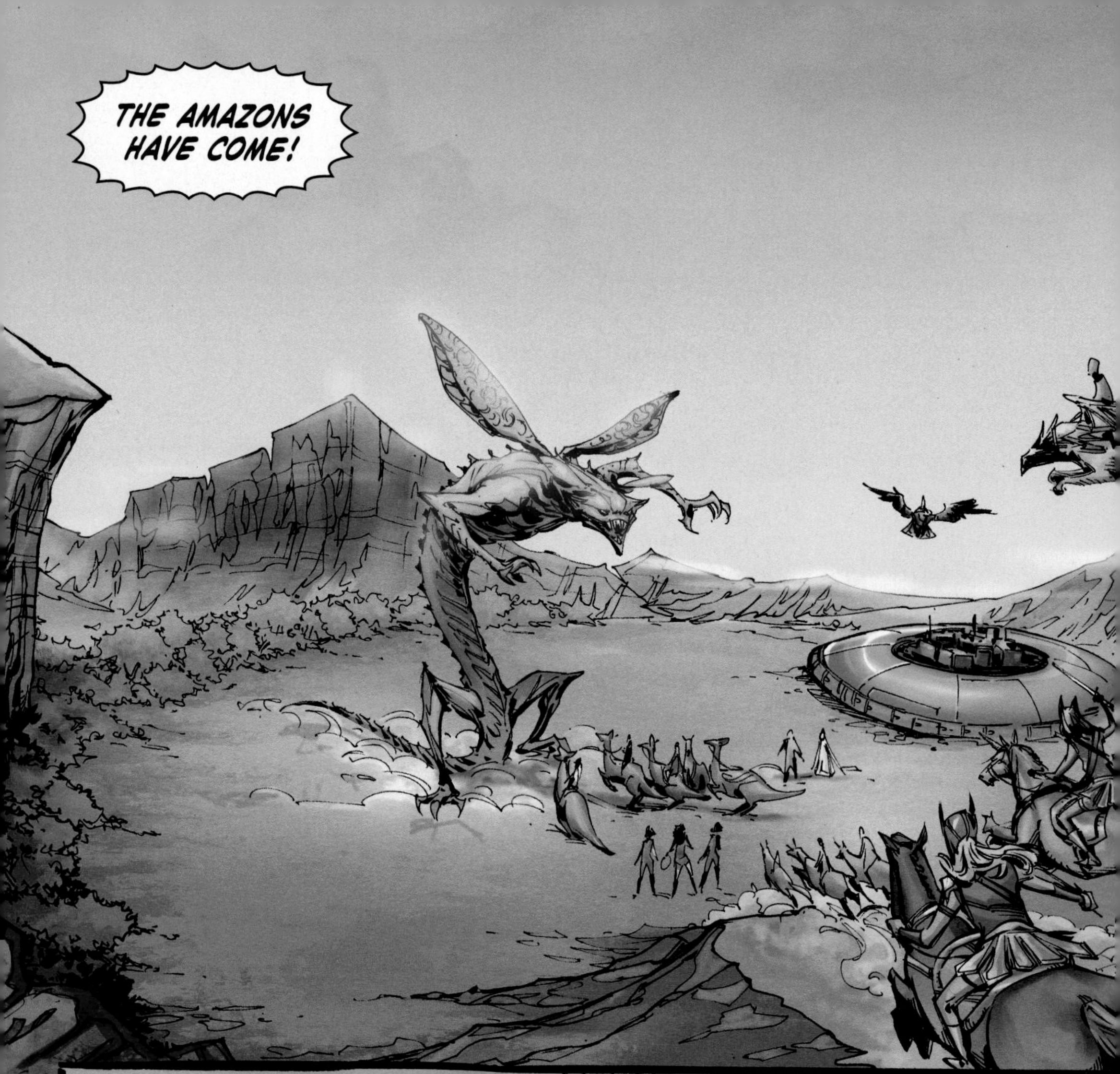
THE AMAZONS HAVE COME!

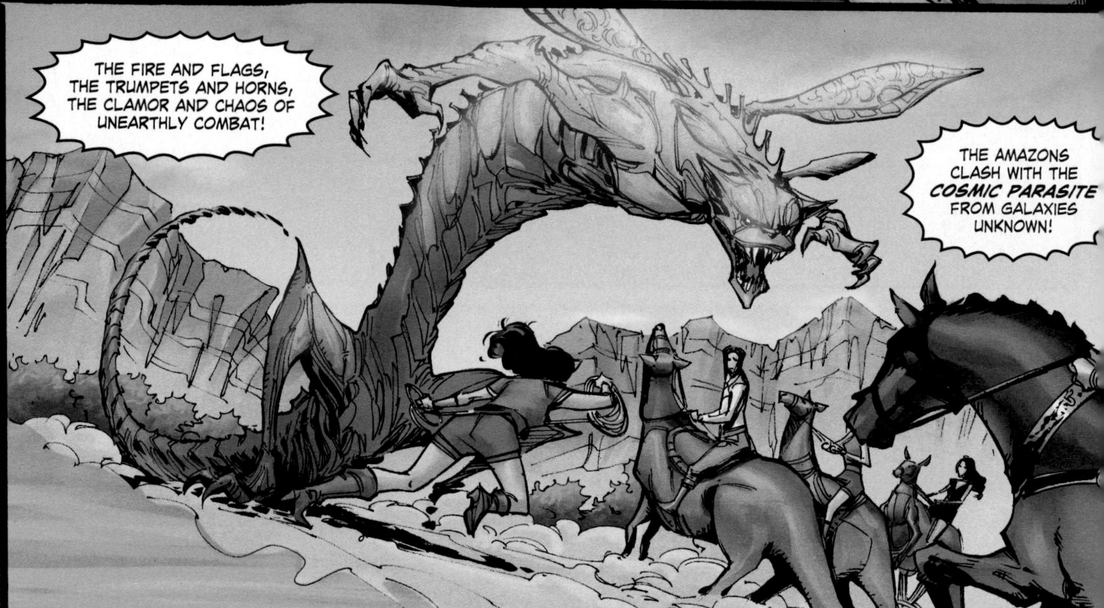
THE FIRE AND FLAGS, THE TRUMPETS AND HORNS, THE CLAMOR AND CHAOS OF UNEARTHLY COMBAT!
THE AMAZONS CLASH WITH THE COSMIC PARASITE FROM GALAXIES UNKNOWN!

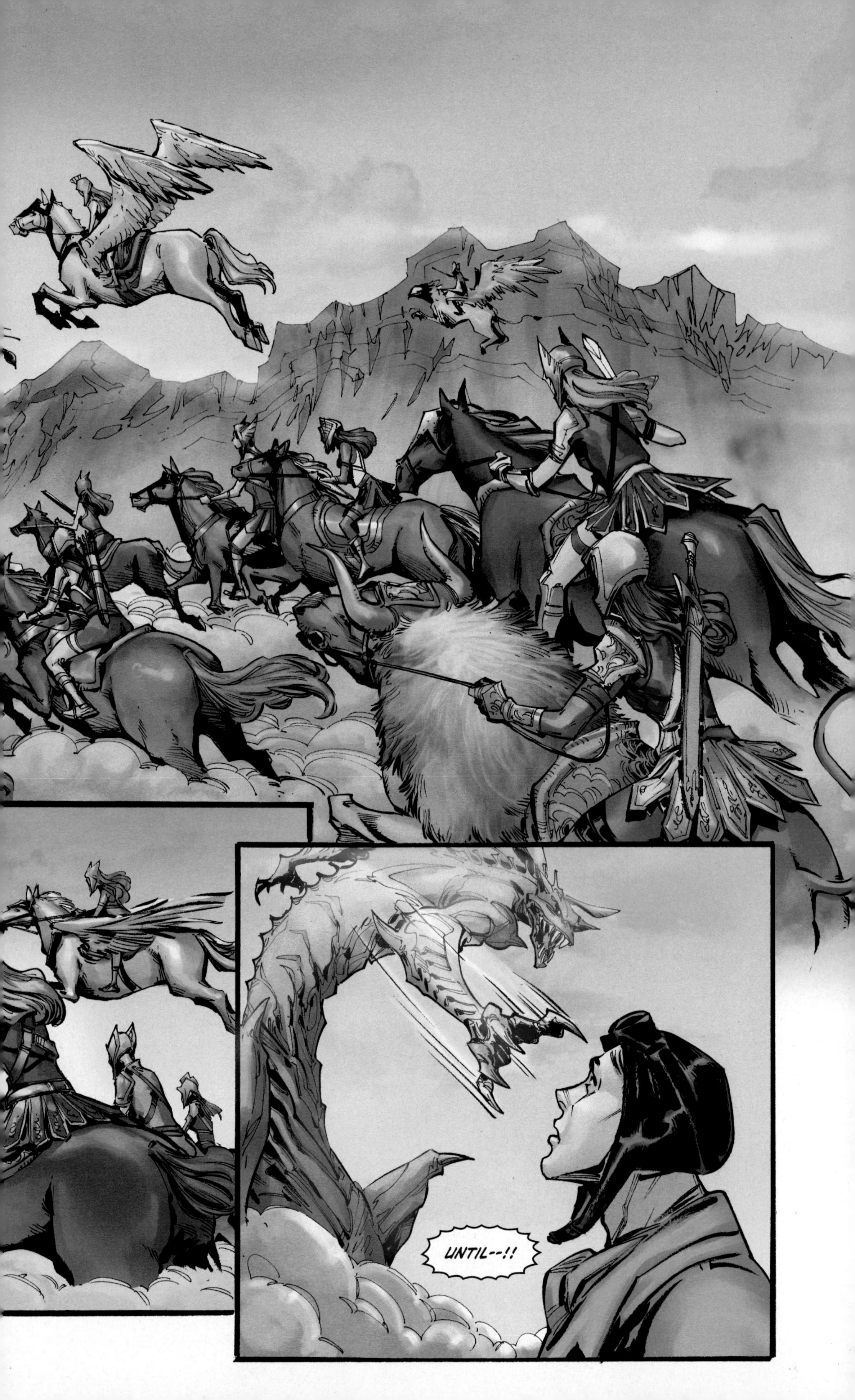
UNTIL--!!

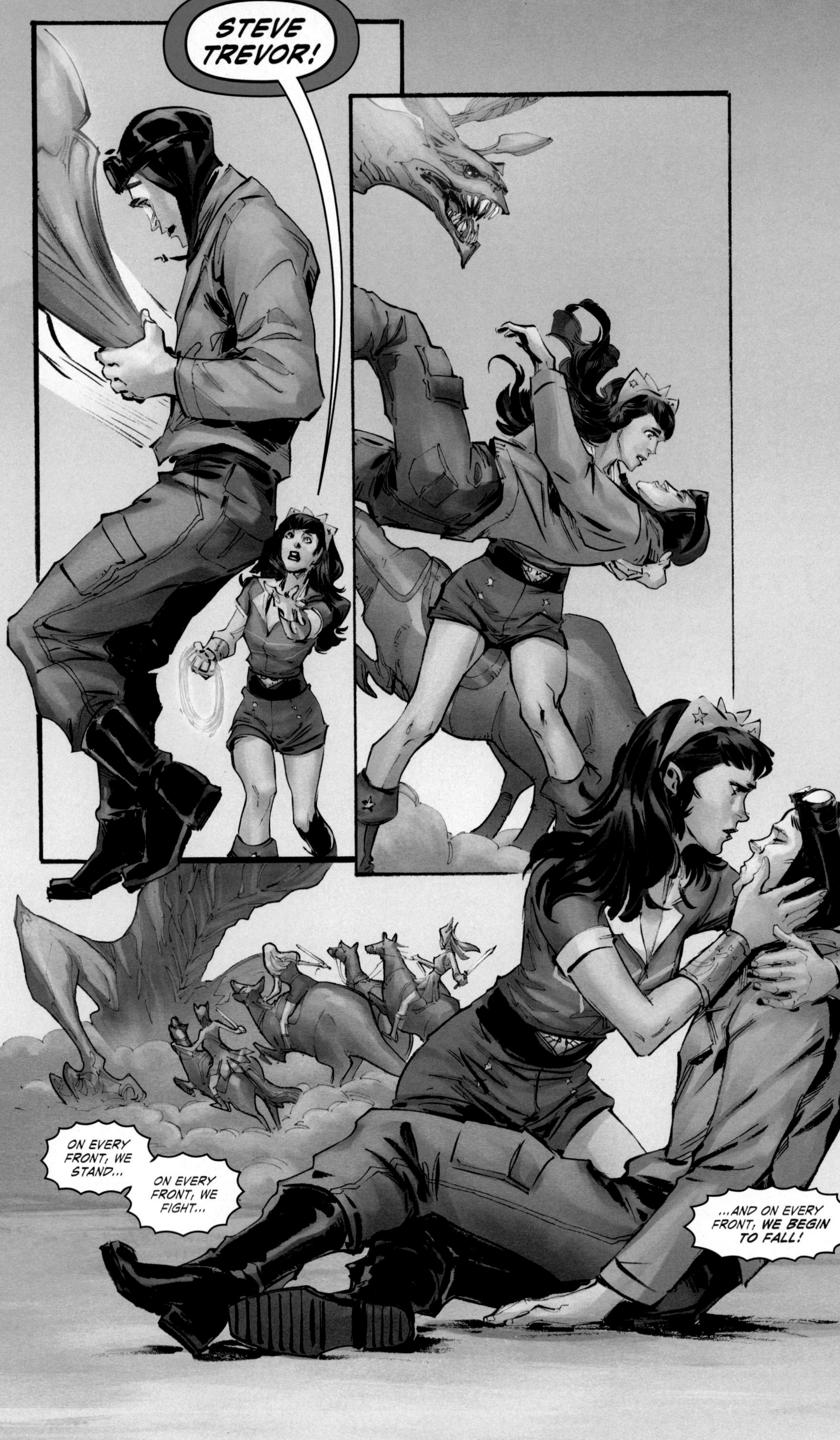
STEVE TREVOR!
ON EVERY FRONT, WE STAND...
ON EVERY FRONT, WE FIGHT...
...AND ON EVERY FRONT, WE BEGIN TO FALL!

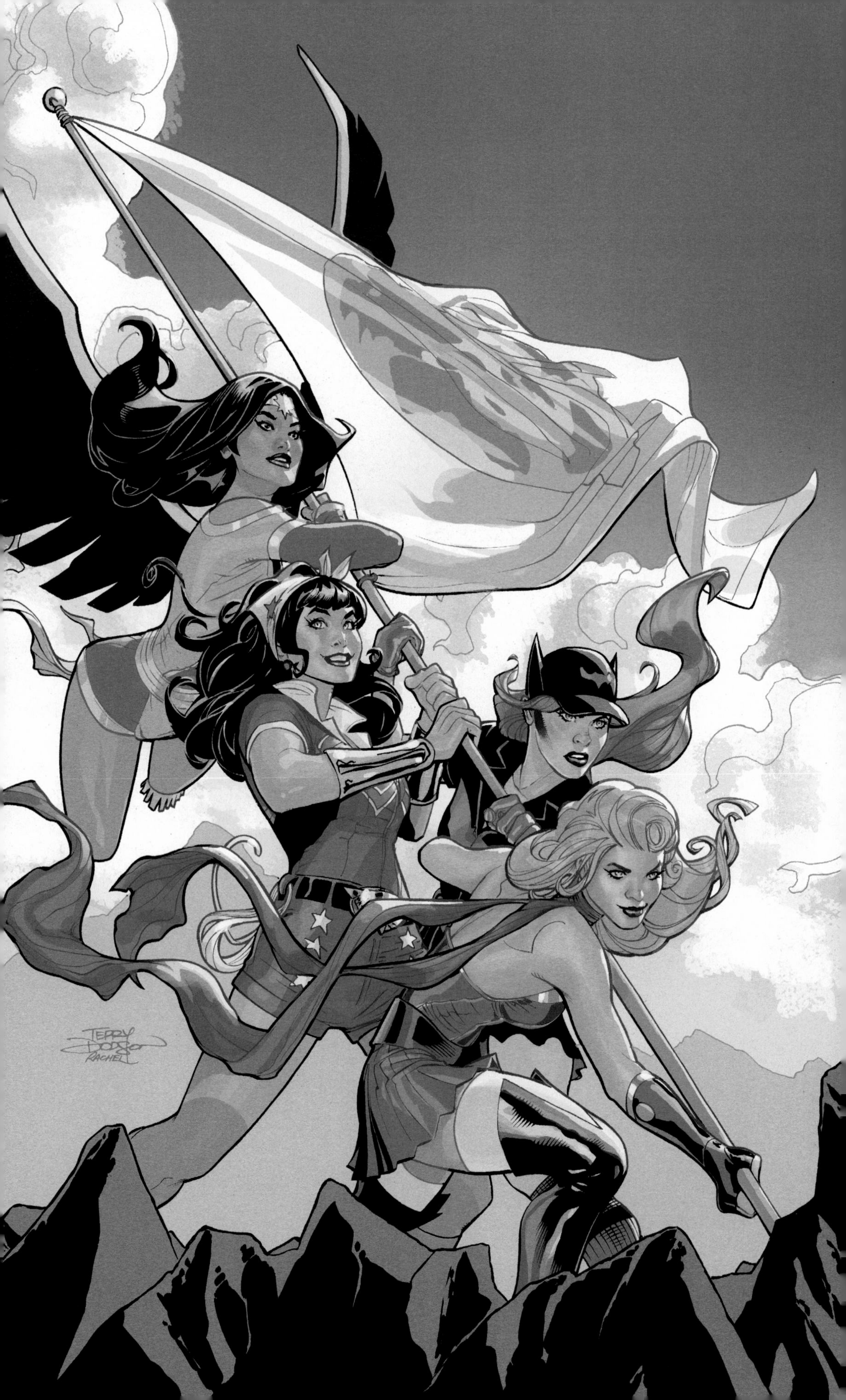
TERRY DODSON
RACHEL

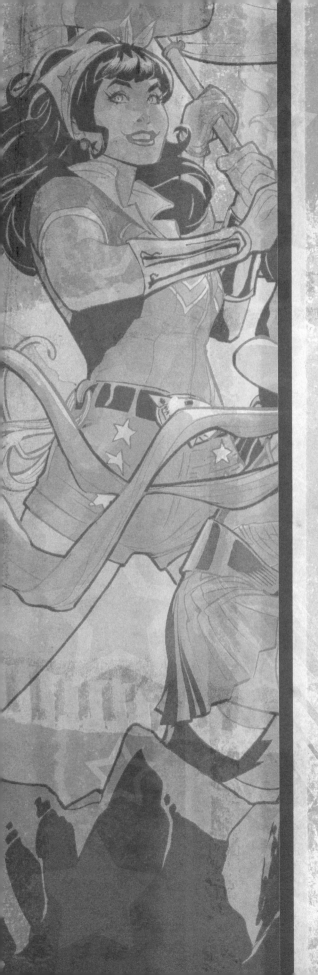

TAPS
PARTS THREE and FOUR

Written by
MARGUERITE BENNETT

Art by
DAVID HAHN

Colors by
J. NANJAN

Letters by
WES ABBOTT

Cover by
TERRY *and* **RACHEL DODSON**

THE VOID.

THE **WORLDS** ARE AT WAR.

THE CONQUEST I FEARED HAS NOW BEGUN, **BY THE HERALD AND HER QUEEN.**

"BUT AS WE SHIELD OURSELVES FROM INVASION WITHOUT...

"...WE HAVE NEGLECTED WHAT WE COULD BECOME FROM **WITHIN.**"

COMMANDER AMANDA WALLER! NEWS FROM-- **EVERY** FRONT!

--**STEVE TREVOR,** SLAIN IN BATTLE--!

--**LIMITLESS FRESH TROOPS** FROM **APOKOLIPS** AS OUR OWN SOLDIERS FALL--

--A SQUADRON OF **BLACK LANTERNS** RAINING AN ANCIENT BURIAL GROUND IN JAPAN, USING THE SPIRITS AS FUEL OR THEIR POWER RINGS--

IF THEY ESCAPE THE ISLAND, **THEY'LL BURN THE WHOLE WORLD,** AND USE THE DEAD FOR THEIR SOLDIERS!

"WHAT WE COULD BECOME, WHEN WE ARE RULED BY FEAR...

"WHEN OUR HUMANITY IS NEGOTIABLE, WHEN **THE ENDS JUSTIFY THE MEANS**--

"BUT IF THE ENDS NEVER ARRIVE AS WE HAD HOPED...

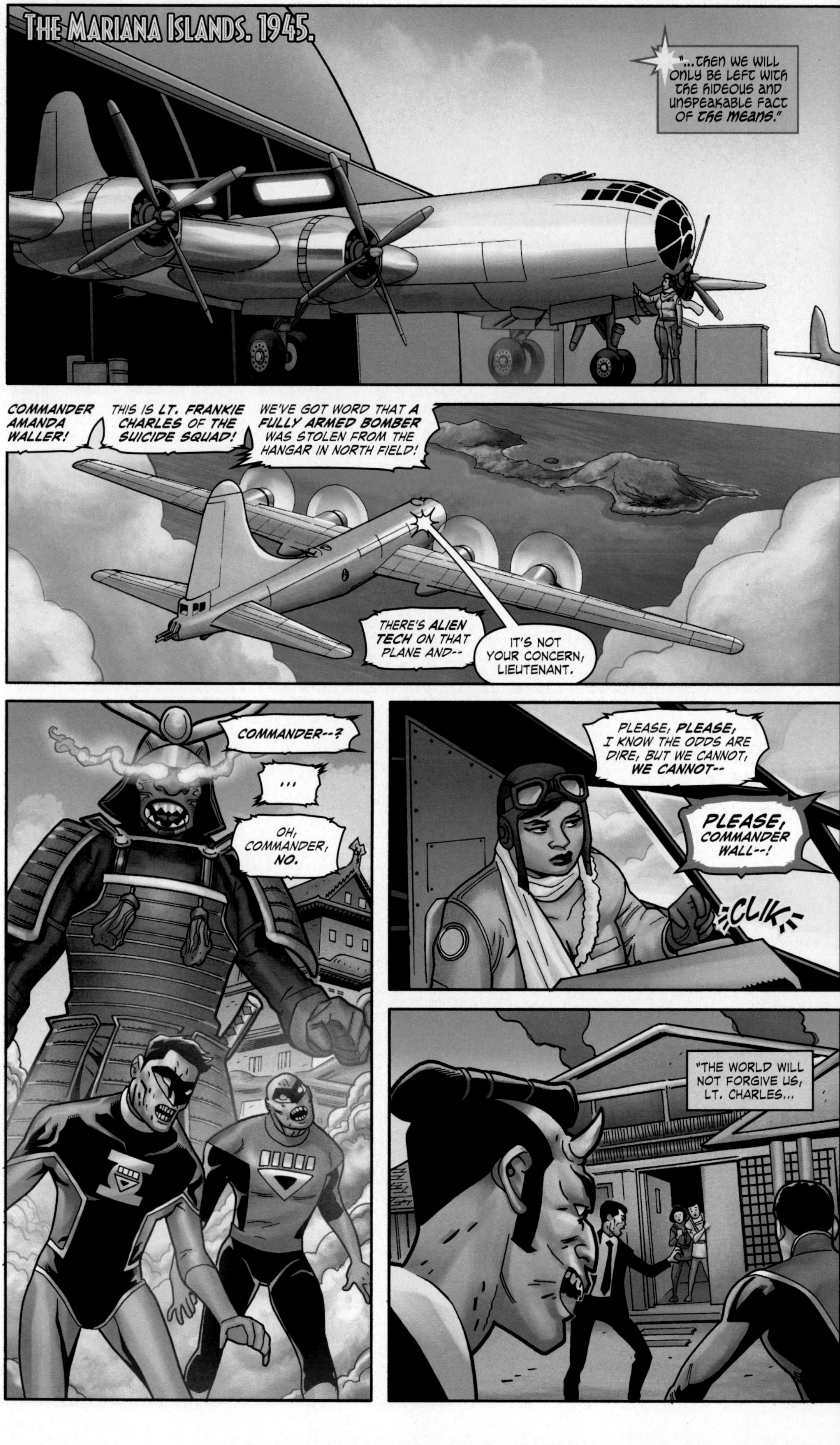
The Mariana Islands. 1945.
"...then we will only be left with the hideous and unspeakable fact of the means."
COMMANDER AMANDA WALLER!
THIS IS LT. FRANKIE CHARLES OF THE SUICIDE SQUAD!
WE'VE GOT WORD THAT A FULLY ARMED BOMBER WAS STOLEN FROM THE HANGAR IN NORTH FIELD!
THERE'S ALIEN TECH ON THAT PLANE AND--
IT'S NOT YOUR CONCERN, LIEUTENANT.
COMMANDER--?
...
OH, COMMANDER, NO.
PLEASE, PLEASE, I KNOW THE ODDS ARE DIRE, BUT WE CANNOT, WE CANNOT--
PLEASE, COMMANDER WALL--!
CLIK
"THE WORLD WILL NOT FORGIVE US, LT. CHARLES...

...AND WE SHOULD NEVER FORGIVE *OURSELVES* FOR WHAT WE DO TODAY.

KER-CHINK

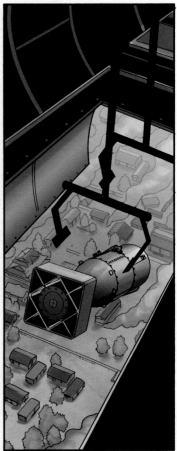

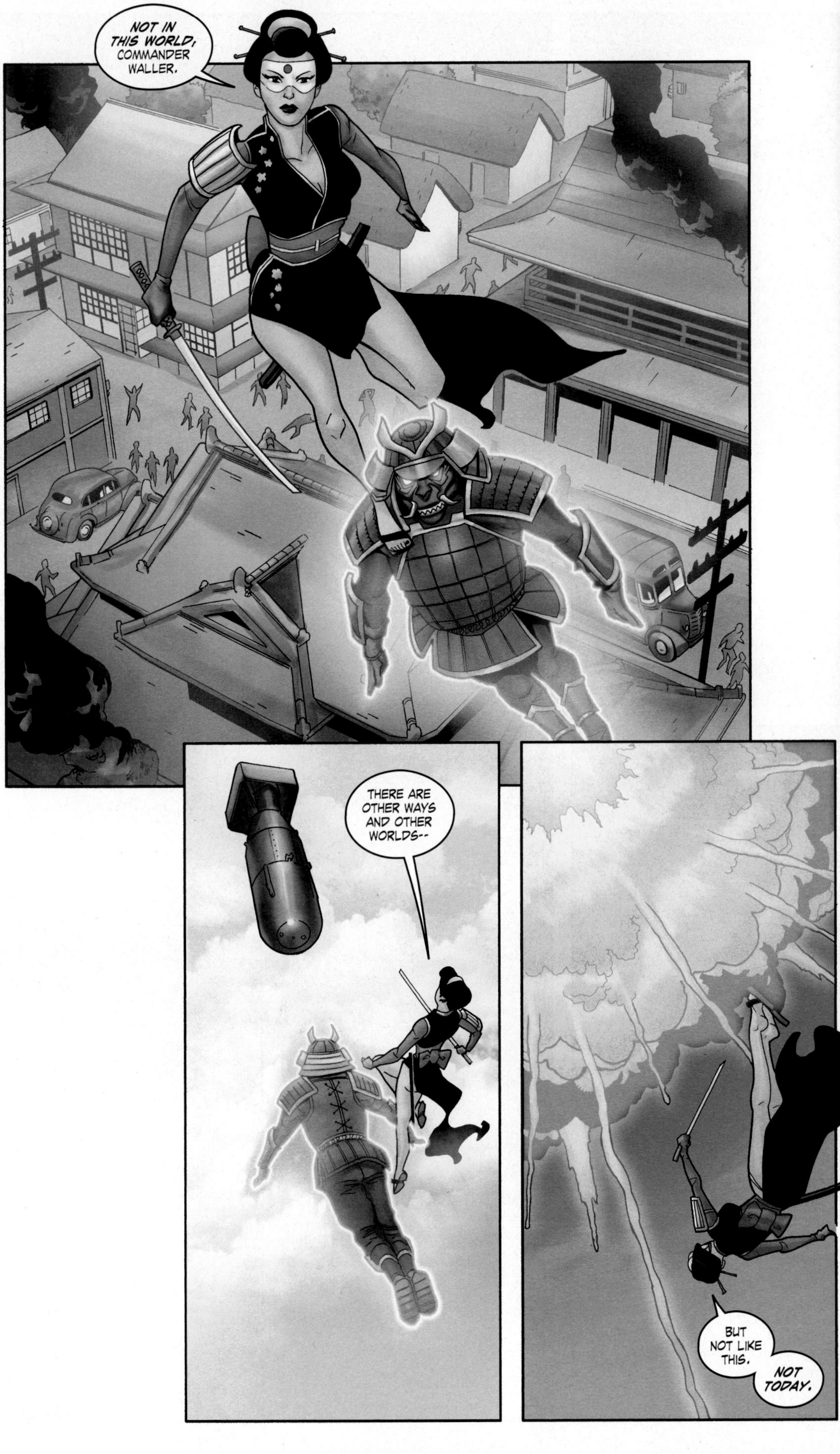
NOT IN THIS WORLD, COMMANDER WALLER.
THERE ARE OTHER WAYS AND OTHER WORLDS--
BUT NOT LIKE THIS.
NOT TODAY.

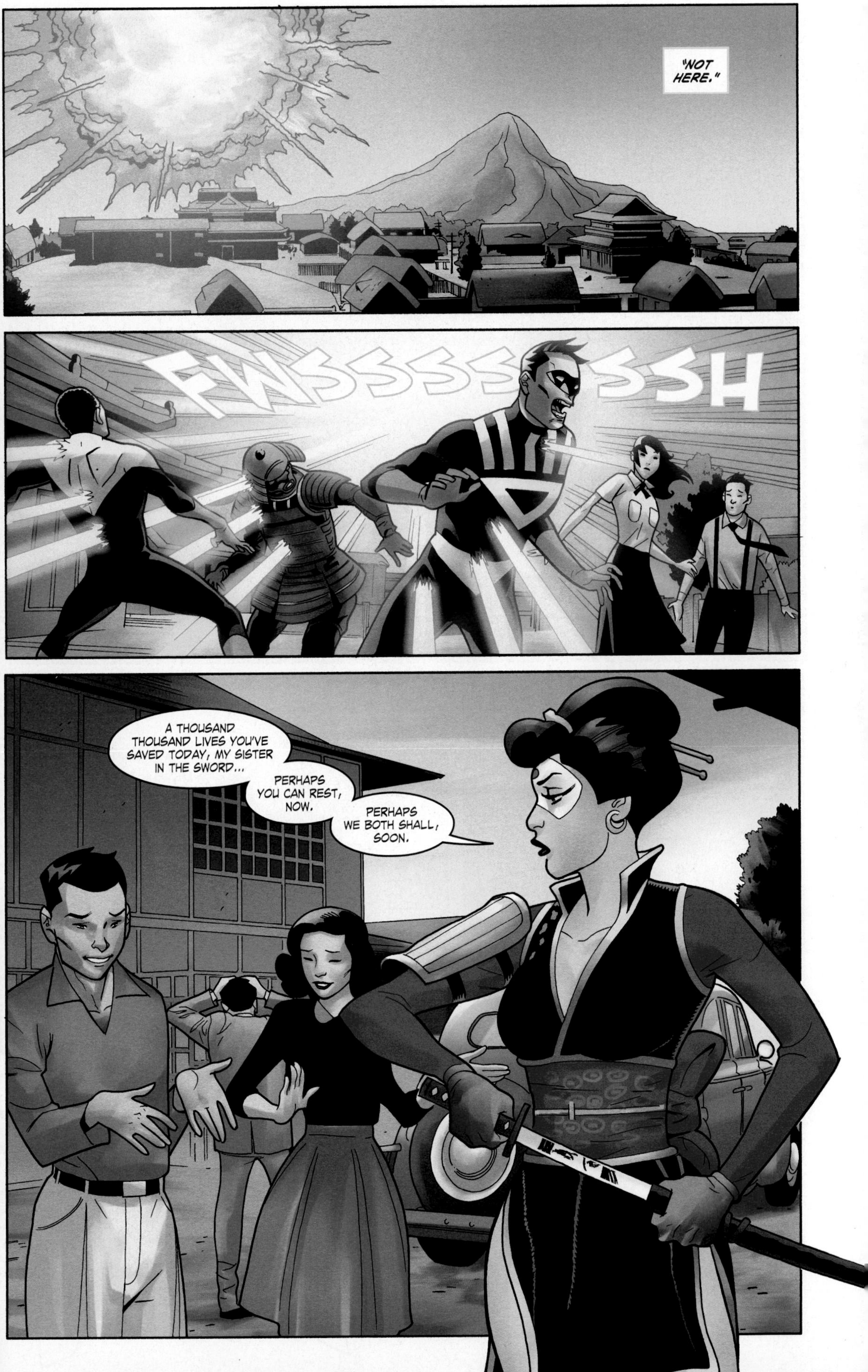
"NOT HERE."
FWSSSSSSSH
A THOUSAND THOUSAND LIVES YOU'VE SAVED TODAY, MY SISTER IN THE SWORD...
PERHAPS YOU CAN REST, NOW.
PERHAPS WE BOTH SHALL, SOON.

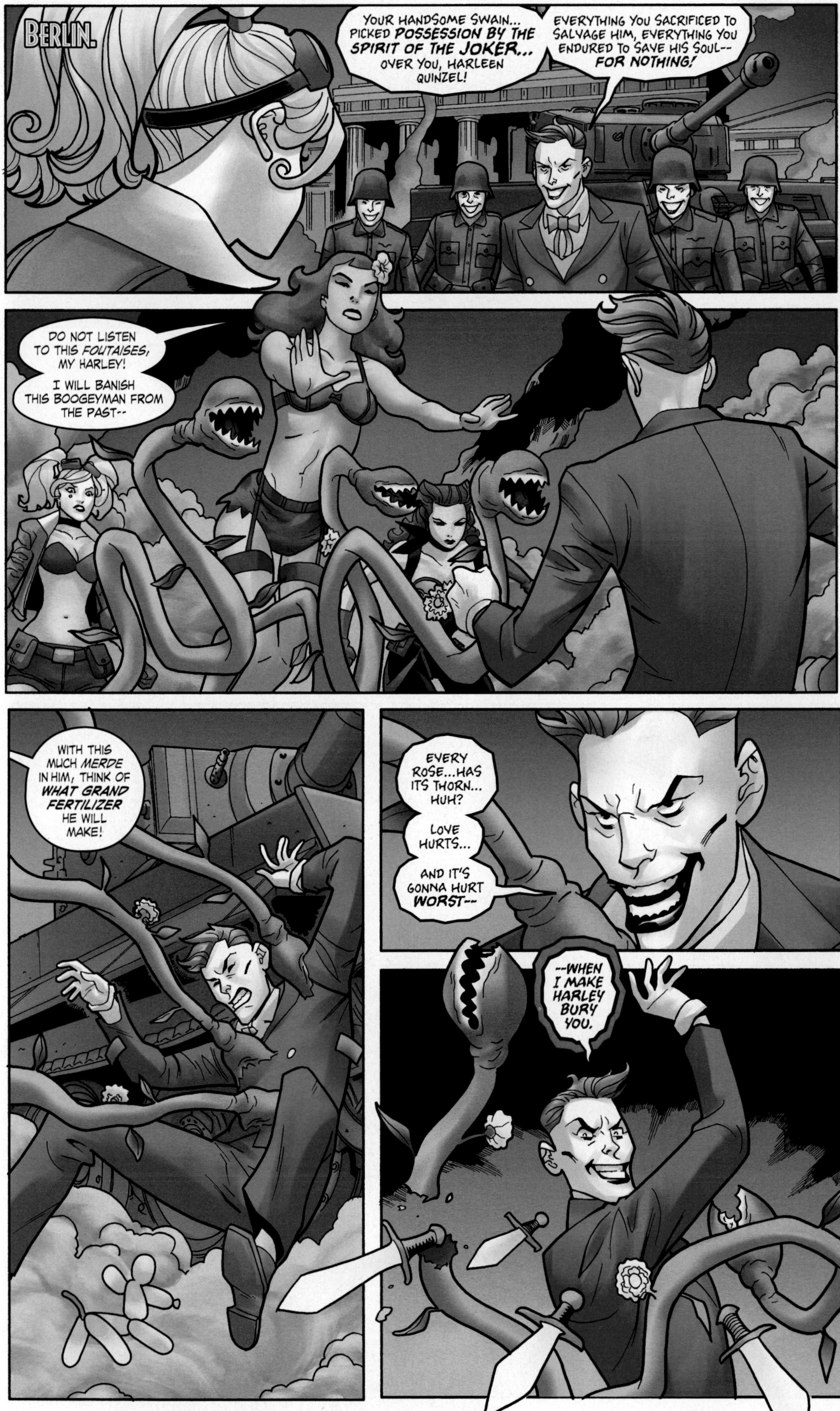
BERLIN.
YOUR HANDSOME SWAIN... PICKED POSSESSION BY THE SPIRIT OF THE JOKER... OVER YOU, HARLEEN QUINZEL!
EVERYTHING YOU SACRIFICED TO SALVAGE HIM, EVERYTHING YOU ENDURED TO SAVE HIS SOUL-- FOR NOTHING!
DO NOT LISTEN TO THIS FOUTAISES, MY HARLEY!
I WILL BANISH THIS BOOGEYMAN FROM THE PAST--
WITH THIS MUCH MERDE IN HIM, THINK OF WHAT GRAND FERTILIZER HE WILL MAKE!
EVERY ROSE...HAS ITS THORN... HUH?
LOVE HURTS...
AND IT'S GONNA HURT WORST--
--WHEN I MAKE HARLEY BURY YOU.

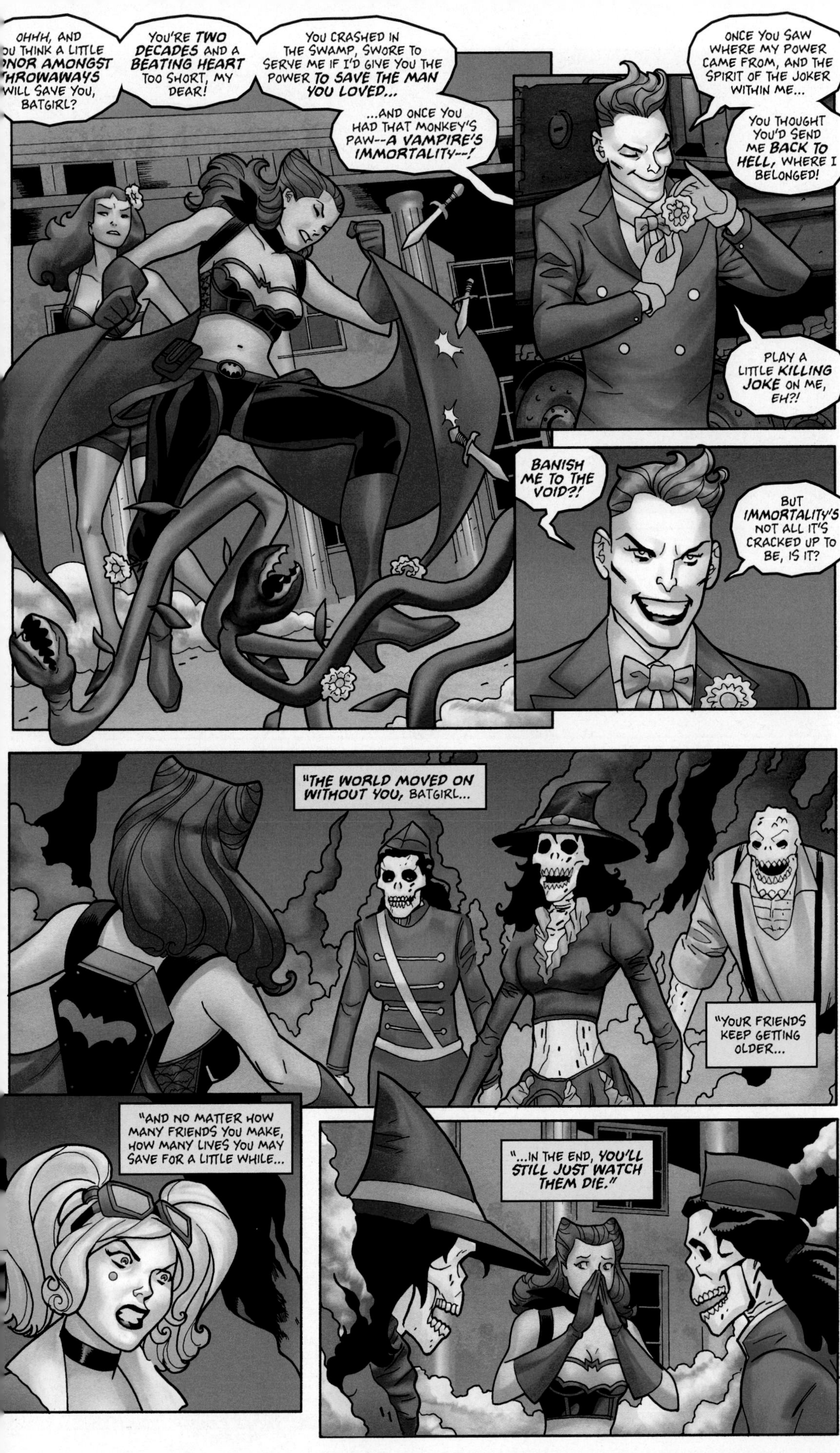

OHHH, AND
OU THINK A LITTLE
ONOR AMONGST
THROWAWAYS
WILL SAVE YOU,
BATGIRL?
YOU'RE TWO DECADES AND A BEATING HEART TOO SHORT, MY DEAR!
YOU CRASHED IN THE SWAMP, SWORE TO SERVE ME IF I'D GIVE YOU THE POWER TO SAVE THE MAN YOU LOVED...
...AND ONCE YOU HAD THAT MONKEY'S PAW--A VAMPIRE'S IMMORTALITY--!
ONCE YOU SAW WHERE MY POWER CAME FROM, AND THE SPIRIT OF THE JOKER WITHIN ME...
YOU THOUGHT YOU'D SEND ME BACK TO HELL, WHERE I BELONGED!
PLAY A LITTLE KILLING JOKE ON ME, EH?!
BANISH ME TO THE VOID?!
BUT IMMORTALITY'S NOT ALL IT'S CRACKED UP TO BE, IS IT?
"THE WORLD MOVED ON WITHOUT YOU, BATGIRL...
"YOUR FRIENDS KEEP GETTING OLDER...
"AND NO MATTER HOW MANY FRIENDS YOU MAKE, HOW MANY LIVES YOU MAY SAVE FOR A LITTLE WHILE...
"...IN THE END, YOU'LL STILL JUST WATCH THEM DIE."

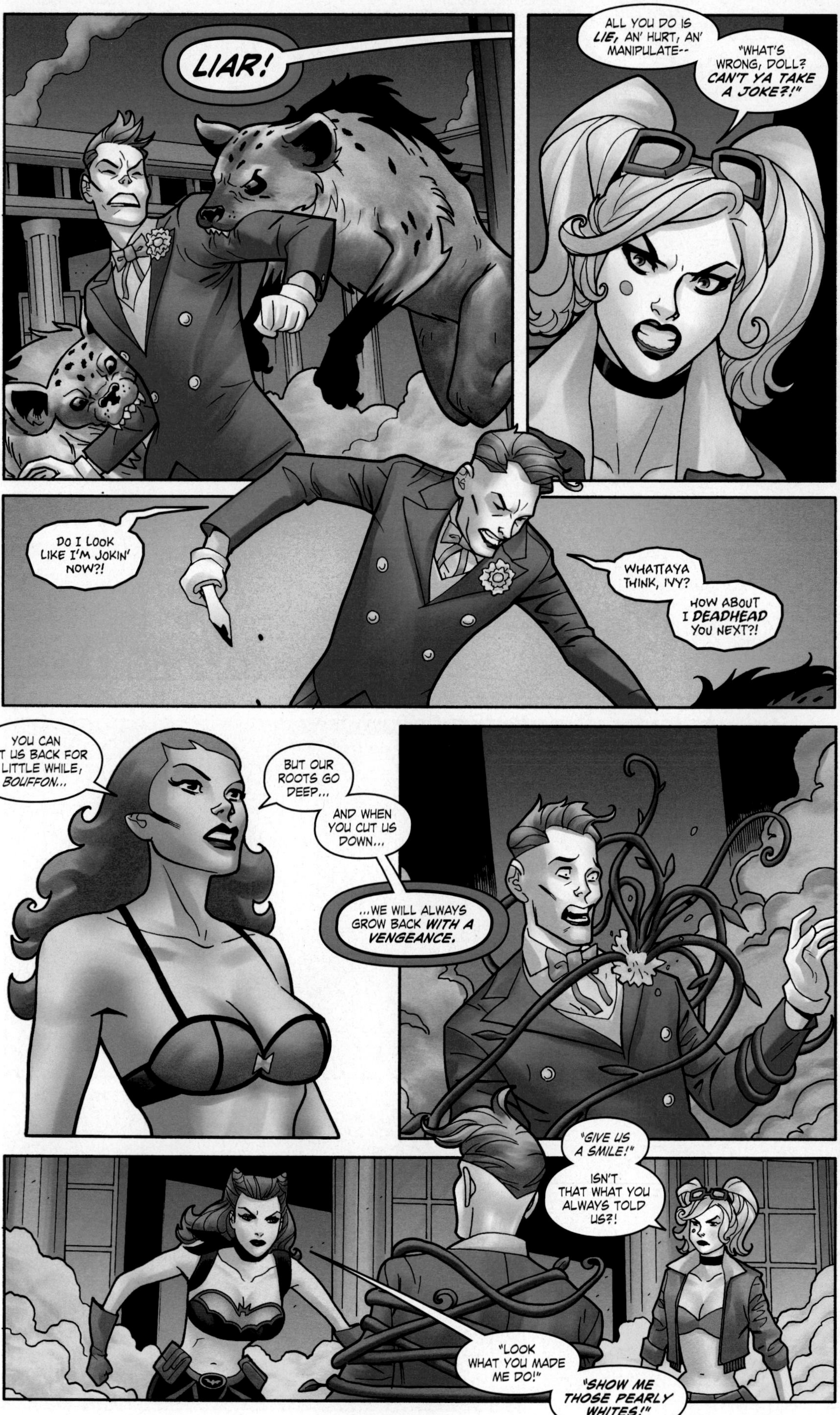
LIAR!
ALL YOU DO IS LIE, AN' HURT, AN' MANIPULATE--
"WHAT'S WRONG, DOLL? CAN'T YA TAKE A JOKE?!"
DO I LOOK LIKE I'M JOKIN' NOW?!
WHATTAYA THINK, IVY?
HOW ABOUT I DEADHEAD YOU NEXT?!
YOU CAN CUT US BACK FOR A LITTLE WHILE, BOUFFON...
BUT OUR ROOTS GO DEEP...
AND WHEN YOU CUT US DOWN...
...WE WILL ALWAYS GROW BACK WITH A VENGEANCE.
"GIVE US A SMILE!"
ISN'T THAT WHAT YOU ALWAYS TOLD US?!
"LOOK WHAT YOU MADE ME DO!"
"SHOW ME THOSE PEARLY WHITES!"

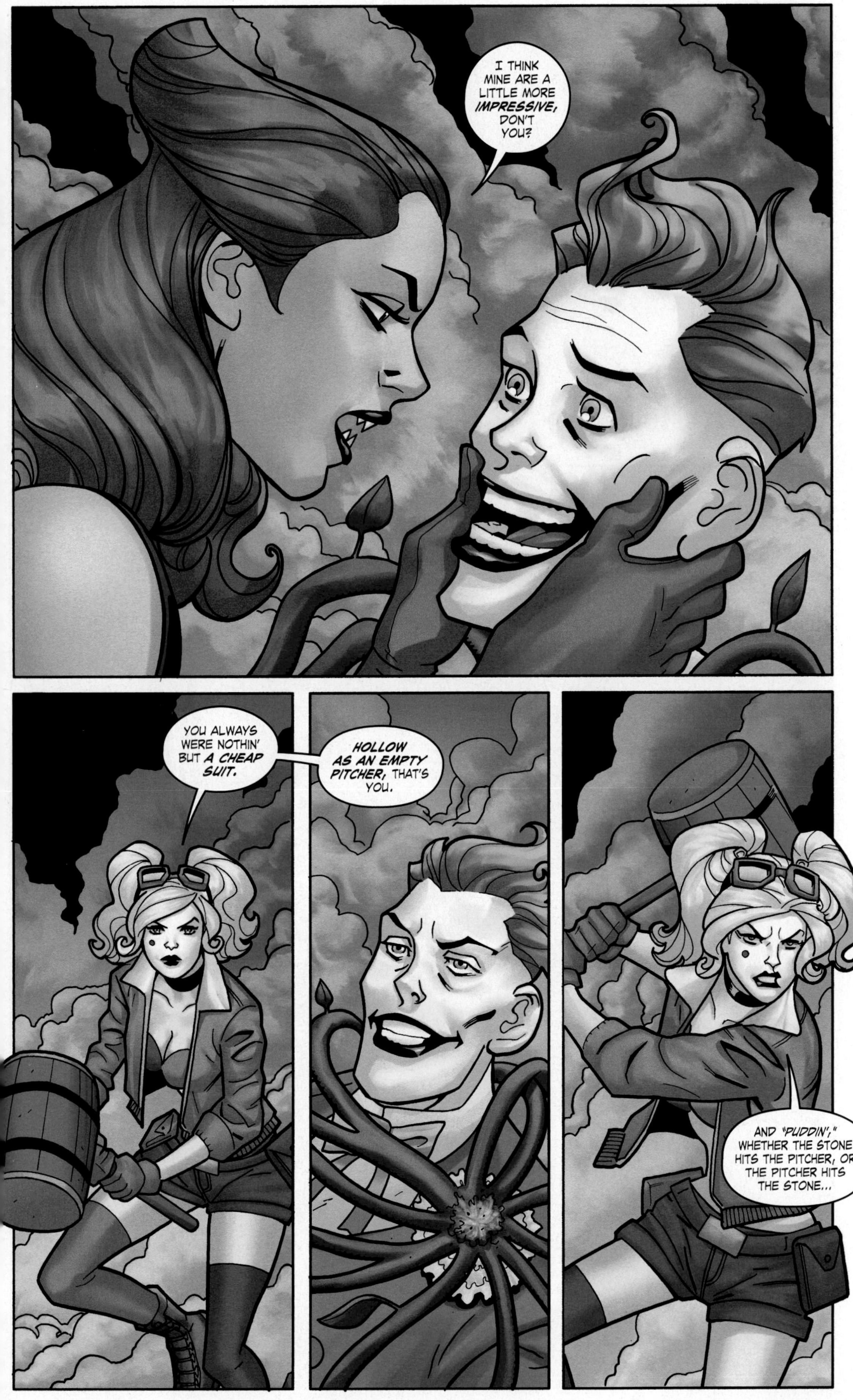

I THINK MINE ARE A LITTLE MORE *IMPRESSIVE*, DON'T YOU?
YOU ALWAYS WERE NOTHIN' BUT ***A CHEAP SUIT.***
HOLLOW AS AN EMPTY PITCHER, THAT'S YOU.
AND *"PUDDIN',"* WHETHER THE STONE HITS THE PITCHER, OR THE PITCHER HITS THE STONE...

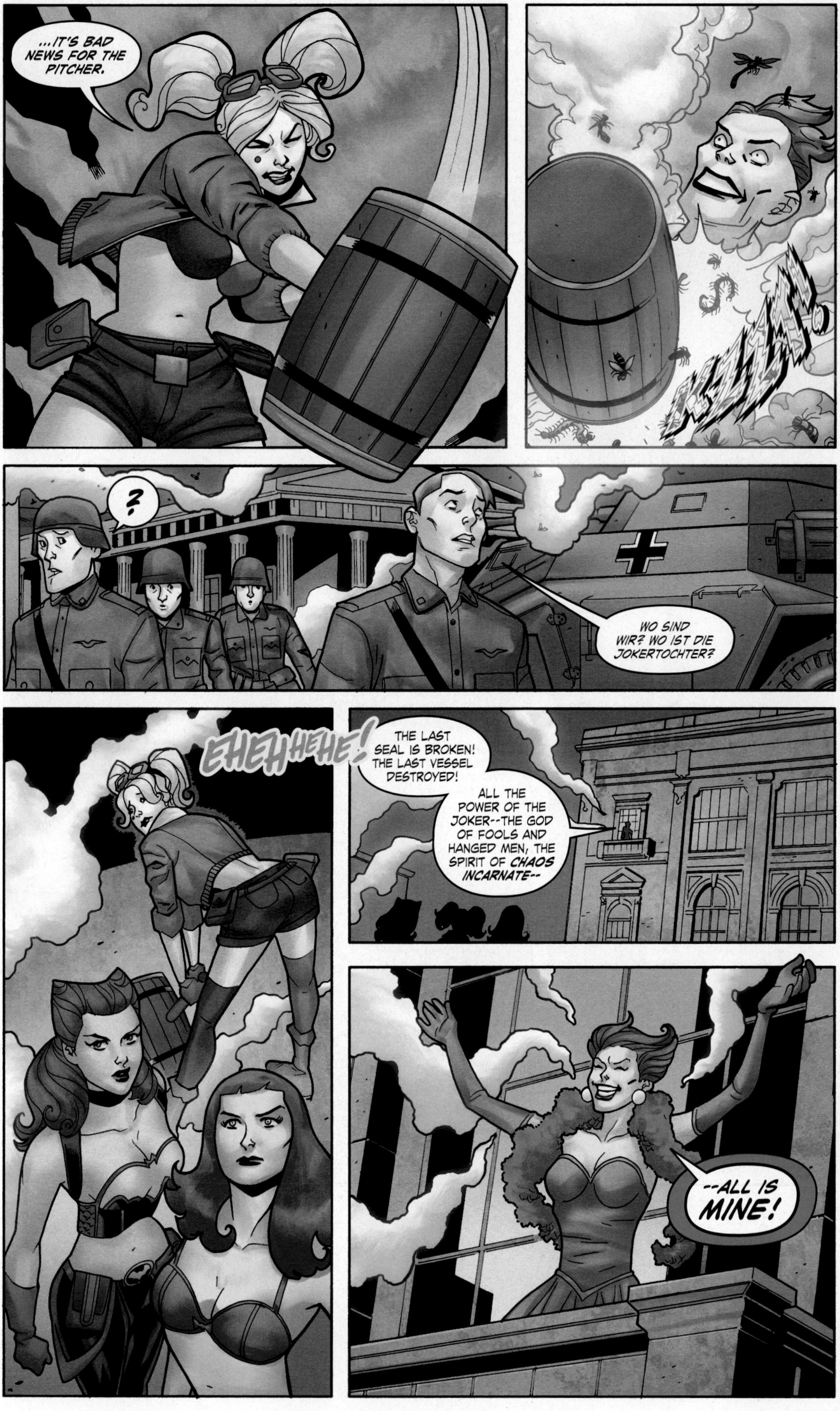
...IT'S BAD NEWS FOR THE PITCHER.
?
WO SIND WIR? WO IST DIE JOKERTOCHTER?
EHEHHEHE!
THE LAST SEAL IS BROKEN! THE LAST VESSEL DESTROYED!
ALL THE POWER OF THE JOKER--THE GOD OF FOOLS AND HANGED MEN, THE SPIRIT OF CHAOS INCARNATE--
--ALL IS MINE!

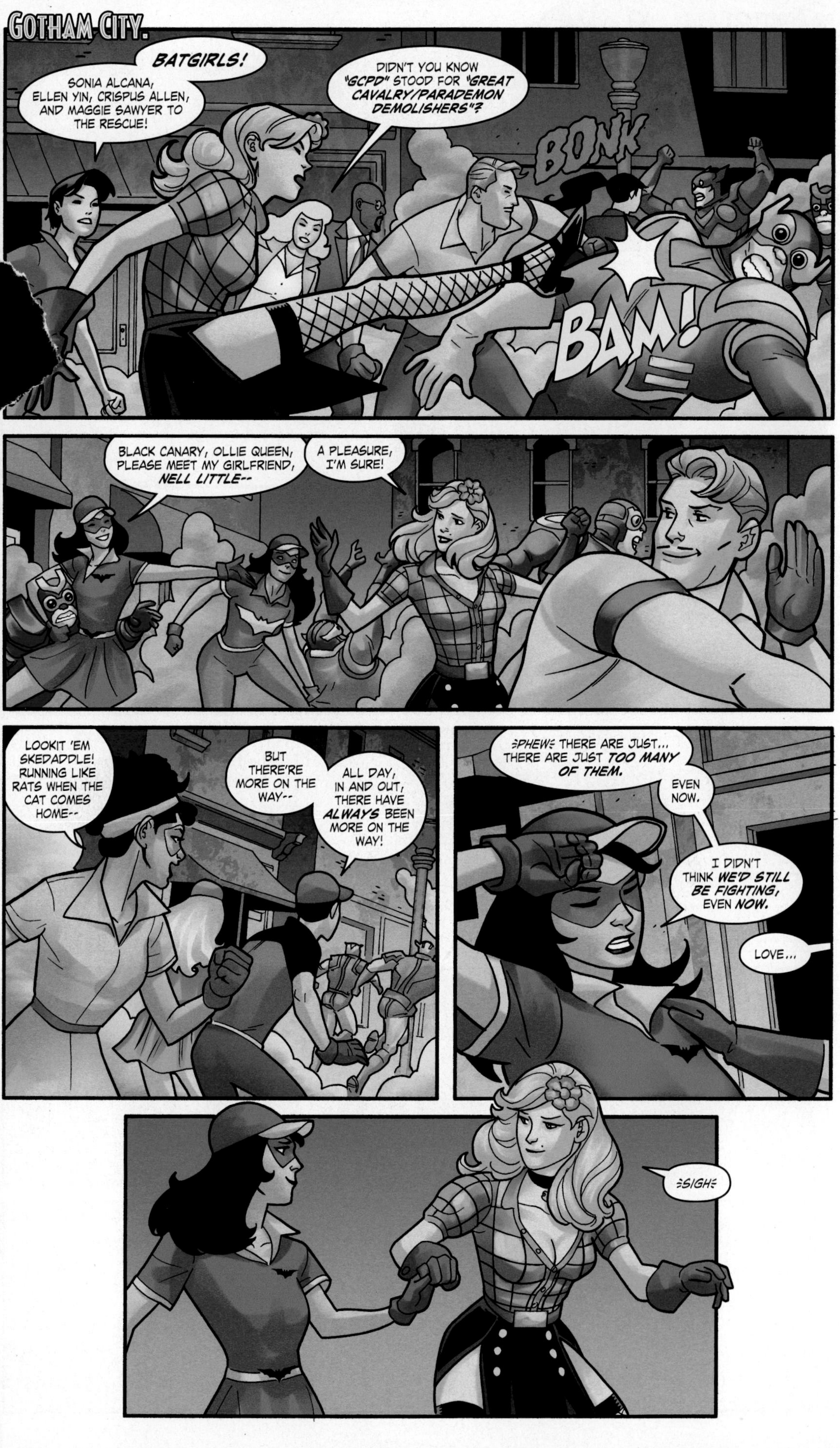
GOTHAM CITY.
BATGIRLS!
SONIA ALCANA, ELLEN YIN, CRISPUS ALLEN, AND MAGGIE SAWYER TO THE RESCUE!
DIDN'T YOU KNOW "GCPD" STOOD FOR "GREAT CAVALRY/PARADEMON DEMOLISHERS"?
BONK
BAM!
BLACK CANARY, OLLIE QUEEN, PLEASE MEET MY GIRLFRIEND, NELL LITTLE--
A PLEASURE, I'M SURE!
LOOKIT 'EM SKEDADDLE! RUNNING LIKE RATS WHEN THE CAT COMES HOME--
BUT THERE'RE MORE ON THE WAY--
ALL DAY, IN AND OUT, THERE HAVE ALWAYS BEEN MORE ON THE WAY!
PHEW THERE ARE JUST... THERE ARE JUST TOO MANY OF THEM.
EVEN NOW.
I DIDN'T THINK WE'D STILL BE FIGHTING, EVEN NOW.
LOVE...
SIGH

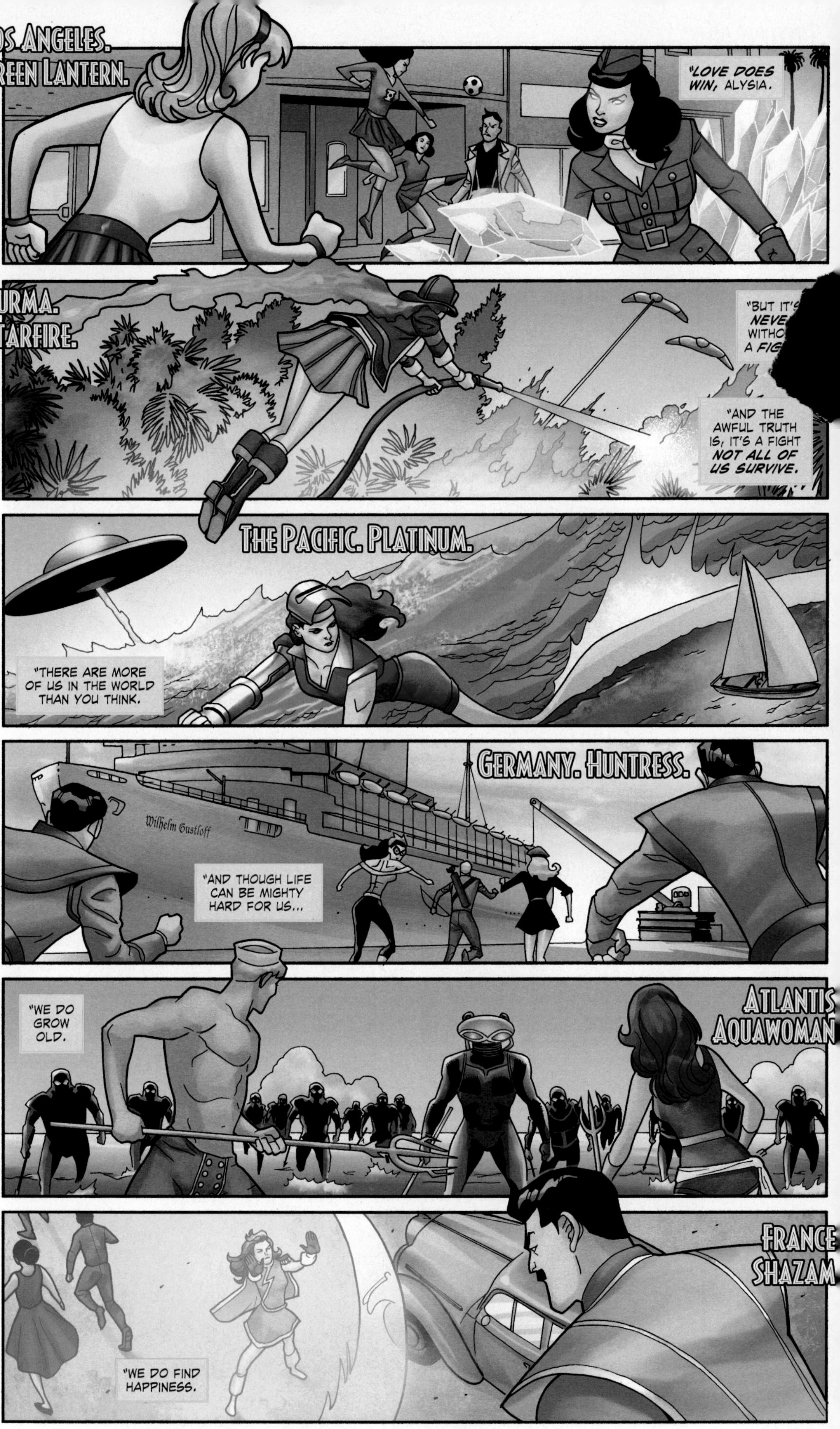
LOS ANGELES. GREEN LANTERN.
"LOVE DOES WIN, ALYSIA.
BURMA. STARFIRE.
"BUT IT'S NEVE WITHO A FIG
"AND THE AWFUL TRUTH IS, IT'S A FIGHT NOT ALL OF US SURVIVE.
THE PACIFIC. PLATINUM.
"THERE ARE MORE OF US IN THE WORLD THAN YOU THINK.
GERMANY. HUNTRESS.
Wilhelm Gustloff
"AND THOUGH LIFE CAN BE MIGHTY HARD FOR US...
"WE DO GROW OLD.
ATLANTIS AQUAWOMAN
FRANCE SHAZAM
"WE DO FIND HAPPINESS.